The One Year® Devotional of
Joy and Laughter

the one year® devotional of joy and laughter

365 inspirational meditations to brighten your day

Mary Hollingsworth

Tyndale House Publishers, Inc., Carol Stream, Illinois

Visit Tyndale online at www.tyndale.com.

Visit Mary Hollingsworth's website at www.MaryHollingsworth.com.

The One Year Devotional of Joy and Laughter: 365 Inspirational Meditations to Brighten Your Day

Designed by Ron Kaufmann

Edited by Susan Taylor and Erin Gwynne

Published in association with Mark Sweeney & Associates, Bonita Springs, Florida.

ISBN 978-1-4143-3639-8

Printed in the United States of America

21 20
10 9 8 7 6 5

Introduction

For everything there is a season, a time for every activity under heaven. . . .

A time to cry and a time to laugh.

ECCLESIASTES 3:1, 4

Welcome to the devotional that offers a small dose of joy and laughter for your spirit every day for a full year. We believe laughter is good for what ails you, so this book is seriously funny. As Solomon, God's wise man, said in Proverbs 17:22, "A cheerful heart is good medicine, but a broken spirit saps a person's strength."

Our world is a serious place in which to live. People are often sad, afraid, worried, depressed, or in physical pain. Perhaps that's where you find yourself right now. I believe that what people need is not another bitter-tasting life lesson. Instead, they need something that will help to lift their spirits, give them hope, and make them smile. They need something that will give them the courage to go on, in spite of their difficulties. We hope this devotional can provide that spark of hope and courage for you day by day.

Perhaps you're wondering how a spiritual devotional can be funny and serious at the same time. That's a good question. Marshall Keeble, a great old African-American preacher I knew, once said, "If you want people to understand something serious, first you've got to get them laughing. Once they're laughing, then you can slap the plaster on, and it'll stick every time."

In other words, as the song from the movie *Mary Poppins* says, "A spoonful of sugar helps the medicine go down." That's why pharmaceutical companies sugarcoat pills and make cough syrup that tastes like cherries or grapes. Doing so makes it easier to take in what's really important. My hope is that while you are enjoying the lighthearted tales in this book, you will also be absorbing important spiritual truths . . . perhaps in spite of yourself.

The One Year Devotional of Joy and Laughter is a delightful collection of funny or joyful stories from which spiritual lessons can be drawn. These stories are told by a variety of contemporary Christian writers or retold from public facts or history so each day will have a unique approach and feeling. Some of the anecdotes and jokes have traveled a considerable path before making their way to this book. They're the kinds of stories that get passed around from friend to friend, from website to website, from one e-mail in-box to another. And that's the way it is with laughter itself, isn't it? By its very nature, joy is contagious. Once we've experienced it ourselves, we can't help but share it with those we love.

In addition to the story for each day, we have provided a related Bible verse to challenge your thinking and remind you of an important teaching in God's Word. We suggest that you read the verse several times throughout that day, contemplate it, and think of ways to incorporate its lesson into your life.

Following each day's story is a prayer to help you begin your daily conversation with the Father. From that short prayer starter, you will likely think of other reasons to praise God and other requests to lift up to him as you focus your heart and mind on things above.

So join us in this day-by-day journey into joy and laughter—at the very heart of God, the eternal joy giver.

Blessings and joy!

—*Mary Hollingsworth*

God loved the world so much

that he gave his one and only Son,

so that everyone who believes in him will not perish

but have "ever-laughing" life.

A FIVE-YEAR-OLD'S VERSION OF JOHN 3:16

Come as You Are!

God showed his great love for us by sending Christ to die for us while we were still sinners.

ROMANS 5:8

On the way home from a fun New Year's Eve gathering, my husband and I decided to pull a prank on some of our friends. About six o'clock on New Year's Day morning, my husband got into our fifteen-seat passenger van, and I got into our car, and we went around town picking up our friends for a come-as-you-are breakfast.

The unsuspecting invitees were allowed only to put on robes and slippers. They couldn't comb their hair, brush their teeth, put on makeup, or do anything else to enhance their "natural beauty." Guys' hair stuck up, women sported curlers, and many wore robes and slippers with holes in them. It looked like Fright Night at a theme park.

We lived on the eighth floor of a large apartment building. So when we herded our pajama-clad crowd into the lobby and up the elevator to our apartment early on New Year's morning, none of the other tenants saw our friends arrive.

We cooked breakfast for everybody and had a great time with an impromptu style show. We gave prizes for the "best dressed" and played games for about three hours.

Then it was time to take everyone home. By that time the other people in our building were awake. The looks on their faces were priceless as we led our strangely garbed parade through the lobby and out to the cars. We especially enjoyed the shocked expressions of one of the elders of our church and his wife, who happened to live on the first floor of our building. It took awhile to explain that nothing sordid or weird had been happening.

Our friends have told us they don't sleep as well on New Year's Eve as they used to. Strange. I sleep like a baby.

Dear Father, thank you for your invitation to come to you just as we are—sinners who are lost without you. Amen.

January 2

Behold! or Not

Look! I stand at the door and knock.

REVELATION 3:20

It was a chilly winter day in Chicago. Snow had fallen during the night, and the streets were still a bit icy. However, the new minister at a community church felt compelled to make a few house calls to members who had not been in church services for a few weeks. So he trekked across town carefully, going from house to house.

When he arrived at the third home on his list, he rang the doorbell and waited, but no one came to the door. He could tell that someone was at home, so he kept ringing the bell. Still, no one answered.

As a final departing act, the minister wrote, "Revelation 3:20: 'Look! I stand at the door and knock. If you hear my voice and open the door, I will come in, and we will share a meal together as friends'" on the back of one of his calling cards and stuck it under the door.

The minister left the house, puzzled as to why the member did not answer the door. He had no recollection of having done anything to upset her. Unsure of what else to do, he returned to his office at the church building, intending to speak to the member about it the next time he saw her.

Two days later, the minister received his calling card back in an envelope with a short note attached that read, "Genesis 3:10: 'I heard you walking in the garden, so I hid. I was afraid because I was naked.'"

Father, I often hear you knocking and wanting to come in and be with me. Please help me to remember that I can never hide from you, no matter what my sin. And please help me always to be ready to welcome you into my heart and life. Amen.

The Perk from Above

I will go to . . . God—the source of all my joy.
I will praise you . . . , O God, my God!

PSALM 43:4

Several years ago I was driving down a rain-swept street in Long Beach, California, on an errand from my office. It was cold, the day was dreary, the sky was overcast, I couldn't find the address I was seeking, and my spirit was out of sorts. I hadn't wanted to leave the comfort of a warm office, but I had no choice. You know how it goes—the demands of duty.

As I was driving along, fretting about a problem that was sapping my emotional energy, I said to God, "Lord, would you please give me a perk? Some little something to lift my spirit? Doesn't have to be big. Doesn't have to be flashy. Just do something creative to cheer me up and to remind me that I'm glad I'm alive. I'd appreciate that very much."

At that moment I turned the corner, looked to my left, and there in the cab of a pickup truck sat two clowns. They were fully decked out in clown regalia, complete with red woolen yarn hair, big bow ties, painted faces, and each holding a helium-filled balloon. As I looked at them, they simultaneously turned, looked at me, and flashed toothless grins from ear to ear.

What a unique answer to prayer! I absolutely *loved* it, and all alone in my car I yelled, "*All right!* Great perk, Lord. What an idea. How clever you are. Who would ever have thought of two clowns in a pickup?"

But we don't have to wonder, do we? God gave us the gift of laughter, so he must enjoy a good giggle now and then too.

—Luci Swindoll

Father, thank you for the surprises and delights you put in my life. Without you life would be such a drag. I love you, Father. Amen.

January 4

All the Way to the Tub

Your word is a lamp to guide my feet
and a light for my path.
I've promised it once, and I'll promise it again:
I will obey your righteous regulations.

PSALM 119:105-106

My husband's Granny Jordan lived to be ninety without suffering a broken bone. But that's not to say she never fell. Whether she had an equilibrium problem or was just clumsy, the family never decided. Suffice it to say, she never hurt herself badly enough to decide to see a doctor for testing. And she never owned up to being clumsy.

It became a family joke even before she became elderly. When her teenagers left for school in the morning, they would say, "Now, Mama, don't go out to get the mail until we get home. We don't want you to fall off that curb—what would the neighbors say about finding you in the gutter?"

Later in life, Granny Jordan lived with her daughter and son-in-law. One night she got up to go to the bathroom, and when she stood up from the toilet, she tipped herself over into the nearby bathtub. Not wanting to wake the "kids" at two o'clock in the morning, she just pulled a towel over her arms and lay there until their alarm clock went off.

When someone teased Granny Jordan about her frequent falls, she would laugh and explain, "I only fall enough to stay in shape."

I wonder how many of us could say the same thing about our spiritual lives. How often do we have to wait for our Father to pull us up out of the problems into which we fall?

—*Dianna Booher*

Lord, thank you for guiding my steps and keeping me safe on the path that leads to you. Help me not to fall for the devil's tricks but to stay on solid footing with you. I know that without your care and grace, I would stumble and fall. Bless me, O Lord. Amen.

You Can't Do That!

Repent of your sins and turn to God, so that your sins may be wiped away.

ACTS 3:19

Sulphur Springs, Texas, where we live, has one of those famous old Texas brick town squares in the middle of downtown. It's a bit like an English roundabout with traffic coming in at all four corners of the square and traveling around the square until drivers get to the appropriate street to exit.

Regardless of where the townspeople are trying to go, they almost always end up on the square at some point. And navigating the traffic on the square can be entertaining.

One busy Saturday morning, an old farmer came into town to get a haircut and do his shopping. He was in an original Model T Ford, which he guided proudly into the traffic on the square. About halfway around the square, he decided he did not want to *be* on the square so he stuck his hand out the window, indicating he was going to make a U-turn right in the middle of the one-way traffic.

Seeing what he was about to do, a policeman yelled, "Hey, mister! You can't do that!"

The old man stopped, poked his head out the window, took a good look around, and yelled back, "Yeah, I think I can make it!" Then he wound up that old Ford and drove upstream through dodging, honking traffic back to the place where he had come in and headed back to the country, where he belonged.

The policeman was so shocked that he just stood there in the middle of the square, laughing his head off.

Although what that farmer did wasn't legal, it *is* biblical. When you realize you are headed in the wrong direction in life, make a U-turn and go the way that will get you back home where you belong.

—Clyde Shrode

Lord, I know I often need to turn around and run to you. Thank you for loving me and for always taking me back. Amen.

Wunny Wace

Sing praises to God. . . .
Father to the fatherless . . .
God places the lonely in families . . .
and gives them joy.

PSALM 68:4-6

When my cousin Donna first learned to talk, she had a bit of difficulty making the *f* sound. She automatically substituted the *w* sound for an *f*. So instead of "foot," she said her "woot" hurt. And in popular fairy tales, things were "war, war away."

Donna loved my brother, who was a teenager at the time. He teased her unmercifully, which she objected to loudly with fake indignation.

My brother would say, "Donna, you're a funny face."

And she would say, "I'm *not* a wunny wace."

He would say, "You're a big, fat elephant."

And she would reply, with feeling, "I'm *not* a big, wat elewant!"

He would say, "Your face is full of freckles."

And she would say, "My wace is *not* wull of wreckles!"

This game went on every time our two families were together until Donna's sixth birthday, when we came to celebrate with her. She opened her gifts. We played games with the children at the party. And we had cake and ice cream.

After the party was over, my brother, in standard form, said, "Donna, you're still a funny face."

And to everyone's surprise, she said, "I am not a funny face"—the *f* sound clear and accurate.

"Well, what happened to my 'wunny wace'?" he asked, laughing.

To our amazement she said, "I'm six years old now. I don't have to talk like that anymore." And she never did again.

Wamilies! Aren't they wabulous?

Father, thank you for creating families, and thank you for my family. They mean so much to me, and I'm so grateful for them. Thank you especially for allowing me to be one of your children and part of your family. Bless you, Father. Amen.

Trading Up

God showed his great love for us by sending Christ to die for us while we were still sinners.

ROMANS 5:8

One night, at the front gate of a large military base in south Texas, a marine private was standing his first guard-duty assignment. Rain was falling gently. It was cold, and the wind was beginning to pick up as a storm moved closer. Still, the new private stood his post staunchly, as a proud marine should.

Presently a two-star general stepped out of his house on base to take his dog for a walk. The nervous young private, wanting to make a good impression, snapped to attention, made a perfect salute, and cried out, "Sir, good evening, sir!"

The general, out for some relaxation, returned the salute and said casually, "Good evening, soldier. Nice night, isn't it?"

It was hardly a nice night, but the private was not about to disagree with a two-star general, so he saluted again and replied, "Sir, yes sir!"

The general walked slowly about with his dog and continued talking to the private. "You know, there's something about a stormy night that I find soothing. It's all really relaxing, don't you agree?"

The private did not agree, but then the private was just a private, so he responded, "Sir, yes sir!"

Indicating the big, friendly dog, the general said, "This is a golden retriever, the best type of dog to train."

The private glanced at the dog, saluted yet again, and said, "Sir, yes sir!"

The general smiled at the private's obvious desire to please him and continued by saying, "I got this dog for my wife."

The private responded, "Good trade, sir!"

O Lord, because of you we have been allowed to "trade up." We have traded our sinful ways for a life of joy and hope through you. Thank you for giving us that chance. We love you, Lord. Amen.

Name That Wife

Moses protested, "If I go to the people of Israel and tell them,
'The God of your ancestors has sent me to you,' they will ask me,
'What is his name?' Then what should I tell them?"
God replied to Moses, "I AM WHO I AM. Say this to
the people of Israel: I AM has sent me to you."

EXODUS 3:13-14

My husband has a variety of pet names for me. I don't know how he comes up with these names (too much caffeine must have something to do with it), but it can become a little embarrassing when he's introducing me to his business associates.

"Captain Buchanan, I'd like you to meet my wife, Honey Biscuit."

"Reverend Salsota, this is my wife, Love Bumps."

"Sugar Bear, this is Congresswoman Stafford. Congresswoman Stafford, this is Sugar Bear."

It would not be so bad, but that is how he fills out my name tags too.

Still, pet names can add a little fun to your marriage. They are something that you, and only you, call your spouse. (Although, an insurance salesman called our house the other day asking to speak with Love Bumps.)

Pet names are an endearing expression of love. Sure, they can sometimes be embarrassing, but when I think about all the names some husbands call their wives, and vice versa, Honey Biscuit doesn't sound all that bad.

But now, Passion Petunia? You just have to draw the line somewhere!

—*Martha Bolton*

O Lord, we praise your wonderful name—the name above all others, and the one we love. It is the name by which we come to the Father, and it is the only name by which we can be saved. Thank you for allowing us to wear it, Lord. It is such an incredible honor and a privilege. Amen.

The Muscle Man

I will praise you, Lord, with all my heart;
I will tell of all the marvelous things you have done.

PSALM 9:1

My dad, Leon Moore Jr., was a train porter. His job was to assist passengers onto the train and handle their luggage, trunks, and boxes. As a result, in my daddy's-girl eyes, he had the biggest, strongest muscles in the world! I would swell with pride when he lifted his arms, tightened his biceps, and allowed me to feel their concrete-like hardness.

One day Dad was startled to see me escorting a long line of kids toward him. "Daddy," I said proudly, "my friends want to feel your muscles."

Needless to say, he was taken aback by the request, but seeing the smile on my face, he dutifully allowed each child to feel his arm. Just as I expected, each one was in awe of his great strength.

After the kids had gone, Dad said, "I had no idea you were that proud of me."

With much satisfaction, I replied, "When I told them how strong you are, they wanted to see for themselves. So I charged them a nickel each and told them to come and see."

"You charged them?" he asked in amazement. "Are you actually saying you made those kids pay you?"

"Well, yes, Daddy," I replied. "They wanted to feel it bad . . . really bad."

To my chagrin, Daddy made me give all the nickels back.

I was just thinking, when was the last time I bragged on the power, strength, and greatness of our heavenly Father? Have I bragged about *his* muscle lately? I must tell others of his great strength—no nickel needed!

—Edith Moore-Parkman

Gracious Father, I will tell others of your power, strength, and love. Help me to be cognizant of each opportunity to freely tell the world of your greatness. Amen.

January 10

Oh, How I Love Jesus!

When Jesus saw what was happening, he was angry with his disciples. He said to them, "Let the children come to me. Don't stop them! For the Kingdom of God belongs to those who are like these children."

MARK 10:14

When I was about ten, an older cousin, her four-year-old daughter, and I were riding a ski lift at an amusement park. As our feet swung gently under the rocking lift, my cousin pointed out various places we could see, waved at people below, and reveled in the cooler breeze from that height.

Suddenly we were aware of faint singing around us and traced it to the small wonder sitting between us. Her little hands were tightly gripping the bar, her shoulders were hunched, and she stared straight ahead as she breathlessly sang to herself, "Oh, . . . how . . . I . . . love . . . Je . . . sus! Oh, . . . how . . ."

She continued to sing the rest of the ride and would not talk to us until we were on the ground. Then she explained with a four-year-old vocabulary and a mature faith that she was really scared up there, but she knew that Jesus was a source of strength and comfort. Her singing was affirmation that she loved and trusted that source.

The rest of the story is that while my cousin thoroughly delighted in the aerial experience, I was actually almost as afraid as her daughter. She concentrated on Jesus, but I concentrated on keeping my shoes on my feet as I silently, desperately, hoped the cable held us up.

The lesson of whom to trust was not lost on me—even a few decades later. Oh, how I love Jesus!

—*Stephanie Terry*

Father God, thank you for the examples of children. Help me to be your little child, one who belongs to your Kingdom. And thank you for your saving grace through Jesus. In his name, amen.

Where Are You Going?

Jesus [said], "I am the way, the truth, and the life.
No one can come to the Father except through me."

JOHN 14:6

When Abraham Lincoln ran for Congress as a Whig in 1846, an evangelical Methodist, Peter Cartwright, ran against him as a Democrat. During the extended and heated campaign, Cartwright was preaching in a religious meeting, and Lincoln decided to attend.

At the end of a long and stirring sermon, Cartwright extended the invitation to all who were in attendance by asking them to stand up if they wished to go to heaven. In response, a few people timidly stood up.

Not to be daunted by the weak response, Cartwright then said with force, "Now, all those who do *not* wish to go to *hell* please stand!"

As one would expect at such an invitation, and not wanting to be in the minority, the rest of the audience rose to their feet, except for Abraham Lincoln, who quietly remained seated and unperturbed by Cartwright's invitation.

Cartwright saw an opportunity to embarrass his political rival and said, "May I inquire of you, Mr. Lincoln, where *you* are going?"

Lincoln then rose to his full, imposing height and said calmly, "I came here as a respectful listener. I did not know I was to be singled out by Brother Cartwright. I believe in treating religious matters with due solemnity. I admit that the questions propounded by Brother Cartwright are of great importance. I did not feel called upon to answer as the rest did. Brother Cartwright asked me directly where I am going. I desire to reply with equal directness: *I* am going to Congress!"

Father, I pray that I will always be aware of where I am going in life. I know that your Son will continue to lead me as I put my trust in him. Thank you for giving me heaven as my eternal destination. Amen.

The Big Snow

We don't look at the troubles we can see now; rather, we fix our gaze on things that cannot be seen. For the things we see now will soon be gone, but the things we cannot see will last forever.

2 CORINTHIANS 4:18

It was one of those winters when the Great Lakes region had record snowfalls. On one occasion, our area received more than eighteen inches of snow in a twenty-four-hour period, a lot of snow even by Michigan standards. But it did not arrive with the usual quiet accumulation to which we were accustomed. This snow came in a raging blizzard with winds that reached nearly forty-five miles per hour.

By the time the howling was over, the storm had delivered mountains of snow, sculpting drifts that reached as high as five feet around the front and back doors of the house.

My brother said, "It's as if the whole storm came ripping straight out of the North Pole, blasted across Lake Superior, and then emptied itself in our yard."

He managed to push the back door open enough to reach the shovel he kept nearby. He dug a path to the side door of the garage; then he used the snowblower to clear the driveway. He headed back to the garage just in time to see the back door open and the top of Mom's head before she reached the bottom step of the back porch. Then she disappeared from his sight! Thinking she had fallen into the deep snow, he started to panic, until a few seconds later he realized she was okay when the side door to the garage seemed to open by itself.

Sometimes it feels as if the storms of life empty themselves right into our lives, too. When that happens, have courage, keep the faith, and by all means, keep your head up!

—*C. Anne Morrison*

Father, please help me to remember not to become overwhelmed by the troubles of this life. I know you are always there to help me carry them. Amen.

Actions Speak Louder

[Paul said,] "You should imitate me,
just as I imitate Christ."

1 CORINTHIANS 11:1

I like to make use of otherwise wasted or imprisoned moments to teach and mold little hearts and minds. The car makes a great classroom when "students" are held captive by door locks and seatbelts. Some of our best conversations take place on the road while we practice math facts and spelling words, recite Scripture verses, share hopes and dreams, provide support and encouragement, or discuss right and wrong behaviors.

One day, when my daughter, Abby, was about three years old, I quizzed her on colors when we stopped for a traffic light.

"What does red mean?" I asked while we waited.

"Stop!" she exclaimed.

"That's right! What does green mean?"

"Go!" she yelled.

"Right. You are so smart. Now, what does yellow mean?"

"Go faster!" she shrieked.

Mouth agape, I snapped my head around to stare at her. She smiled broadly, so proud of herself. The car behind me honked when the light turned green.

"Green light! Go!" shouted Abby happily.

As I quickly turned back in my seat and drove forward, I realized that although my body sat in the driver's seat, my heart was sitting in a corner wearing a dunce cap. And I marked my lesson well.

Abby might not always have learned from my words, but she had certainly learned from my actions. Sad to say, what people see us do sometimes shouts so loudly that they cannot hear what we say. The problem always comes when our words and our actions don't match. *Sigh.*

—Sandra Heska King

Father, I know my actions do not always please you and that I might be the only "Bible" another person reads. I want to be more like Jesus. Help me to grow closer to you so that I can be a good example to others. Thank you. Amen.

January 14

I Have a Great Plan!

"My thoughts are nothing like your
thoughts," says the Lord.
"And my ways are far beyond
anything you could imagine."

ISAIAH 55:8

I was running errands with our three-year-old son, who was happily chattering away in the backseat. Suddenly he announced, "I have a great plan, Mama!"

Driving along, I humored him. "Okay, honey. What's your plan?"

"When we get home, you can give me some cookies," he said. "And you'll say I can have them and not 'Wait till after dinner'—but you be nice to me and let me eat them, okay?"

Trying not to laugh, I said, "Honey, I *am* being nice when I say wait till after dinner, because if you eat cookies now, you'll get a tummy ache and won't be hungry for your good food."

"But, Mom!" he wailed. "Don't say no! *No* is not my favorite!"

"I know you want some cookies," I assured him. "But trust me. It's better to wait till after dinner."

More often than I would like to admit, God uses my kids' antics to spotlight how I have been relating to him.

All too often in my prayers, I approach God with, "I have a great plan!" Then I casually suggest to the sovereign God of the universe how *he* could accomplish *my* plan. And say (or at least think), "You be nice and don't say no, God. Because *no* is not my favorite."

But God, like a good parent, knows what is best for me. Sometimes he says no to my plans, not because he is "not nice" but because he has in mind something infinitely better for me. And his plans are not just great—they're perfect.

—Jennifer Stair

God, help me to wait and seek what you have in store for me. Instead of telling you my great plan, teach me to trust in your perfect plan. Amen.

Senior I.D.

Don't think you are better than you really are. Be honest in your evaluation of yourselves, measuring yourselves by the faith God has given us.

ROMANS 12:3

After retiring from teaching school for many years, I decided to take a long-term job substituting for a teacher on maternity leave. Before returning to work, though, I took time to hide my advanced years. I cut and colored my hair and purchased trendy clothes and up-to-date teaching materials. I was ready!

At the orientation meeting, the principal stressed a school rule: no cell phones in use during teaching hours. I had not planned to use mine, but I still carried it to school with me inside my purse for emergency use. To my surprise, one day during class I heard the phone ring. I quickly gave an assignment and turned my back to the class to open my purse under my desk and retrieve the ringing phone.

As I glanced at the phone, and before I could turn it off, I heard a student say to another, "I didn't know old people had cell phones!"

I'm sure my face turned red, but I simply returned the phone to my purse and resumed teaching. Although I had convinced myself that I was still young enough to handle the strenuous job of teaching, I had not fooled any of the students about my senior status.

Surely our Father God sees everything in secret and knows us better than we know ourselves. He sees our efforts at pretending to be more than we are and winks at our humanity. And I am sure he gets a good laugh out of our wasted efforts to be someone we're not.

—*Grace G. Booth*

Father, let me recognize my own frailties and look to you for help in my time of need. Allow me to be transparent so that others can see your goodness in my life. Amen.

January 16

How Do We Define Ourselves?

In Christ lives all the fullness of God in a human body. So you also are complete through your union with Christ.

COLOSSIANS 2:9-10

It was my first week back with my favorite first graders, and we were sitting around the table catching up when one of them asked, "Are you in college?"

"No, I've finished college."

"Oh, then you're married."

Grin. "No. I'm not married."

The situation was full of intrigue, and everyone began to tune in. Many guesses at my age flew around the room, and someone chimed in, "Are you in high school?"

With help and with proud smiles they finally guessed my age and were willing to believe I was indeed old enough to have finished college. The girl sitting next to me was catching up. "Wait, you're not married?"

"No."

"Do you have a boyfriend?"

"No."

"How do you *live*?" she exclaimed, eyes wide, arms stretched out toward the sky in desperation.

I couldn't help myself. That was the funniest thing I had heard in a week! I laughed a little as I replied, "I have *lots* of friends." I was resigned also to respond, "And I have a job," not wishing to further instill the idea that we are defined by what we do, but not knowing how else to assuage their confusion about my young, out-of-college-but-not-married status as a person. That did seem to satisfy them, even the wide-eyed girl whose flair for the dramatic completely made my morning. My hope is that she will continue to encounter holistic examples and ideas of what it means to be a woman and a complete person.

—Renea McKenzie

Father, may we find our identities in your Son alone, for only he has the words of abundant and whole life. And as we learn, by your grace, to live fully, may we better bear your image before a lost world. Amen.

Credit Where Credit Is Due

Do not steal.
Do not deceive or cheat one another.

LEVITICUS 19:11

The letter read, "Congratulations! Your article 'Gold Cross' will appear in a future issue. A check will be mailed upon publication."

This would be my third "accepted" article. I had promised myself that I would frame every published story and a copy of its check as reminders that I am a paid writer. More than once, seeing those helped me during times when nothing flowed from my brain to the keyboard.

I searched through my word processing files for "Gold Cross." I could not find it.

Had the editor changed the title? That would explain why it didn't sound familiar, but what if I hadn't written that article? Was it possible the editor had my name mixed up with the true author's name? My taking credit would not be fair to the original author; besides, it would jeopardize my integrity and the magazine's. The words of Leviticus 19:11 weighed heavily on my mind.

I wrote to the editor, apologizing and saying that I did not write "Gold Cross," so I could not take credit for it.

When he did not reply, I wondered whether I had blown it and ruined any future chance of being published with the magazine.

Sometime later, I got the check from the magazine, then an envelope with four contributor copies. Torn between regret and anticipation, suspense and anxiety, I scanned the contents for "Gold Cross" and the byline with my name.

I quickly turned to page 38. As soon as I had read the first sentence, I remembered writing the article. A copy of the check and article now hang on the wall of my study.

Months later I found the missing manuscript on a portable flash drive I use for work. And I'm thankful that since then I have had forty-three more articles accepted by that same editor.

—Al Speegle Jr.

Lord, thank you for your promise that you will withhold no good thing from us if we do what is right. Amen.

January 18

Marshmallow Wars

You have turned my mourning into joyful dancing.
You have taken away my clothes
of mourning and clothed me with joy.

PSALM 30:11

I stood in the kitchen, cleaning up after dinner, deep in a begging prayer for help. Eight months before my husband was to receive lifetime medical benefits, his job had been outsourced. Now, a year later, my husband continued in his job search. Our son was in his junior year of high school, and my chronic illness was a constant worry. Should we put the house on the market? If we did, where would we go? What if we moved to an apartment and then my husband found a job in another state? How long would our savings last? *Whimper.*

Just then a big white marshmallow zipped past my shoulder, *thwapped* against the cabinet, and fell to the counter. The deep laugh of our teenage son reverberated from around the corner. I scooped up the fluffy morsel and threw it back, then dodged and weaved through the kitchen to avoid enemy fire.

My husband joined in the chase, and we raced through the house pelting (or attempting to pelt) one another with marshmallows. Our little Shih Tzu ran wide-eyed from room to room, wondering what on earth had happened to his normal, even-keeled family.

Finally we collapsed in the family room, exhausted from playing and our stomachs sore from laughing. It was funny how the problems and worries no longer seemed as large and life seemed much brighter. How like God to answer my prayers with something fun and imaginative! Our situation did not immediately change, but during the course of our wait, we surely did have some fun marshmallow wars.

Are there troubles troubling you? Give them to God, grab a bag of big marshmallows, and enjoy a respite from your worries.

—Lisa Buffaloe

Father, thank you for reminding us that our problems are in your hands, not in ours. And that is a good place for them to be. Amen.

On My Way!

Who can find a virtuous and capable wife?
She is more precious than rubies.

PROVERBS 31:10

A family was watching TV when Mom said, "I'm tired, and it's getting late. I think I'll go to bed."

She went to the kitchen to make sandwiches for the next day's lunches, rinsed out the popcorn bowls, took meat out of the freezer to thaw, checked the levels of the cereal boxes, filled the sugar container, put spoons and bowls on the table, and programmed the coffeemaker for brewing the next morning.

Next she transferred some wet clothes from the washer to the dryer, put another load into the washer, ironed a shirt, and secured a loose button.

She picked up the newspapers strewn on the floor, gathered the game pieces left on the table, and put the telephone book back into the drawer.

She watered the plants, emptied a wastebasket, and hung up a towel to dry.

She yawned and stretched and headed for the bedroom. She picked up two pairs of shoes in the hall and put them in the closet. Then she stopped by the desk and wrote a note to the teacher, counted out some cash for a field trip, and pulled a textbook out from under the chair. She signed a birthday card for a friend, addressed and stamped the envelope, and wrote a quick list for the grocery store. She put both near her purse on the table by the front door.

Mom then creamed her face, brushed and flossed her teeth, and trimmed her nails.

About that time, Dad called, "I thought you were going to bed."

"I'm on my way!" she said.

O Lord, we are on our way to you. Sometimes the path seems long and fraught with endless "detours." Please help us to stay focused on you as we take care of the myriad details and tasks that make up our lives. We love you, Lord. Amen.

A Little Push

If you had faith even as small as a mustard seed, you could say to this mountain, "Move from here to there," and it would move. Nothing would be impossible.

MATTHEW 17:20

For many months the huge ship had been under construction by the bay of the small New England town. Now she was finished and ready to launch. Her deck was polished and gleaming. The crew in their starched white uniforms stood at the rail and saluted as her flags were raised to the top of the mast. The entire city had gathered on the dock to see the ship slide down the slip into the bay.

At the moment of the scheduled launch, the giant blocks were removed, and the people collectively held their breath . . . but nothing happened. The big ship did not move. No one could figure out what to do. The captain scratched his head, and the crew remained at attention. Still, for several minutes the ship did not budge.

Finally, from the middle of the crowd, a little boy escaped from his mother and ran down the dock. When he reached the ship, he put his tiny hand on the bow of the massive ship. Then he gave it a push with all the might his little body could muster.

Of course, all the people laughed at the comical sight. The idea of a small boy pushing a ship as big as a city was ludicrous. But the whole crowd suddenly stopped laughing as the huge ship groaned and slowly began to slide down the slip. When it splashed into the bay, a mighty cheer went up—not for the ship but for the little boy who had given it a push.

Like that small boy, we can move mountains if we have faith. God promised we could, and he does not lie. Believe it!

Father, thank you for your promise. Please help me to believe that with your help I can accomplish great things for you in my life. Increase my faith, Father. Amen.

T-H-E-A-T-R-E

The very hairs on your head are all numbered. So don't be afraid; you are more valuable to God than a whole flock of sparrows.

MATTHEW 10:30-31

Conversations with other people can sometimes be less than satisfying. *Theatre Arts Magazine* records one of the most confusing and frustrating conversations in all of theatrical history.

It seems that one of the magazine's loyal subscribers dialed "information" to get the phone number for the well-known drama industry magazine. But the conversation did not go exactly as he had hoped. Instead, it proceeded as follows:

"Information. What city and state are you calling, please?" asked the operator.

"New York City, please," answered the subscriber.

"Thank you, and what listing are you seeking?"

"Theatre Arts, please."

After a few seconds, the operator drawled, "Sorry, but there is nobody listed by the name 'Theodore Arts.'"

"It's not a *person*; it's a publication. I want *Theatre Arts*," said the subscriber patiently.

A little aggravated, the operator repeated, "I told you, sir, we have no listing for Theodore Arts."

Now a little more than impatient, and with his voice rising a few decibels, the subscriber said loudly, "Confound it, ma'am, the word is *Theatre*: T-H-E-A-T-R-E."

The operator came back with crushing finality: "Sir, that's *not* how you spell Theodore!"

Isn't it great to know that God knows all about you? He knows how many hairs are on your head, and he never forgets your name. He even records it, spelled correctly, in the Lamb's Book of Life for all eternity.

Thank you, Lord, for knowing me and loving me, in spite of the sins in my life. Please show me the role you want me to play in the eternal drama you have written for humanity. Help me to learn my lines well and to deliver them at just the right moment so that those who hear them will be touched with your love. Amen.

January 22

Lunch with the President

Come! Gather together for the great
banquet God has prepared.

REVELATION 19:17

It is always an honor to be invited to have a meal with someone important. Former Secretary of Labor Raymond Donovan once told about a special invitation he received on board *Air Force One.*

Donovan was in the back compartment of the plush jet. President Ronald Reagan was in the front in his personal compartment. The phone rang in the back compartment, so Donovan answered.

"Mr. Donovan?" said a formal voice.

"Yes?"

"The president would like you to join him for lunch," said the voice.

"Oh, well, thank you! I'll be right there," stammered Donovan.

Thinking how important he must be to receive an invitation to lunch with President Reagan, Secretary Donovan straightened his tie and walked toward the front of the huge plane. When he arrived, the president's aide met him and escorted him forward. Just as he walked through the doorway into the president's private compartment, the red phone rang—the presidential hotline!

The president picked up the phone and said, "Yes—uh-huh—yes. What are my options?"

Donovan's heart almost stopped. His mind raced: What world leader must the president be talking to? What military commander? What world crisis must he be discussing at this very instant? And he was there! What a moment!

Then the president continued. "Okay, then I'll have the iced tea," and he hung up.

So much for ego.

We are invited to join the Lord for supper regularly, too, but it is not about us and how important we think we are—it is all about him and what he did for us.

Father, thank you for inviting us into your presence to partake of the memorial supper for your Son. We are honored and humbled to take the bread and wine that remind us of his great sacrifice and love for us. Amen.

Chem-Tone and a Roller

I am trusting you, O Lord,
saying, "You are my God!"
My future is in your hands.

PSALM 31:14-15

Every day I get up, get dressed, do my hair, and put on my makeup whether I feel like it or not. Why do I do those things even when I don't feel like it? Because Frances did.

My husband and I lived in Pittsburgh, Pennsylvania, where he was a personal evangelist. In the church was an amazing older lady named Frances. She was funny, sweet, and altogether delightful. I admired her so much for her wonderful attitude, no matter what might have been going on in her life.

Believe it or not, during her lifetime Frances had already been through forty-three surgeries. And there she was, facing major surgery again. The week before, she was really frightened—not of the surgical procedure but of the terrifying hallucinations she experienced under anesthetic. Still, she stuck out her chin, smiled brightly through eyes brimming with tears, and said, "Now, don't you worry, honey; old Frances will be just fine. Always have, and there's no reason to think the Lord will let me down this time. I trust him."

The next day we went to see Frances, expecting to find a pale, languishing, older woman in a white hospital gown and sound asleep. We were happily shocked to find Frances sitting up in bed laughing and talking, in a beautiful pink bed jacket, with her hair combed and her makeup done to perfection.

"Well, look who's here!" she exclaimed when she saw us. "Come here and give Frances a big hug."

"Frances, how wonderful you look!" I said, hugging her carefully. "How do you do it the day after surgery?"

"Oh, honey," she said as she laughed, "I just use Chem-Tone semigloss and a roller. It goes on a lot thicker and faster, and it covers a multitude of sins!"

Every day I get dressed and do my hair and makeup. Why do I do it even when I don't feel like it? I figure, if Frances could do it, I can do it.

Father, thank you for taking care of us in our most difficult moments. Help us to trust you more with the problems and struggles of our lives, because we know only you can really handle them. Amen.

January 24

It's All in Your Perspective

You aren't in the dark about these things, dear brothers and sisters, and you won't be surprised when the day of the Lord comes like a thief.

1 THESSALONIANS 5:4

I heard a story about a general and his lieutenant during World War II who were traveling from their base to a base in another state. Their orders meant they would travel with civilians aboard a passenger train. They found their berth, where two other folks were already seated—an attractive young woman and her grandmother. For most of the trip, they conversed freely.

The train entered a long and rather dark tunnel. Once inside the tunnel, the passengers in this particular car heard two distinct sounds—the first, a kiss; the second, a loud slap.

Now, the four people in this berth possessed four completely different perspectives on what happened.

The young woman was thinking to herself how glad she was that the young lieutenant got up the courage to kiss her, but she was somewhat disappointed that her grandmother slapped him for doing it.

The general was thinking how proud he was of his young lieutenant for being enterprising enough to take this opportunity to kiss the attractive young woman, but he was flabbergasted that she slapped him instead of the lieutenant.

The grandmother was flabbergasted to think that the young lieutenant would have the gall to kiss her granddaughter, but she was proud of her granddaughter for slapping him in return.

The young lieutenant was trying to hold back his laughter, for he had found the perfect opportunity to kiss an attractive young girl and then slap his superior officer!

—Michael Hodgin

Father, thank you for the unexpected opportunities you place before us. They often surprise us and delight us. But we ask you to give us wisdom from above as we identify which opportunities are good and helpful for us. Then, please help us to use those well to glorify you. Amen.

Waiting for God

Wait patiently for the Lord.
Be brave and courageous.
Yes, wait patiently for the Lord.

PSALM 27:14

I heard recently about a man who was extremely punctual. It was his hallmark. You could set your watch by him because he followed a specific schedule every day.

His alarm sounded at 6:30 a.m. He got up quickly, shaved, showered, ate his breakfast, brushed his teeth, picked up his briefcase, got into his car, drove to the nearby ferry landing, parked his car, rode the ferry across to the downtown business area, got off the ferry, walked smartly to his building, marched to the elevator, rode to the seventeenth floor, hung up his coat, opened his briefcase, spread his papers out on his desk, and sat down in his chair at precisely 8:00 a.m. Not 8:01 or 7:59. Always exactly at 8:00 a.m.

For eight years he followed this routine without variation, until one morning his alarm did not go off, and he overslept by fifteen minutes. When he finally awoke, he panicked. He rushed through his shower, nicked himself shaving, gulped down his breakfast, barely brushed his teeth, grabbed his briefcase, jumped into his car, sped to the ferry landing, jumped out of his car, and looked for the ferry. There it was, already a few feet out from the dock.

I think I can still make it, he said to himself. He ran down the dock at full speed. Reaching the edge of the pier, he gave an enormous leap out over the water and miraculously landed with a loud *thud* on the ferry's deck.

The captain rushed down to make sure he was all right. "Man, that was a tremendous leap!" he exclaimed. "But if you had just waited another minute, we would have reached the dock, and you could have walked on."

Lord, I know that you have a plan for my life. And you know how hard waiting is for me, Father. Please help me to be patient and wait for your timing and your leading so that your plan for me can be successful. I love you, Lord. Amen.

Save Me!

The Lord has heard my weeping.
The Lord has heard my plea;
the Lord will answer my prayer.

PSALM 6:8-9

It was a bright Sunday morning in northern Arkansas, and my friend James was wrapping up his sermon of the day. He had done an excellent job with his topic, he was thinking to himself, when the disruption occurred.

One of the older men in the church had been sitting about halfway back. He and his wife were parents of a tiny, two-year-old surprise package that had been divinely delivered to them later in their lives. The wife was out of town for a day or two, and the husband had spent the entire sermon trying to keep that little bundle of energy under reverent control.

Finally, just as James was ready to make his concluding point, the man could take no more. So he picked up the little girl and started toward the back of the auditorium. Walking out, he had his back to James, but the tot, being carried in typical over-the-shoulder fashion, was facing James.

Now, little Betsy was familiar with this exit routine and fully aware of its coming "reward." So just as her father pushed through the double doors of the auditorium, she threw her arms out to James and wailed plaintively, "Save me!"

The congregation attempted to stifle its laughter, of course, and James later confessed that by that time, the rest of his sermon was strictly anticlimactic.

We could all take a lesson from Betsy, though. When you are up to your ears in trouble in this life and it looks as if the worst is yet to come, don't be afraid to throw your arms out to God and call for help. He will hear you, and he will answer.

Lord, please hold me tightly in your arms throughout my life, and when the end of my earthly life comes, please take me to be with you. You are my only hope and my greatest joy. You are my salvation. I love you, Lord, and I praise your holy name. Amen.

Am I Driving?

Your word is a lamp to guide my feet
and a light for my path.

PSALM 119:105

Does your life sometimes seem as if it is out of control? Does it feel as if someone else is in charge and you are just along for the ride? You do not know where you are headed; you do not know when you will get there; and you do not know in what direction you should even be going.

Well, you are not alone. I think a lot of people feel that way at various times in their lives. And I know personally just how you feel.

The story is told that in Cape Coral, Florida, two elderly women were out driving in a large car; both could barely see over the dashboard.

As they were cruising along, they came to an intersection. The traffic light was red, but they just went on through the light. The woman in the passenger seat thought, *I must be losing my mind; I think we just went through a red light.*

After a few more minutes, they came to another intersection where the light was red. But again they sailed right through it.

This time Bessie, the passenger, was almost sure the light had been red, but she was really concerned that maybe she was mistaken. She was getting nervous and decided to pay very close attention to the road and the next intersection to see what was going on.

Sure enough, the next light was definitely red, and still they sailed right through. Turning to her friend in the driver's seat, Bessie said, "Shirley! Did you know we just ran through three red lights in a row? You could have killed us!"

Shirley turned to her with a look of surprise and said, "Oh, am I driving?"

—Lowell D. Streiker

Dear Father, thank you for being in charge of my life. Help me to remember that life always works better when I let you do the driving. Amen.

What's Your Line?

No one can know a person's thoughts
except that person's own spirit.

1 CORINTHIANS 2:11

Two pictures—which one tells the real story? Imagine each of us on the old television show *What's My Line?* trying to guess who the contestants really are. My Bible study group is ready for this game show.

A group of women were sitting in a circle around me, and I began to analyze them. Ellie is a bright person with bold, big eyes, blonde hair, and an extremely curvaceous figure; perhaps she is an assertive and loud person.

Lee is slim, and everything about her seems more than perfect—graceful smile and speech, an outfit of immaculate style and taste on a perfect figure. She has an amazing necklace collection, which she displays regularly. Maybe she is all about herself and being the best.

Holly is quiet and careful about her words and dress. My guess is that she may be judgmental.

Jamie forcefully states her opinions. Perhaps she needs more humility.

After a few months of getting to know these women, I took another look at each of them. Ellie has Scripture in her DNA. I listen in rapt attention as she boldly shares her faith.

Lee, the fashion plate, is the kindest, gentlest person on earth and has some self-esteem issues. I can cry on her shoulder if I need to.

Holly is the most accepting person I know.

Jamie, who has been widowed twice, just tries to find her voice again after tragedy by sharing her thoughts a lot.

It was then I finally realized that my Bible study group is a "gotcha" trick of God. He put a group together that no one could know just from looking at its outside cover.

Before we jump to conclusions about others, we need to take time to discover what's on the inside.

—Diane E. Kay

Father, help me to see your genius in the wonder and variety of people you bring into my life. Please make me humble and able to see others as better than I am. Amen.

Staying Over until Sunday

Fix your thoughts on what is true, and honorable, and right, and pure, and lovely, and admirable. Think about things that are excellent and worthy of praise.

PHILIPPIANS 4:8

George was walking along the street in Colorado Springs, Colorado, one day on his way to his weekly meeting of the Kiwanis Club. It was a glorious fall day. The chill of coming winter was in the air, a slight breeze was blowing, and the sun was reluctantly giving up the blue sky to encroaching gray clouds.

Then George noticed an old man coming toward him from the edge of town. He looked as if he had just wandered down from the mountains. He was dressed in his Sunday finest, and he was carrying a big Bible under his arm.

"Hey, Samuel, old friend, what's happening? Where are you headed all dressed up fit to kill?"

"Oh, hey, George. I've been hearing about New Orleans, and I'm thinking of going on down there. I hear there's a lot of free-runnin' liquor and a lot of real good—or maybe I should say *bad*—shows."

George looked him over and said, "But Samuel, if you're really thinking about going to New Orleans for all the bad things there, why are you taking your Bible with you?"

Samuel looked up with a mischievous grin on his face and said, "Well, if it's as good as they say it is, I might just stay over until Sunday!"

Sunday-only Christianity. It is a malady many folks suffer from, isn't it? We like to keep our toes in both worlds, even though the Bible cautions us against that. We can overcome this tendency by concentrating on "what is true, and honorable, and right, and pure, and lovely, and admirable." Then we can become Sunday-through-Saturday Christians.

O Lord, help me to concentrate on you and your Word and not be pulled away by thinking about foolish things. I love you, Lord. Amen.

January 30

Cleansing and Clothespins

Let us go right into the presence of God with sincere hearts fully trusting him. For our guilty consciences have been sprinkled with Christ's blood to make us clean, and our bodies have been washed with pure water.

HEBREWS 10:22

Grabbing the plastic coffee container filled with food scraps from its hiding place under the sink, I headed to the backyard to empty it into the compost bin. As I went through the utility room, I set the compost can atop the dryer and stopped to add fabric softener to the washing machine.

Then, grabbing my red container, I went out the back door and headed across the yard. I yanked open the lid of the compost bin. Its depths teemed with little creatures scurrying to and fro through the debris. I popped off the container's black lid and without a second glance dumped its contents inside.

Clothespins rained down on the decaying vegetable matter and squirming insects. I recoiled in disgust, then leaned forward to get a closer look. I had grabbed the wrong container! I *needed* those clothespins.

Careful not to touch the slimy mess, I retrieved every wooden pin. I hosed them off, then doused them with bleach water to disinfect them. After spreading them on an old towel to dry, I retrieved my compost container and carried it to the compost bin. This time I looked twice before I emptied it.

God cares for people immeasurably more than I care about my clothespins. He rescues us from the filth and decay of sin and cleanses us of all unrighteousness when we turn to him. And he does it over and over again, demonstrating his unbounded love.

—*Mary A. Hake*

Dear Lord, thank you for forgiving me and cleansing me from sin. Help me to live a life pleasing to you and to be strong when faced with temptations to sin. I want to remain clean and pure for your glory. Amen.

Good Morning, Master Jesus!

It will happen in a moment, in the blink of an eye, when the last trumpet is blown.

1 CORINTHIANS 15:52

Abraham Lincoln, the only US president who is considered a natural humorist, told many funny stories to illustrate points in the speeches he made and in conversations with other politicians, friends, and family. He once related this story:

A hot-air balloon ascension occurred in New Orleans, Louisiana, before the War between the States began. After sailing in the air for several hours, the aeronaut, who was bedecked in bright-colored silks and sparkling spangles like a circus performer, descended in his giant balloon onto the cotton field of a large plantation where a group of slaves were hard at work picking cotton.

The frightened slaves, who had never seen anything like this amazing balloon before, took to the woods in alarm—all but one venerable old man who had rheumatism and could not run.

Frozen in place and seeing the resplendent balloonist having apparently just dropped straight out of heaven, the old man grinned broadly and hailed the strange visitor from the sky with the cry, "Good mornin', Massa Jesus! How's yo' pa?"

Someday the resplendent Jesus will indeed descend unexpectedly straight out of heaven. Like the old slave, we will be frozen in place by the surprise and thrill of it all. But if we are ready for Jesus' return, we will, no doubt, shout with joy, "Good morning, Master Jesus!"

What a glorious day that will be!

Lord, although we can't know the day or the hour of your return, please make us ready to meet you. We can't wait to see you in all your majesty and splendor and to be in your presence, surrounded by your glory. Please come quickly! We love you, Lord. Amen.

February 1

Where Is God?

My enemies continually taunt me, saying,
"Where is this God of yours?"

PSALM 42:3

A couple had two little boys, ages eight and ten, who were extremely mischievous. The two were always getting into trouble, and their parents could be sure that if any mischief occurred in their town, their two young sons were in some way involved. The parents were at their wits' end as to what to do about their sons' behavior.

The mother had heard that a clergyman in town had been successful in disciplining children in the past, so she asked her husband if he thought they should send the boys to speak with him.

The husband said, "We might as well. We need to do something before I really lose my temper!"

The clergyman agreed to speak with the boys, but he asked to see them individually. The eight-year-old went to meet with him first. The clergyman sat the boy down and asked him sternly, "Where is God?"

The boy made no response, so the clergyman repeated the question in an even sterner tone, "Where is God?"

Again the boy made no attempt to answer. So the clergyman raised his voice even more and shook his finger in the boy's face, "*Where is God?*"

At that the boy bolted from the room and ran straight home, slamming himself in the closet. His older brother followed him into the closet and said, "What happened?"

The younger brother replied, "We are in *big* trouble this time. God is missing, and they think *we* did it!"

God often seems to be missing in our world today too. I wonder if we, as silent Christians, did it.

—*J. John and Mark Stibbe*

Father, please help me to open my mouth and speak up when others are trying to make you disappear. Without you in our world, we are lost indeed. Give me courage, Father. And help me to remember that you are always with me in what I say and how I live. Amen.

Surprise!

Those who worship the Lord on a special day do it to honor him. . . . [Whatever we do,] it's to honor the Lord.

ROMANS 14:6, 8

Over breakfast one morning, Jenny said to her husband, Rhett, "I'll bet you don't know what day this is."

"Of course I do," Rhett answered, as if he were offended.

"Really? Okay, so what day is it?" she teased.

Thinking he had forgotten some important date, such as their anniversary or Jenny's birthday, Rhett scrambled around and said, "Well, if *you* don't know, I'm certainly not going to tell you." And he left for work.

Jenny grinned as he left, knowing full well that he had no idea what special day it really was.

About ten thirty in the morning, the doorbell rang, and when Jenny opened the door, she was handed a box containing a dozen long-stemmed red roses.

Early in the afternoon, a foil-wrapped, two-pound box of Jenny's favorite chocolates arrived.

Later, a boutique delivered a designer dress in just the right size and color for Jenny, along with a card inviting her to dinner at the restaurant where Jenny and Rhett had become engaged.

Jenny could hardly wait for Rhett to come home from work. When he did, she ran into his arms with a huge smile.

"Honey, first the flowers, then the chocolates, and then the dress and dinner invitation!" she exclaimed. "Wow! I've never had a more wonderful Groundhog Day in my life!"

Father, thank you for the laughter and surprises you place in my days. Please help me to share that joy with others today. Amen.

Out of Sight

Nothing in all creation is hidden from God.
Everything is naked and exposed before his eyes,
and he is the one to whom we are accountable.

HEBREWS 4:13

Sacha, my two-year-old granddaughter, and her baby brother, Llewellyn, lived with their parents in Lesotho, a small country located inside South Africa. One day their parents went on a shopping expedition, and I had the children to myself for the day.

I put the baby down for a nap and sat Sacha on a pile of cushions on a chair at the dining-room table. I took out my collection of rubber stamps and ink pads and gave her some scrap paper. Soon we were happily creating colorful designs.

Sometime later, the baby started to cry. I moved everything out of Sacha's reach, leaving her with one stamp and one ink pad. I also gave her a clean piece of paper.

"Make something special for Mommy and Daddy," I said. "But don't move until I get back, okay?"

Her red curls bounced as she nodded. Her forehead puckered, and her tongue peeked out from between her lips as she concentrated on inking the stamp.

I changed the baby quickly and hurried back to the table with him in my arms. Sacha, her cheeks flushed, was scrambling back onto her chair.

"Sacha, what did you do?" I asked.

"Nuffing," she assured me. Then, to be sure I understood, she added, "I didn't stamp under the table!"

I put the baby down and dropped to my knees. Sure enough, the underside of the table was brightly decorated with small red hearts.

Sacha watched me anxiously for a moment and then said, "I did make something special for Mommy and Daddy."

—Shirley M. Corder

Heavenly Father, sometimes I think my sins are so small that no one will notice them, yet I can't hide them from you. Please help me to make something special of my life for you. Amen.

The Whistling Preacher

Take control of what I say, O Lord,
and guard my lips.

PSALM 141:3

When I was in high school, my family lived in a small town in central Texas. The sign at the city limits said, "Welcome to Grandview—home of 964 nice people and one old grouch." (We all knew who the old grouch was, too.)

My dad was the preacher for one of the local churches, and we lived in the preacher's house next door to the church building. Dad also worked part time for the local funeral home. He liked to say he was a full-service preacher—he blessed you at birth, spoke at your graduation, performed your wedding, blessed your children when they were born, preached for you every Sunday, and delivered the eulogy at your funeral.

Dad was an upbeat, cheerful guy who whistled happily most of the time. Mom said if Dad was not whistling, you knew something was wrong.

One day Dad went to the only grocery store in town to get a few things for Mom. He wandered through the aisles, shopping and whistling quietly. Then he took his purchases to the checkout register at the front of the store. Whistling away as he waited for the clerk to total his bill, the boy bagging Dad's groceries started laughing.

"What's so funny, Tommy?" Dad asked, smiling.

"Well, sir, I just thought it was funny to hear a preacher whistling a beer commercial."

Dad stopped whistling. He thought about it for a second and realized he had, indeed, been whistling the Hamm's beer theme song: "From the land of sky blue waters . . ."

Oops!

Father, help me to be careful about what I say and do (and even whistle), knowing that others are always listening to me and watching what I do. I want my life to be a beautiful reflection of your glory, and I need your help to do it. Guard my lips, O Lord. Amen.

February 5

Have a Nice Day

I am convinced that nothing can ever separate us from God's love. Neither death nor life, neither angels nor demons, . . . indeed, nothing in all creation will ever be able to separate us from the love of God that is revealed in Christ Jesus our Lord.

ROMANS 8:38-39

A woman was gliding along the interstate in her new convertible on a relaxing spring evening drive. With the top down and the breeze blowing through her hair, she decided to see just how fast her new car would go.

The speedometer needle jumped to eighty, then ninety, then one hundred miles per hour. Suddenly she saw flashing red-and-blue lights coming up behind her. She sighed and pulled over.

The officer asked for her driver's license and examined it and the car.

"Look," he said wearily, "it's been a very long day. This is the end of my shift, and it's Friday night. I really don't feel like creating more paperwork, so if you can give me an excuse for speeding that I haven't heard before, you can go."

The lady thought for a second. Then she looked up at the officer, smiled, and said, "Last week my husband ran off with one of your lady officers. When I saw your flashing lights, I was afraid she was trying to give him back."

The policeman handed back her license and turned toward his car, saying with a slight smile, "Have a nice night."

Have you ever wondered if God sometimes looks at those of us whom he has rescued from sin, sees us committing the same offenses over and over again, and thinks maybe he should just give us back to the devil? Fortunately for us, he never does. Instead, he continually lavishes his astonishing love on us, renewing his forgiveness and salvation every morning as he says, "Have a nice day."

Father, we do not deserve your patience and long-suffering care, but we accept it greedily, because we know we need it so badly. Thank you for loving us so completely through your Son, Jesus. Amen.

What Powdered-Sugar Doughnuts?

You may be sure that your sin will find you out.

NUMBERS 32:23

I grew up in a family with seven children. Food wasn't necessarily in short supply, but you did not want to wait around for seconds, because there might not be any. And when it came to a delicacy like powdered-sugar doughnuts, a guy could not be too careful.

On one particular day, my mother brought home a big bag of those snow-white temptations. I watched as she opened a cabinet above the kitchen counter and placed the bag on the top shelf.

"Can I have one?" I asked.

Mom shook her head. "They're for tomorrow."

No matter how hard I tried, I could not get those delicacies out of my mind. So later that night, when the house was quiet, I crept into the kitchen, slid a chair over to the counter, climbed up, and opened the cabinet. I felt as if I were cracking a safe. I reasoned that, even if I opened the bag, no one would know who did it, and I could get away with the caper. But who can eat just one powdered-sugar doughnut? I lost count after three.

Then, without warning, all the lights in the kitchen came on. I spun around to see my father standing in the doorway.

He stared up at me as I quivered on the countertop. "What are you doing? Eating the powdered-sugar doughnuts?"

I held out my hands and said, "What doughnuts?"

Unfortunately, there was powdered sugar all over them, my face, and the front of my jeans.

I was so busted!

—Max Elliot Anderson

O Father, please teach me to be transparent today, before you and the others around me. Help me to know that you are aware of everything I do, both good and bad, and that I can never hide my sins from you. Amen.

Serving with Grace

[The Lord said,] "My grace is all you need.
My power works best in weakness."

2 CORINTHIANS 12:9

William was our family's first and only cat, a scrawny fuzz ball of a kitten rescued from behind an auto-parts store. In a rush of sympathy, we adopted him without consulting our miniature dachshund, Alexandra.

At first William caused Alexandra no trouble. He slept in a cardboard box and drank kitty formula from a doll-sized bottle. But when he began stretching his paws to the top of the box, I knew that soon, instead of waiting to be lifted, he would hop out on his own to explore the backyard. *Alexandra*'s backyard. It had always been her exclusive domain, and she was becoming a cranky old lady. I feared for William's safety should he decide to cut his teeth on her tail instead of my beleaguered index finger.

One rainy day I went outside to fetch William for his feeding and found the box empty. I thought the worst when I saw Alexandra across the yard, with four kitty legs and a bedraggled tail hanging from her jaws. My panicked orders, "No! Drop him, Alex!" went unheeded. But before I could get to her, Alex brought William to me, dragging him carefully across the wet grass, his head completely but gently enclosed in her jaws.

Alexandra had no previous experience in motherhood; she just did her best. Though she never got the hang of the scruff-of-the-neck grip, William never seemed to mind her bad breath and the temporary blindness she thrust on him. Until he was taller than she was, whenever Alex decided William needed help, she pulled him to safety—headfirst.

—*Kathleen Brown*

Lord, let me step up each time you call me to serve, even if I feel afraid and unqualified. When the world looks at me, may it see not my fear, but your loving care and grace; not my weakness, but your glorious power at work. Amen.

Lighting My Lamp

I had to talk as though you belonged to this world or as though you were infants in the Christian life. I had to feed you with milk, not with solid food, because you weren't ready for anything stronger. And you still aren't ready.

1 CORINTHIANS 3:1-2

Back in the early days when electricity was first being introduced to a little Scottish village, almost everybody in a particular church switched from their long-used propane lanterns to the new electricity just as soon as it could be hooked up. Most of them could hardly wait to flip the switch for the first time.

However, the oldest couple in the congregation could not get their electricity as quickly as everyone else because they were waiting for the poles to go up and the wire to be strung. So they continued to use their propane lanterns without complaining.

The day finally came when the electricity was brought into their home. Everyone came for the festive event. The old man waited with anticipation for it to get dark; then he told his wife to go turn on the switch. When she did, the bright new electric light filled the room, and everyone cheered.

The old man grinned from ear to ear, picked up a propane lamp, and said, "It sure makes lighting my lamps easier." And with that, he lit one of their old faithful lamps, and then his wife turned off the electricity.

Sometimes we're just like that, aren't we? We resist change, even when change would make life altogether better for us. But life *is* continual change, one day at a time, from the cradle to the grave. And the wise accept the changes for good that come into their lives.

O Lord, help me embrace the changes you send to help me grow up in wisdom and faith. Please give me a double portion of your wisdom so that I will always follow you with joy and hope. Amen.

Laughing in the Pits

Sarah declared, "God has brought me laughter.
All who hear about this will laugh with me."

GENESIS 21:6

When we received an invitation to attend dinner with new church friends, we were asked to bring a fruit salad for twenty-two people.

Watermelons and a bevy of other fruits were purchased. Someone (whose name is not being used, to protect the guilty) decided that because children would be in attendance, we could cut the watermelons in half, hollow out both pieces, save the melon to eat, place cherries in one end, and use the other to capture seed spittings.

The morning of the party we went to the sand dunes and returned home with limited time to get ready to leave for dinner. I finished my shower and found the watermelon more mauled than sliced.

With no time to waste, we grabbed the fruit, threw it into plastic mixing bowls (our only options in our furnished apartment), and then in plastic shopping bags for carrying, and jumped in our filthy car.

On the way, panic set in. What if we were attending a formal dinner party? *Gasp!* By now our son was contemplating exiting the moving car. Surely Martha Stewart would shudder in disgust at our redneck version of a fruit salad.

In a sweat, we hightailed it to the nearest grocery store and bought nice platters and several "real" fruit salads. In the parking lot, we assembled a new, more dignified creation by hiding our mauled melon pieces on the bottom.

We arrived at the host home—an absolutely stunning, huge, gorgeous home with pool and veranda, overlooking a lake with waterfalls. Can you imagine the response if we had walked in with our plastic bags and hollowed-out watermelons and had suggested a cherry-spitting contest?

Later, that evening—home safe and disaster averted—we laughed until our insides hurt.

—Lisa Buffaloe

Father, thank you so much for laughter! Thank you for saving us from making pitiful mistakes. And thank you for forgiving us when we go ahead and make the mistakes anyway. What would we do without you, Lord? Amen.

Life's Rhapsody

The LORD is my strength and my song.

EXODUS 15:2

The fair-haired composer sat at her piano, working carefully on her new and, she hoped, finest rhapsody. The work of composing this piece was not easy; she struggled with the melodies, and the chords did not seem complete somehow. At the end of the frustrating day, the tired young woman laid down her pencil and left the unpolished music on the piano. She sighed as she slowly went to bed, thinking, *It's just not right.*

Later that evening, the composer's old, white-haired father came home and noticed his daughter's work on the piano. Being a composer himself, he sat down and played through his daughter's rhapsody. He smiled because he had taught her to love and write music. Then he took up her pencil and began filling in the missing notes to complete the full, rich chords his daughter had imagined but was unable to write. He worked long into the night adding minor strains and lilting melodies to the music. Finally, with a nod of satisfaction, he left the piece where he had found it and went to bed.

The next morning the daughter sat down at the piano to begin polishing her work from the day before. As she played through the beautiful music, she was amazed at how thrilling it was. She congratulated herself on producing a much more glorious composition than she had remembered from the night before. It was, indeed, the finest rhapsody of her career.

And so it is with life. We compose our lives as we go along, but the strains of a masterpiece are often hindered by our human frailty and weakness. Then the Master Composer comes along and fills in the missing notes. He adds the lilting melodies and minor chords so that the finished life plays like a symphony. He does not write a new song; he just enhances and polishes the basic rhapsody we have written through the years until it is a joy for others to hear.

Thank you, Father, for finishing my song. What more can I say? Amen.

One of the Ten

Peter came to [Jesus] and asked, "Lord, how often should I forgive someone who sins against me? Seven times?"
"No, not seven times," Jesus replied, "but seventy times seven!"

MATTHEW 18:21-22

My mom and dad were happily married for seventy years. They did not argue or fight, and they kept up a continual, affable conversation throughout the day. Dad read to Mom from the newspaper. Mom reminded Dad about things that had happened on that same day in years past from the daily journal she has kept for more than thirty years.

My parents were great forgivers, which is what made it all work for such a long time. Their marriage reminds me of a story pastor and author Paul Lee Tan tells.

At her golden wedding anniversary party a wife told guests the secret of her happy marriage:

"On my wedding day, I decided to make a list of ten of my husband's faults that, for the sake of our marriage, I would overlook."

As the guests were leaving, a young woman whose marriage had recently been experiencing some difficulties asked the older woman what some of the faults were that she had seen fit to overlook.

The older woman said, "To tell you the truth, my dear, I never did get around to actually listing them. But whenever my husband did anything that made me hopping mad, I would say to myself, *Lucky for him that's one of the ten!*"

That woman could have been my mother. Mom and Dad surely understood Jesus' direction about forgiveness, because I'm sure they had to forgive each other more than seven times during every one of their seventy years together.

O Lord, thank you for forgiveness. It is the healing oil that keeps life working smoothly. I pray that I will be more forgiving and that others will forgive me freely, because I know I will always need it. I love you, Lord. Amen.

Is Anybody Listening?

Again [the Lord] listened to me.

DEUTERONOMY 9:19

Public records reveal that President Franklin D. Roosevelt was constantly having to go to large receptions and stand while endless lines of people filed by just to shake his hand and speak a few words to him. This sometimes went on for hours at a time, and the president grew tired and impatient with it. The brief conversations he had with people as they came by were mindless and repetitive.

Finally one evening at such a reception, so the story goes, Roosevelt decided to find out whether people were really paying attention to what he was saying to them as they filed by.

As each person came up to him with extended hand, he flashed that big presidential smile and said, "I murdered my grandmother this morning." Then he smiled again and waited for that person to move on.

As Roosevelt suspected, people automatically and unthinkingly responded with comments such as "How lovely!" or "Continue with your great work!"

Nobody actually seemed to listen to what the president was saying. So Roosevelt continued his game, which added an element of humor and fun to his typically boring routine.

After dozens of people had passed by, one foreign diplomat approached Roosevelt with hand outstretched. Roosevelt said, smiling, "I murdered my grandmother this morning."

Without missing a beat, the diplomat shook Roosevelt's hand and replied, "I'm sure she had it coming."

Do you ever wonder if anybody is listening to you? In our noisy society, it is often difficult to know whether we can be heard over the din of daily life. And yet the Bible assures us that God is always listening to our prayers and the petitions of our hearts. We are never without a listening audience.

O God, thank you for listening to me, even when it seems no one else is. I am so grateful for your constant attention and sweet grace. Help me to listen carefully when you are speaking to me, too. Amen.

February 13

Sing to the Lord

Make a joyful noise unto God, all ye lands!

PSALM 66:1 (KJV)

Our niece Sara was in her pajamas and ready for bed when my husband came home from a long trip. Sara had been looking forward to this evening for weeks. Since Len had been away "supply preaching" every Sunday since she had come to live with us, she was very concerned that he did not go to church as we did. The five-year-old did not understand that when Len, a recent seminary graduate, was away, he was in churches preaching or teaching. She knew only that she liked going to church and her Uncle Len was not enjoying that experience with her.

Sara rearranged the furniture in our living room for a church service of our own. She sat in her little rocking chair and used the footstool as her pulpit. Her Bible storybook was opened to the picture of the baby Moses. She had practiced telling the story from memory while pretending to be reading from her Bible. She would face the chair, which held the congregation of one—Len. I was the choir, sitting in a chair behind her.

At first she asked me to hold the songbook. Then she thought her uncle might want to be included, so she handed the songbook to Len and asked him to lead. But Sara had never heard this notorious monotone sing. After only one verse, in her sweet, innocent way, she took the songbook away, saying, "Uncle Len, I forgot you don't know what we do in church. Maybe Aunt Barbara should lead the singing."

I could laugh, because I was behind her, but Len did not dare laugh, since Sara was so serious. This was the kindest way anyone had ever told him that he had no musical ability.

Fortunately, God doesn't require trained voices. He asks us only to make a joyful *noise* in praise to him, and all people can do that, even if they have no musical talent.

—Barbara Ferguson

Father, thank you for accepting the gratitude of our hearts, even when we lack musical quality. Amen.

Know What Day This Is?

Do to others as you would like them to do to you.

LUKE 6:31

My husband and I had been separated for several months when I realized that Valentine's Day was just a couple of weeks away. Talk about awkward! When two people are separated, they are not really apart, but they are not really together, either. So what is the appropriate thing to do on Valentine's Day—send a card, don't send a card, send a gift, don't send a gift? It's a real head-scratcher.

I contemplated the dilemma for several days. I even asked a friend or two what they thought about it. But an obviously right answer escaped me. Finally, I ran out of time to think about it anymore. I had to make a decision.

Always the optimist, I decided to keep it light. Do something nonthreatening. Don't be maudlin or sentimental. Don't make him feel bad. Don't get mushy or be critical.

I decided not to buy a gift—that seemed just a bit too much, considering the situation. So I went to my favorite Hallmark store to see whether I could find a card that could, in any way, be appropriate. I looked for about half an hour and finally stumbled on one that I thought was perfect.

On the outside of the card was a picture of an ape scratching his (her?) head. Under the picture was the question "Know what day this is?" And on the inside was the answer: "Me neither!" It made me laugh, and I hoped it would make him smile too.

A couple of days before Valentine's Day I addressed the card, signed it, and mailed it to my not-really-ex-yet husband. And for two days I chuckled about the card and his possible reaction.

Then, on Valentine's Day morning, I received a dozen long-stemmed red roses at my office . . .

Dear Father, please help me to show more sensitivity toward the people in my life. Give me wisdom in how I interact with others so that they feel your kindness and care. Amen.

Anatomy 101

You must teach these things . . . to correct [believers] when necessary.

TITUS 2:15

In fourth grade science, my son, Shaefer, spent months studying the human body. One evening we reviewed all the information he had learned.

"Femur, patella, tibia, and fibula," he said, pointing to his leg.

"That's great," I said. "Now what about the bones in the arm?"

He moved his finger down his arm. "Humerus, radius, ulna."

"Good job, Dr. Shaefer," I said, beaming. "Let's go over the digestive system."

Beginning with the mouth, he recited each body part that our food passes through. But when naming the organs south of the belly button, he got stuck.

To unglue his mental block, I asked where the food goes after the small intestine.

After a long pause, his older sister chimed in. "Cologne," she whispered.

"What'd you say?" I asked.

"Cologne. The tube coming from your small intestine."

"It's not pronounced *cologne*," I laughed. "It's colon, *'kō-len.*"

Jumping on the correct-his-sister bandwagon, my son informed her that the tube connected to the intestines is, in fact, the *sarcophagus*, not the colon.

"And in case you didn't know, that thingy at the back of the throat is called your *anus*," he said, laughing.

Confusion unleashed, Celeste fervently disagreed while I tried to regain control of the science lesson gone awry.

"You guys, stop!" I opened the science book, pointing out the path that food travels through the body.

"It passes the *uvula* after you swallow, then goes down the *e-e-e-sophagus*, not the *sarcophagus*, see."

We followed the food trail until it reached the *'kō-len*, then out the body through the *anus*. Shaefer giggled at that word, as he always did.

Thinking the anatomy lesson was over, my daughter pointed to her forearm.

"Hey, Mom, that was really *humerus*, wasn't it?"

—Christine Thomas

Lord, when I pray, help me to get the words right. May I not spend all my time asking for things I think I need. But when I forget and do that, please gently impress upon me your will. Amen.

How to Fix a Ford

I was a stranger, and you invited me into your home.

MATTHEW 25:35

The great carmaker Henry Ford once traveled to Dublin, Ireland, on an extended vacation. He enjoyed the glory of the vibrant-green Emerald Isle, the standard tourist sites, and the wonderful food prepared by local cooks and chefs. Before he left, he also paid a visit to an orphanage where a building project was being planned.

Hearing that Henry Ford, who was both famous and rich, was coming for a visit, the director of the fund-raising committee for the orphanage decided to pay him a call. Ford welcomed him. After their discussion, Ford decided the project was indeed a worthy one, and he took out his checkbook and gave the man a check for an amount equal to two thousand British pounds. In those days, two thousand pounds was quite a generous gift, and the man thanked him profusely.

In fact, Ford's generosity was so unusual that it made the headlines in the local Irish newspaper. There was just one problem: The paper reported, "Ford Gave 20,000 Pounds to Local Orphanage."

Embarrassed by the huge mistake, the director of the orphanage called Mr. Ford to apologize. In fact, he offered, "I'll be happy to phone the newspaper editor right away and ask them to print a retraction."

Ford knew a retraction would be a bit awkward, and perhaps he felt a little guilty. So he said there was no need for the retraction. Instead, with a sigh, he took out his checkbook again and said to the director, "I'll give you a check for the remaining eighteen thousand pounds." But he added one request. "When the new building opens, I want this inscription put on it: 'I was a stranger and you took me in.'"

O Lord, I know that you are the most generous benefactor ever. You lavish your wonderful blessings on us every day. Please help me to reflect your glory into the dark corners of the world by being generous too. Amen.

Who's Steering This Thing, Anyway?

Remember that you also have a Master—in heaven.

COLOSSIANS 4:1

One of my favorite quotes is an old Jewish proverb that says, "If you want to give God a good laugh, tell him your plans." In other words, we are not in charge of our lives. Unfortunately, most people seem to think they are, and they give God little credit for being the Master of the universe.

That reminds me of a newly elected politician who was visiting Washington, DC, to get his bearings before moving there to take office. During his visit he had dinner in the home of one of the longtime senior senators. After dinner, they walked outside to the edge of the Potomac River and stood there, taking in the familiar sites of the nation's capital and talking about the wonder of it.

From where they stood, they could see several landmarks, including the Capitol building, that instill a feeling of quiet awe and wonder in those who view them. As they watched the powerful river flowing by, the senator pointed out a rotten log.

The old-timer said, "This city is like that log out there."

The fledgling politician asked, "How's that, Senator?"

The senator replied, "Well, there are probably more than a hundred thousand grubs, ants, bugs, and critters riding along on that old log as it floats down the river. And that river is taking that log straight to the ocean, where it will likely be lost forever. But I imagine every one of those critters thinks he's steering it."

O Lord, I know that you are the Creator and Master of the world and of my life. I give you praise and glory for your astonishing works. And I willingly place my life in your hands. Please guide me, protect me, and love me, Lord. Amen.

No Quitter

I will tell of the LORD's unfailing love.
I will praise the LORD for all he has done.

ISAIAH 63:7

My great-aunt May was in her late eighties when her husband, my uncle Frank, died. And because they had no children, she had to move into a nursing home for her remaining years.

Aunt May was no quitter. She never quit on my uncle Frank, even when he was ill for several years before he died. And she did not quit on life when she moved into the nursing home. She was always happy and laughing when I went to see her. I would stop in, thinking I would cheer her up, but I always came away encouraged myself.

After a few months in the nursing home, Aunt May and an elderly gentleman there became interested in each other. And at ages ninety and eighty-eight, they decided to get married. They held the ceremony in the large living room of the nursing home, and my preacher dad performed the wedding. It was a happy time for everyone, especially Aunt May.

Since Aunt May and her new husband had separate rooms, the director of the nursing home decided something should be done about that. So to celebrate their marriage, the director hired some workers to take out the wall between the two rooms, creating one large suite for the two of them.

Somehow the local newspaper found out about the event, and on the following Sunday a large photo of Aunt May and my new uncle in their suite appeared on its front page. They were both grinning, as my dad would say, "like a mule eating briars."

Father, thank you for your unfailing love. I am so grateful that love is ageless. I pray that I will emulate your sweet love to others. Amen.

Standing In for God

[He] is the messenger of the LORD of Heaven's Armies.

MALACHI 2:7

An active member of the United States Marine Corps was attending some college courses between deployments. He had completed extended missions in both Iraq and Afghanistan and expected to return to the Middle East in a few weeks. One of the courses he was taking was taught by a professor who was an avowed atheist.

One day the professor shocked the class when he came into the room, looked up at the ceiling, and issued this challenge: "God, if you are real, then I want you to knock me off this platform. I will give you exactly fifteen minutes." The lecture room fell silent. You could have heard a pin drop.

Ten long minutes dragged by and nothing happened. Then the professor stood up, held out his arms, and proclaimed, "Here I am, God. I'm still waiting."

It had finally come down to the last couple of minutes when the marine suddenly got out of his chair, walked to the front of the room, and clobbered the professor in finest marine fashion, knocking him completely off the platform and onto the floor. The professor was out cold.

The marine went back to his seat and sat there silently, waiting. The other students were dumbstruck and looked on in silent anticipation of what would happen when the professor woke up.

The professor eventually regained consciousness. Noticeably shaken, he got to his feet as he rubbed his bruised jaw, looked at the marine, and asked, "What is the matter with you? Why did you do that?"

The marine calmly replied, "God was busy protecting American soldiers, who are protecting your right to say stupid stuff and act like an idiot. So he sent me to stand in for him."

Father, if the time ever comes for me to act as your messenger in this world, please give me the courage and faith to do it without question. I want to be your faithful servant. Amen.

Grandma-saurus

Gray hair is a crown of glory;
it is gained by living a godly life.

PROVERBS 16:31

They say parents are the first educators, and I agree. But as a grandmother of five, I like to think grandparents can get a few lessons in, too, before the children's formal schooling begins. When I watch our grandson, Sam, and his little sister, I make sure we talk about colors, numbers, nature, and music.

Sam is a quick study with a great attention span, and he also has the ability to retain all the details of his favorite subjects. When he loved trains, he knew about coal tenders, the difference between diesel and steam engines, and the names and functions of all his plastic train cars. Next came pirates, then airplanes, and most recently dinosaurs. He knew about books, movies, and computer games with dinosaur themes. This included knowing the various dinosaurs' names and weights, whether they were herbivores or carnivores, and in what time periods—Jurassic, Triassic, or Cretaceous—they had lived. Smart boy!

One day on our way to the library, I was lamenting that he would soon be in kindergarten and how much I would miss him. But I also told him he would be learning more things than he could ever imagine.

"Oh, Sam," I said, "you're going to learn so much in kindergarten. You'll know more than Grandma ever knew, from day one!"

There was a thoughtful pause from the backseat of the car, and then he responded, "Grandma, I think it will be day ten. You're pretty smart."

I'm sure going to miss him.

—Susan Sundwall

Father, help me to remember that old age is a gift and to humbly see the blessing and wonder of young lives around me. Help me to welcome gray hair as it comes my way and to see it as a blessing from you. In Jesus' sweet name, amen.

Comfort Zone

Do not be stubborn . . . but submit yourselves to the Lord.

2 CHRONICLES 30:8

I was eating dinner with my dad and several other family members one night, when he broached the subject of Internet connections.

"When I try to send an e-mail, I keep getting this error message that something has reached capacity," he said.

Everybody else kept eating; maybe they were thinking or trying to figure out the problem.

"The hamster gets tired, so he gets off the wheel," I explained.

He looked at me. "What are you talking about?"

"When the hamster gets tired, he gets off the wheel, and that dial-up service you have goes down until he rests up and gets back on the wheel." I took another bite.

"What can I do?"

"Get another Internet provider. That way you can get a DSL and download attachments, something the hamster won't let you do now."

He took another couple of bites. "Will it cost more than eight dollars a month for me to change?"

"Yes."

"No way."

"Okay, but one day the hamster will die, and you will have *no* Internet service."

I just love that look he gives me—the "why did I ask her when it's only going to end up costing me more money" look.

I understand his reluctance. A new provider would take him out of his comfort zone. He would have to learn new tricks, new ways of doing things. But isn't that what God wants, too—to roust us out of our comfort zones so that we have only his hand to guide us? He wants us to depend totally on him, not on ourselves.

—*Stevie Stevens*

Father, take me out of my comfort zone more often so that I can reach more people with your love and mercy. And, Lord, please make me more willing to go wherever you lead me. Amen.

Who's That Knocking?

Look! I stand at the door and knock. If you hear my voice and open the door, I will come in, and we will share a meal together as friends.

REVELATION 3:20

Donna was a pediatric nurse who worked in one of the children's wards in a large hospital. She loved her work, and she adored the children she treated every day. They added such life and delight to her days, and she thrilled at seeing them get well and go home.

As the children's nurse, she often had to use her stethoscope to listen to their lungs and hearts. So that the kids would not feel frightened by the stethoscope, before Donna used it, she would ask if they would like to listen first. Then she would put the earpieces in their ears and let them hear their own hearts beating. Their eyes would light up in surprise and awe, and she would get excited responses.

"Wow! What's that?"

"It sounds like someone's playing a drum."

"Is there a woodpecker in there?"

One day she let little four-year-old David listen to his heart. She gently tucked the stethoscope into his tiny ears and placed the round disk on his chest over his heart.

"Listen, David," she said quietly. "What do you hear? What do you suppose that is?"

Concentrating really hard, little David pulled his eyebrows together in a puzzled look and stared up at the ceiling as if lost in the mystery and wonder of the soft tap, tap, tapping. Then, suddenly, a huge grin broke out on his cherubic face, and he asked excitedly, "Is that Jesus knocking on the door of my heart?"

Father, I pray that I will constantly listen for your gentle tapping on the door of my heart. Help me to open that door and daily welcome you into my life. I can't make it without you, Lord. Amen.

Camels

"I know the plans I have for you," says the LORD. "They are plans for good and not for disaster, to give you a future and a hope."

JEREMIAH 29:11

One of my favorite quotations is from Isaac Bashevis Singer: "Life is God's novel. Let him write it." And it seems to me that life would run a lot better if each of us could only do what God, in his great wisdom, planned for us to do.

For instance, a mother camel and her offspring were talking one day when the young camel asked, "Mom, why do I have these huge three-toed feet?"

The mother replied, "Well, Son, when we trek across the desert, your toes will help you stay on top of the soft sand."

"Okay," said the son.

A few minutes later, the son asked, "Mom, why do I have these great long eyelashes?"

"They are there to keep the sand out of your eyes on the trips through the desert."

"Thanks, Mom," replied the son.

After a short while, the son returned and asked, "Mom, why do I have these great big humps on my back?"

The mother, now a little impatient with all the boy's questions, replied, "They are there to help us store water for our treks across the desert so we can go without drinking for long periods of time and not get thirsty."

"That's great, Mom. So we have huge feet to stop us from sinking into the sand, long eyelashes to keep the sand out of our eyes, and these humps to store water for long trips in the desert, right?"

"Yes, Son, that's right."

"Well, then, why in the world are we living in the San Diego Zoo?"

Father, I'm thankful that you already know the path I am on. Please help me to follow your lead and trust that you know what is best. Amen.

A Dog Named Cool Whip

The LORD came down in the cloud and stood there with Moses, and the LORD called out his name: the LORD.

EXODUS 34:5 (NCV)

All right," his mother said, relenting. "You can keep a puppy. But just one."

A litter of seven small puppies nuzzled next to their mother, Duchess, a registered gold-and-white collie. Duchess had been bred so that the family would benefit from the extra money the puppies would bring. Eleven-year-old Ryan protested as soon as he saw the newborn creatures.

"You can't sell them! You just can't," he protested.

Even though the puppies would go to good homes, it would indeed be hard to let them go. Ryan was close to tears, and so his mother's heart softened. She finally agreed to let him keep one of the puppies as his very own.

Kneeling next to Duchess, Ryan cupped one of the small animals in his hands. Duchess allowed him to hold each one until he decided which he would keep.

"This is the one," he said, holding a fine male with the same beautiful coloring as Duchess.

Ryan's mother agreed that this puppy would not be sold and would belong to Ryan. "What about a name?" she asked.

Without hesitation Ryan replied, "Cool Whip. I am going to call him Cool Whip!"

A smile on her lips, his mother had to ask the obvious question: "Why would you name a dog Cool Whip?"

"Because," Ryan answered calmly, "I've always wanted a dog that had his name on his bowl!"

Ryan was right—calling people, animals, and other things by their correct names is very important.

—*Cathy Phillips*

O Lord, your name is the greatest name of all, and I want my words and my life to bring honor and praise to your holy name. Help me, Lord, to remember to call things that you do in my life by the right name—not coincidence or fate, but blessings from your hand. Amen.

February 25

To Kiss a Frog

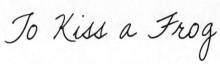

Greet each other with Christian love.

1 PETER 5:14

Do you ever feel like a frog? Frogs feel slow, low, ugly, puffy, drooped, pooped. I know. One told me.

The frog feeling comes when you want to be bright but feel dumb; when you want to share but are selfish; when you want to be thankful but feel resentment; when you want to be great but are small; when you want to care but are indifferent. Yes, at one time or another each of us has found himself on a lily pad, floating down the great river of life. Frightened and disgusted, we are too froggish to budge.

Once upon a time there was a frog, only he was not really a frog; he was a prince who looked and felt like a frog. The wicked witch had cast a spell on him, and only the kiss of a beautiful maiden could save him. But since when do cute chicks kiss frogs? So there he sat, an unkissed prince in frog form.

One day a beautiful maiden gathered him up and gave him a big smack! *Zap!* There he was, a frog turned handsome prince, and they lived happily ever after.

So what is the task of the Christian? Kissing frogs, of course!

Well-known minister Rick Atchley says, "Jesus didn't come to make freaks out of people; he came to make people out of freaks." And each of us, as sinners, is a freak (or frog) until we are kissed by the love of Jesus Christ, touched by his grace and beauty, redeemed and blessed. Then, and only then, can we look into the mirror and see a prince or princess who reflects the glory of Christ.

So, pucker up, honey! Get out there and kiss a few frogs for the Lord.

—Bruce Larson

O Lord, I love you, and I want to help you touch the lives of sinners and help to draw them into your Kingdom of love. Please give me the courage to share your love with others. Amen.

Read the Instructions? You're Kidding!

All Scripture is inspired by God and is useful to teach us what is true and to make us realize what is wrong in our lives. It corrects us when we are wrong and teaches us to do what is right.

2 TIMOTHY 3:16

My husband's work shift begins at 5 a.m. Since we can easily sleep through regular alarms, I bought a talking alarm clock, thinking a soothing voice would awaken us.

After reading the first page of the lengthy instructions, Bernie tossed them aside and said, "Hello, clock."

"Say a command," replied a mechanical voice.

"Set alarm for 4 a.m."

"Alarm set," a female voice cooed.

The next morning at 4 a.m., we were startled awake. "Wake up! Beep, beep! Four a.m."

"I'm up," grumbled Bernie. The clock repeated its chant.

"Turn that thing off," I snarled.

"Shut up, clock!" Bernie yelled. As an afterthought, he added, "Please."

As the clock squawked messages, I stumbled across the room for the instructions. After several minutes, I said, "Turn off the alarm now."

"Alarm off." The clock was silent.

"When all else fails, read the instructions" is a clever motto that applies not only to gizmos but also to our lives. When stress and problems overwhelm us, we moan, seek the advice of friends, and scream that life is not fair, instead of reading the Bible, God's instruction manual for our lives. His Word, as spoken through the prophets, apostles, and his only Son, Jesus, will comfort and guide us in all situations.

Don't wait until life is out of control and screaming like a pesky alarm clock before you seek God's answers. Begin each day by seeking God's guidance and reading his instructions and end the day with a prayer of thanks and praise.

—*Rebecca Willman Gernon*

Heavenly Father, too often I think I can manage my life without reading your Word. Increase my desire to let your wisdom guide my life by daily reading of the Bible. Amen.

With Love to Jennifer

Be kind to each other.

EPHESIANS 4:32

In about 1970 singer Pat Boone came to Abilene Christian University to do a concert. A girl named Jennifer in my dorm was absolutely *nuts* about Pat. She even had a huge photograph of him hanging in her room over her bed.

Pat was coming to our dormitory to lead our evening devotional after his concert. As president of the dorm, it was my privilege to meet him and guide him to the parlor for the devotional. The other 360 girls in the dorm were all atwitter.

When Pat arrived, I told him about Jennifer and the photograph. He asked where her room was, and since it was near the parlor, I took him there first. I used my master key to let him in. He got on his knees on her bed and autographed the photograph with something like "With love to Jennifer. Your boy, Pat." He loved doing it, and I thought it was a very kind thing for him to do.

When the devotional time was over, Jennifer was ecstatic at having seen her hero. I followed her back to her room, wanting to see what she would do when she saw the newly autographed photo. Before she even saw the beloved photograph, she threw herself down on her bed, kicked her feet, and screamed like a little child. Then she glanced up at the photo, did a double take, and froze. She slowly got to her knees and read the inscription. Then, realizing he had actually knelt on her bed to sign the photo, she fainted dead away. It was several minutes before she came to.

I think it was also several months before she washed her bedspread. She was both horrified and happy! And I suspect Pat had a good laugh for a few days too.

Father, thank you for the many kindnesses you do for me every day. I am grateful to you for your generous blessings. They add such richness to my days, and my life would not be the same without them. Amen.

Number, Please

Be humble, thinking of others as better than yourselves.

PHILIPPIANS 2:3

As humorist Robert Henry walked up to a counter, he noticed that he was the only customer in the store. Behind the counter were two salespersons. One was so preoccupied talking to "Mama" on the telephone that she refused to acknowledge that Robert was there.

At the other end of the counter, a second salesperson was unloading inventory from a box onto the shelves. Beginning to grow impatient, Robert walked down to her end of the counter and just stood there. Finally she looked up at Robert and said, "You got a number?"

"Do I have a what?" asked Robert, trying to control his astonishment at such an absurdity.

"You got a number? You gotta have a number."

Robert replied, "Lady, I'm the only customer in the store! I don't need a number. Can't you see how ridiculous this is?"

But she failed to see the absurdity and insisted that Robert take a number before agreeing to wait on him.

By now, it was obvious to Robert that she was more interested in following procedure than in helping a customer. So he went to the take-a-number machine, pulled off number 37, and walked back to the salesperson.

At that, she promptly went to her number counter, which revealed that the last customer waited on had been holding number 34. She screamed out, "35! . . . 35! . . . 36! . . . 36! . . . 37!"

"I'm number 37," said Robert.

"May I help you?" she asked, without cracking a smile.

"No," replied Robert, and he turned around and walked out.

—Michael LeBoeuf

O Lord, thank you for always being there when I need your special attention. I am grateful that I don't need to take a number and wait in line before you tune your ear to my every need and prayer. Please help me to listen to others when they need my attention, too, so that I can show them your love and care. Amen.

The Race

Let us run with endurance the race
God has set before us.

HEBREWS 12:1

My friend challenged our grandma-filled Sunday school class to enter a race that would raise funds to help feed the homeless. After checking to make certain we would be allowed to walk the one-mile segment instead of run it, we accepted her challenge.

Since all good athletes spend time training before an event, we came up with a plan. My friend lives a half mile from McDonald's. Meeting at her house and then walking to the restaurant and back would be the perfect workout for us. On two occasions we walked, treated ourselves to senior coffees, and visited. It took two hours—one and a half to visit and savor our coffee, and thirty minutes to walk.

Race day arrived, and six of us loaded into our vehicles and headed to the event. Arriving forty-five minutes early, we stood in line to register as our teeth chattered from the cold. We had not counted on how harsh the morning wind would be. As soon as we had our T-shirts and our big blue numbers, we raced back to our cars to warm up. We eagerly layered on our new shirts for added warmth and helped one another pin our numbers on our backs. We really looked official!

Then, as we sat inside our cars and watched other people fight the cold, we began to dread leaving our warm spots. Fortunately, our "training" kicked in. Hot coffee was what we craved, so we ditched the race and headed to McDonald's. *Un*fortunately, as we sat inside the restaurant, still wearing our T-shirts and numbers and enjoying our coffee and fellowship, people looked at us and smiled—and one person even congratulated us on running the race. Uh-oh!

—*Pam Whitley*

O Lord, may I never just look as if I'm in the race—the race you have set before me. Instead, let me be running with all my heart. And may I never allow myself to be detoured by the difficulties of life. Amen.

Soggy Seats

Now we see things imperfectly, like puzzling reflections in a mirror, but then we will see everything with perfect clarity.

1 CORINTHIANS 13:12

Seated in the church service beside my son's family, I watched proudly as the baptistery curtains opened. There stood blond-haired, seven-year-old Jack, looking quite angelic in his white baptismal robe. I cried with joy at seeing my firstborn grandson declare his faith.

His four-year-old brother, Will, seated next to me, was proud too, but for different reasons. He wanted to know all about how Jack had gotten up there in that water. His parents had tried to prepare Will for the service, but obviously he had not understood. He did, however, think he would like to get in that water sometime too.

When the baptism was over, Jack came and sat next to me, and my son took Will back to the nursery. At the end of the service, I planned to take their family out to eat to celebrate Jack's baptism.

As the last song concluded, Jack looked up at me and asked innocently, "Mimi, can I get some dry underwear before we go eat?"

He had not pulled off his wet undies following the baptism. No wonder he had squirmed throughout the whole service!

I told my son about the crisis, and Jack and I headed off in search of "drier ground" while my son went to get Will. Jack was usually with his parents when they picked up Will, so on this day when they arrived without Jack, Will looked at them matter-of-factly and asked, "Jack gone to heaven?"

—*Pam Whitley*

O God, may I be as trusting as Will when I do not understand your ways. Please help me to see you and your plan for me more clearly as I mature. I want to be perfect in your sight, Lord, and I want to spend eternity with you in heaven. I love you, Lord. Amen.

The Frantic Fowl

The temptations in your life are no different from what others experience. And God is faithful. He will not allow the temptation to be more than you can stand. When you are tempted, he will show you a way out so that you can endure.

1 CORINTHIANS 10:13

The day had been hot and tiring, and my wife and I were looking forward to a good night's sleep. Being Tasmanians on a short-term mission project in northern Ghana was a "climate change" experience. Sleep was intermittent at best, but as the sun was waking up, even our rest was shattered. A frantic, screeching guinea fowl was just outside our window.

Stumbling to the window and rubbing my bleary eyes, I saw the bird running up and down the wire fence seeking an escape hole. The panic was not caused by human activity. Rather, I spied three vultures on a tall tree stump looking intently at the distressed bird. From our vantage point, we could see what the bird could not: Just beyond the length it had run was a huge break in the fence.

My going out to help the bird find the hole seemed to make it more frightened. Perhaps it thought I wanted it for the cooking pot. Finally, after some frustration, I herded it toward and through the gap. Freedom for the bird! Silence for us. Disappointment for the vultures.

Later I reflected on the times I have felt as the guinea fowl did. In my panic over some issue, I have run about aimlessly squawking, if not aloud, definitely in my soul, not seeing the "hole" that will solve my problem. I wonder how much interrupted sleep I have caused others by my fretting and lack of trust in the faithfulness of the Lord?

—Raymond N. Hawkins

Lord, when the spirit of that frantic fowl stirs within, may I put it on the chopping block! Don't let it blind me to your answers or directions, please. Amen.

Request a Shower from God

Let us go right into the presence of God with sincere hearts fully trusting him. For our guilty consciences have been sprinkled with Christ's blood to make us clean, and our bodies have been washed with pure water.

HEBREWS 10:22

When my son Micah was four, he did not like it when I took showers because he could not be with me. He complained each morning and sat outside the bathroom door waiting for me and calling, "Are you done yet?"

One morning as I headed to the bathroom, he asked, "Why do you have to take showers anyway?"

I responded, "We take showers to stay clean and smell nice."

He seemed satisfied with that answer. He lay down on the floor outside the bathroom, pushing a Hot Wheels car in and out under the bathroom door while he waited. After my shower, Micah and I went on with our day, and I completely forgot about the morning's exchange.

That evening at bedtime, we finished our story, and then he prayed, "Dear God, thank you for today. Thank you for all my things. Please help Mommy to stay clean and smell nice. Amen."

Ah, yes, there is more than one way to solve a problem, and there is nothing like going straight to the source for answers. We were created by God, so surely he can keep us clean. Even though physical life does not work quite that way, I had to admire Micah's sincere heart and how he fully trusted God with his problem. I only hope I can be half as relaxed in my relationship with God as Micah is in his relationship with the Creator.

—*Janelle Shantz Hertzler*

Dear God, I pray that you will help me to come into your presence with a sincere heart, fully trusting in you. Help me to remember that I can bring all my problems to you because you care for me. Amen.

Moving

The LORD had said to Abram, "Leave your native country, your relatives, and your father's family, and go to the land that I will show you." . . . So Abram departed as the LORD had instructed. . . . Abram was seventy-five years old when he left Haran.

GENESIS 12:1, 4

Moving is something I know intimately, having moved almost thirty times in my life. I can remember my minister dad coming home one day and asking my mom if she could be ready to move in three days. She never flinched but said, "Well, I guess so, if that's what we need to do."

Moving always makes me think of Sarah, the time when Abraham came home and said, "Honey, guess what? We're moving."

Now, to a desert nomad, moving was really nothing new, but this time was different.

"Really?" says she. "Why?"

"Well, I don't really know."

"When?"

"In three days."

"Three days! Where are we going?"

"I don't know that, either."

"When will the moving vans arrive?"

"Uh, that's a bit ahead of our time, sweetheart. You'll have to load everything on the camels."

"You're kidding, right?"

"Uh, no."

"And just exactly what made you decide to do this crazy thing, Abraham?"

"God told me to."

"Oh." Pause . . . two . . . three. "Okay, please back that camel up to the front door!"

When God tells us to "move," we need to get packing!

Father, help me to always be ready to move when you urge me to do it. I know you're either moving me away from something I need to leave, or you're moving me toward a place I need to be. Help me to follow your lead and to go willingly. Thank you, Lord. Amen.

The Rs Have It

You will show me the way of life,
granting me the joy of your presence
and the pleasures of living with you forever.

PSALM 16:11

I sat with my friend Maria, planning the Sunday-morning worship service for the upcoming women's retreat. Things seemed to be falling into place. However, the most bizarre thing kept happening. Words beginning with the letter *r* were finding their way into the conversation.

"Maria, do you see and hear what is going on here?" I asked.

"I guess I don't know what you're talking about," she replied.

"We're using a lot of words beginning with the letter *r*."

We continued to discuss ideas, and "*r* words" continued to pop into the conversation. I began writing them down—words like *repent, repeat, rut, road, righteousness, rejoice,* and *revelation.*

"This is funny. Do you think maybe God wants us to use these words?" I asked.

The plan became to write one *r* word on a three-by-five-inch card for each woman attending the retreat. Then we would pray over the cards and randomly give each woman her *r* word on the first night.

Wow! One woman at the retreat actually wanted to leave because her word was too uncomfortable. But she decided to stay and later laughed at her initial reaction. God gave us joy with one letter from the alphabet.

After I returned home from the weekend, the *r* words raised their unruly heads one more time. At five o'clock Monday morning I woke up laughing. As I was giggling, my husband roused from sleep and said, "Are you all right?"

The laughing continued. "Go back to sleep, honey. I'm okay. I was just thinking of something that tickled me."

But as he lay back down, my giggles continued. "I think I'm addicted to *r* words."

—*Mary Brawner*

Abba Father, thank you for teaching me in simple ways to rejoice. Amen.

And a Cherry on Top

Be careful not to forget the Lord. . . . You must fear the Lord your God and serve him.

DEUTERONOMY 6:12-13

President Ronald Reagan once told a story about an elderly couple getting ready for bed one night.

The wife said, "Oh, I am so hungry for ice cream, and there isn't any in the house."

And the husband said, "I'll get some."

She said, "You're a dear. Vanilla with chocolate sauce." And she added, "Write it down, honey, or you'll forget."

He said defensively, "I *won't* forget."

Then she said, "With some whipped cream on it."

And he said, "Vanilla with chocolate sauce and some whipped cream. Got it."

"And a cherry on top. Please write it down," she said, "because I know you'll forget. Your memory is just not what it once was."

He reiterated, "I *won't* forget. Vanilla with chocolate sauce, whipped cream, and a cherry on top." And away he went to the store.

By the time he got back, the wife was already in bed, reading her book and waiting patiently for him to return.

So he handed the paper bag to her, smiling. She opened it, and there was a ham sandwich.

She said, "I told you to write it down—you forgot the mustard!"

I can relate to that story. Some days my memory works great, but other days I have to work hard to call up people's names, events from the past, or details about my work that I cannot afford to lose. Still, when all is said and done, the most important thing for us to remember in this life is God. If we remember him, fear him, and serve him, whatever else we forget is incidental.

Dear Lord, thank you for always remembering me and protecting me. Please help me to keep my mind focused on you and to never forget to praise and worship you. Amen.

Football in Heaven?

I saw a new heaven and a new earth, for the old heaven and the old earth had disappeared.

REVELATION 21:1

Two buddies, George and Harvey, were avid football fans. They watched, played, and talked about football endlessly. As we say in the South, "They were *ate up* with it." They attended more than fifty games each year—Pee Wee games, high school games, university games, and every pro game they could get to. They were so dedicated to the sport they even agreed that the one who died first would try to let the other one know if there was football in heaven.

After watching a Dallas Cowboys victory one night in October, George passed away in his sleep. His wife said he went peacefully, with a smile on his face, because the Cowboys had won that night.

Harvey was terribly upset and really missed his football buddy. About a week later, Harvey was awakened by what he thought was George's voice, saying, "Hut one, hut two, Harvey!"

Harvey sat up and ventured, "Hey, George, is that you?"

"Yes, it's me," replied the eerie-sounding voice.

"Wow! I can't believe you actually came back. I really miss you, buddy."

"Right. Well, this is harder than you might think," said George.

"Okay, I understand. So tell me, is there football in heaven?"

"Well, Harvey, I have some good news and some bad news for you. Which do you want first?"

"I guess the good news."

"The good news is that, yes, there is football in heaven. And it's amazing! Nobody ever misses a catch. The kicker never misses a field goal. And, oh yeah, the cheerleaders are real angels."

"That sounds great, George! So what's the bad news?"

"You're playing quarterback tomorrow night."

Like George and Harvey, I think we will all be surprised at what we find in heaven. God loves surprises!

O Lord, thank you for the promise of heaven and the gift of living with you for all eternity. I am so grateful for your saving grace and love. Amen.

March 9

The Painful Truth

Honest words can be painful.

JOB 6:25

Children are the most honest people I know. If you want a completely honest answer, ask children, and they will tell you "the whole truth and nothing but the truth."

But sometimes children can be *too* honest, leaving the recipient of their honesty blushing with embarrassment. My three-year-old daughter, Holly, was no exception to the rule. She spoke whatever she was thinking, and it was not always pretty.

When I became pregnant with my second child, a boy named Christian, Holly was not short of questions about her soon-to-be baby brother or about my protruding belly. It was getting bigger and bigger, and of course, Holly took notice.

When I was six or seven months pregnant, I was taking a walk with my mother and little Holly. My mother and I were discussing my pregnancy, and I reminded Holly about the baby growing inside me. She looked at my belly to observe the size and then turned to look at Grandma's belly, which is somewhat protruding as well, although for a totally different reason. Then, without missing a beat, she asked, "Is Grandma having a baby too?"

My mother and I chuckled as we were reminded of both the honesty and the innocence of children.

The truth can at times be painful to both the speaker and the hearer, but it is what it is—the truth! And although telling the truth to someone is often necessary and the right thing to do, we must deliver that message with love and kindness. Otherwise, the truth may be lost in the telling.

—Naomi Cassata

Dear heavenly Father, thank you for teaching us the value of honesty through the example of little children. Help us to be honest in our speech, even though at times it can be painful to the hearer. And always help us temper our language with love. In Jesus' name, amen.

Imagination? No Problem

When I was a child, I spoke and thought and
reasoned as a child. But when I grew up,
I put away childish things.

1 CORINTHIANS 13:11

Grandmothers like me are worrywarts; my condition was handed down to me from my own mother. I cannot help it. I worry about the mind-numbing effect of television, video games, the Internet, and peer pressure on my grandchildren. But helping them to learn the benefits of thinking for themselves is a goal worth reaching, and whenever they are in my care, I do my best to ensure that their imaginations get plenty of stimulation.

We have made forts from couch cushions and chair throws, battled dinosaurs in the wilds of Montana, and had tea parties on the living-room rug. I always hope I am doing my part, but I still wonder how much these activities are really helping my grandchildren's developing minds.

One busy afternoon I had to give my four-year-old grandson a time-out for shoving his baby sister. He sat with his arms crossed, pouting on a dining-room chair where I had told him he had to sit for five minutes. Of course, for the first three minutes he bargained and begged for a reduction in his sentence, but I would not give in. I ignored his yowling while I soothed his sister in the adjoining room, until he suddenly grew quiet. I was relieved that he had settled down to wait out his time, but then he spoke.

In his best boy voice he said, "Grandma? You know, everybody has to listen to their legs, and mine are telling me I need to walk!"

His ability to reason and use his imagination no longer concerns me.

—Susan Sundwall

Father, help us to love all the stages of our lives so that we may grow into full adulthood with you. Help us to eventually put away our childish ways and mature into the leaders you need us to become. Amen.

Remember Names

The gatekeeper opens the gate for him, and the sheep recognize his voice and come to him. He calls his own sheep by name and leads them out.

JOHN 10:3

Many people share a common problem: They cannot remember names. It is annoying to look into the eyes of people you know and suddenly go blank. You know you should remember, but you cannot recall their names even if your life depended on it. It is not only frustrating; it can also be embarrassing.

Individuals use many different tricks to try to jar their memories. I go through the alphabet, searching for a reminder of the first name by its first letter. Maybe the name will be triggered by something special, such as a color: brown. His last name is Brown.

It causes real trouble for pastors when they are unable to remember names of church members because they may be offended. Visitors also like the special recognition of being called by name. Leaders in the church deal with a real handicap when their memories fail them.

Our church members knew very well that our loving pastor frequently forgot names. We overlooked that flaw and appreciated his honesty about the situation. One Sunday as I sat in the choir facing the congregation, the pastor began to share something involving his wife. And, you guessed it, he forgot her name! I could see only the back of the pastor's head, but embarrassment turned it beet red.

Smiles and laughter filled the church. This time he really needed help, and nobody came to his rescue. He would, no doubt, face the wrath of Zelma when they got home. Aren't you glad that God never forgets your name?

—Pam Ford Davis

Lord, thank you for calling me by name. Help me to recall the names of your children and especially to always honor your name. Amen.

God Moves in a Mysterious Way

Can you solve the mysteries of God?
Can you discover everything about the Almighty?

JOB 11:7

Some time ago I lost enough weight that my clothes did not fit anymore. So I cleaned out my dresser, taking a bag of like-new pajamas and bras to an organization that serves abused women and children. A few days later the following e-mail was forwarded to me from the woman who had received my castoffs:

I picked the clothes up tonight. I don't know how to say this, but pajamas and more than two bras for me have been out of the question, because they were not necessities. I am beside myself with appreciation for the person who donated the bras and pajamas.

You know . . . the girls came home from their dad's and have been adjusting to being back home with me and to my rules. I realize God can use all situations to minister, and I saw that firsthand tonight. I had been praying he would give me an opportunity to be a mom and have some girl time with my daughters. I never dreamed a bag of bras would do it.

Jennifer had been very guarded and closed . . . until today. She asked if we could go to church tonight, even though she has not wanted to do anything with me. Then, after church, the girls ripped into the bag of clothes. After finding the treasure inside, they burst out laughing and had a bra fight in the car.

They said, "It's raining bras!"

It was priceless. They talked nonstop all the way home about a lot of normal stuff. I never thought God would use bras as an icebreaker. I am grateful to be so blessed.

Hymnist William Cowper so eloquently wrote, "God moves in a mysterious way, his wonders to perform." But who would have thought God would use bras and pj's?

Father, thank you for allowing my castoffs to become someone else's treasure and to open the door for a mother and her daughters to reconnect. You are amazing! Amen.

March 13

Love Your Neighbor

The whole law can be summed up in this one command: "Love your neighbor as yourself."

GALATIANS 5:14

For six months or so, my husband and I had been teaching our two-year-old daughter to say "I love you." Early in this process, we emphasized the words at bedtime and anytime either of us left the house, hoping to hear those three sweet little words in return.

Also, with her grandparents living more than seven hundred miles away, hearing her say, "I love you" to them seemed like a good way to close the emotional distance between us, and it has become a valuable part of our phone conversations with them. Confession time, though: We had to trick her into saying those words the first few times. The tactic went something like this:

"Guess what?" my husband or I would ask. We would then follow with "I love you."

Isabelle picked up on that game pretty quickly, answering, "I love you" almost before we could ask the question. Now when we say, "Guess what?" she almost always answers, "You love me," instead of "I love you." Perhaps we taught her too well.

When my husband left the house for his seminary class one day recently, he said to her, as usual, "'Bye, Isabelle, I love you."

Without hesitation, Isabelle shouted in reply, "I love me too!"

Well, she has half of the Golden Rule down. Now, if only we can teach her to love others as much as she loves herself. And, oh yes, if only we can learn that lesson ourselves!

—*Lisa Bartelt*

Father, I confess that sometimes I love myself too much. Perhaps I learned that lesson too well. Please help me to love others as much as or more than I love myself and to never be shy or hesitant to say to others, as I say to you now, Lord, "I love you." Amen.

Keep Good Company

Since we are surrounded by such a huge crowd of witnesses . . . let us run with endurance the race God has set before us. We do this by keeping our eyes on Jesus.

HEBREWS 12:1-2

Cary Weisiger III, a retired pastor, was invited to participate in the ceremonies celebrating Fuller Seminary's fortieth anniversary and the inauguration of the president's lectureship. The event took place in early November.

The four speakers on the program included the scholarly giants Carl F. H. Henry, theologian; Samuel Hugh Moffett, professor emeritus of ecumenism and mission at Princeton; and Mary Stewart Van Leeuwen, professor of interdisciplinary studies at Calvin College, as well as Weisiger.

When Weisiger got up to deliver the opening address, he was characteristically humble in the company of such academic luminaries:

> *I have been a pastor, by the grace of God. If I could do it all over again, I would be a pastor. I have never, frankly, regarded myself as a scholar. I have tried to be studious, and I want to thank Dr. David Hubbard for including me in this program today.*
>
> *A farmer once put his mule in a horse race, and his friends said to him, "Silly, that mule can't run with those thoroughbreds."*
>
> *The farmer said, "I know it, but you have no idea how good it makes him feel to run with those great horses."*

Like that mule, I know I can't run with all those biblical heroes listed in Hebrews 11, but I know they are there cheering me on as I run my own race, and I just *love* being in such great company.

Thank you, Father, for allowing me to stay in the race. I know I am still running only because of your sweet grace and long-suffering kindness. Give me the heart and courage to keep running, no matter what may happen in this life. Heaven is my goal, and I won't stop until I get there. Amen.

Wash Your Hands!

My child, pay attention to what I say.
Listen carefully to my words.

PROVERBS 4:20

In the summer after my first year of teaching, at age forty, the only kinds of trips we could afford to take were car trips. So our blended family hopped in our minivan in Fort Worth, Texas, and headed south along Interstate 35 toward the beautiful rolling hills and wildflowers of the Texas Hill Country.

We rode along for a couple of hours, enjoying the familiar scenery. Then everyone needed a break, so we stopped at a roadside bakery in West, Texas—the name of the town, not the direction we were headed—a Czechoslovakian community known for its delicious and authentic freshly baked kolaches.

When we walked in, the bakery was crowded with at least two dozen people waiting in four different lines to get the famous kolaches. I needed to visit the ladies' room, but when our five kids got in a couple of different lines, I said to them, apparently in my newly developed "teacher" voice, "Okay, everyone! You need to wash your hands before you get your kolaches!"

At that moment, all the customers in the store got out of their kolache lines and headed for the restroom! Needless to say, I found myself at the end of the restroom line.

So much of the time it seems that people do not listen to our words, but in this case, everyone did! Just as we pay attention to God's words because they are wise, righteous, and just and will steer us in the right direction, we should also be careful in what we say and in how we say it, because we never really know who may hear us, quote us, or do what we say to do.

—Cynthia Phagan Bittick

Dear Lord, please give me wisdom so that my words help, encourage, and give trustworthy advice to those who listen. And, Lord, please help me to listen more carefully to your words. Through Jesus I pray, amen.

Bleating Buffaloe

In panic I cried out,
"I am cut off from the LORD!"
But you heard my cry for mercy
and answered my call for help.

PSALM 31:22

Have you ever watched a movie in which the hero or heroine, in utter agony, lets out a primal scream? The cry echoes across time and space. Shortly before my husband would have received lifetime medical benefits, he lost his job. More than a year later, the job search continued. Emotionally drained and frustrated, I decided I really needed a deep, cathartic scream.

Standing in the backyard, I called up all those nasty, desperate emotions from the depths of my soul, took a deep breath, pulled in oxygen from several surrounding counties, and then opened my mouth and let it out.

Unfortunately, the release sounded more like a bleating sheep, which caused my throat to freeze tight, the dogs in the neighborhood to bark uncontrollably, the squirrels to fall off tree limbs, the cats to screech, and an elderly neighbor to call animal control.

Bummer. No relief and only a sore throat to show for my pitiful efforts. I tucked in my proverbial tail and went back inside, up the stairs, and into my office, where I plopped down in my chair and stared at my computer screen.

After a while, I finally did what I should have done in the first place—I picked up my Bible. Thumbing through the verses, I found that God is ready to listen, in spite of my guttural shrieks. Our situation did not immediately change, but my attitude did. With several more months of waiting before more work arrived for my husband, and then a ten-month wait to sell our house, I felt that some days those primal screams would have come in handy. But they wouldn't help, not like running into God's strong arms.

—Lisa Buffaloe

Thank you, Father, for hearing our cries. Whether we think, whisper, or bleat like sheep, your ears are always open, you hear our whimpers, and you give us the answers we need the most. I know I can always depend on you, Lord. Amen.

Golden Words

Timely advice is lovely,
like golden apples in a silver basket.

PROVERBS 25:11

On the day of March 17, I awoke to glorious sunshine and a few wispy clouds floating through an azure sky. That was a very special day for the Walker family. Parents Tom and Lucy were in their seventies, and today they were celebrating their fiftieth wedding anniversary. Unfortunately, Tom had lost much of his hearing through the years. And yet he and his wife were still getting along together and celebrating this great anniversary—a fitting tribute to their lasting love and commitment to one another.

Their large extended family had come for the celebration, sleeping all over the house—in the guest room, on sofas, in sleeping bags on the floor. Lots of friends from Tom and Lucy's neighborhood, community, and church came to offer their good wishes. Everyone enjoyed the gala event and family reunion through the midmorning and into the afternoon. Finally, about sundown, the remaining family members reluctantly went home, leaving Tom and Lucy alone.

Tired but happy, Lucy and Tom decided to walk out onto the front porch and sit down on the swing to watch the beautiful sunset together. It seemed symbolic somehow to end such a special day that way.

The old gentleman pulled his tie loose and leaned back, not saying much to his bride of fifty years. Lucy looked at him somewhat in wonder and said to him, "You know, Tom, I'm real proud of you."

Tom turned and looked at her rather quizzically. After a moment of studied silence, he finally said, "Well, Lucy, I'm real tired of you, too!"

Father, sometimes I say things I regret. Please just shut my mouth, Lord, and help me to be more careful about the words I choose. I never want to hurt anyone's feelings, and yet I know I'm guilty of unwittingly doing that at times. Please forgive me for words poorly chosen or poorly said. Amen.

Sunrise at Evening

Weeping may last through the night,
but joy comes with the morning.

PSALM 30:5

It had been a long day—a day full of problems and frustrations and difficult decisions. I was tired, so very tired. My work was finished. I had done my duty. I had performed all the tasks, completed all the projects planned for me that day, run all the errands, and worn myself to a frazzle trying to keep up with a hectic schedule. I was ready to go home and relax. I just wanted to curl up in my big recliner with a good book and let what was left of the day go by peacefully, quietly.

As I turned toward home, the sun was low in the sky, and pink cotton-candy clouds floated in front of the darker ones lined in glistening silver. I was awestruck at the incredible beauty God could create with streaks of sunlight and puffs of moisture. The day was finally over, and I was almost home.

Then I suddenly realized—the sun was not going *down*; it was coming *up*!

"Wait, Lord! How can that be? It's evening. The sun doesn't come up in the evening unless—" I had worked all night!

Then I heard the wind seeming to whisper in the rustling autumn leaves, "It's a new day for you. Yesterday is gone, but today's a brand-new day. Now is your chance to do what you've always wanted to do. Go for it!"

I turned to look out the side window of my car, saw my own face reflected, and realized that I was smiling.

Sunrise at evening—the unexpected thrill and joy of life.

O Lord, you are the sunshine of my heart, the source of my joy, my hope, and my laughter. Thank you, Father, for shining on me. Please help me to reflect your joy into the dark corners of others' lives too. Amen.

The Critic

How can you think of saying, "Friend, let me help you get rid of that speck in your eye," when you can't see past the log in your own eye?

LUKE 6:42

It was a beautiful March day. The sun was shining, the breeze was blowing gently, and the early spring flowers were beginning to bud. It was much too beautiful to stay at home. So George and Wendy decided to spend the day out and about, doing things they loved to do, just the two of them.

Wendy packed a nice picnic lunch; they put the top down on their old Thunderbird convertible and headed into the city. They would visit a favorite museum and then have lunch in the downtown park, where they could feed the ducks and walk along the tree-covered paths by the lake.

After wandering through the history museum and looking through a few shops along Main Street, they stopped at the car for the picnic basket and walked to the park, where they indulged in chicken salad, fruit, French bread, and chocolate cake for dessert.

Putting the basket back in the car, George suggested they visit the nearby art gallery. George considered himself an expert on fine art. So as they entered the lobby, he looked at the image hanging there and began to analyze it.

"First of all, that frame is not fit for a fine painting. Second, the matting around the edge is the wrong color. And third, the subject is not even worthy to be painted. Look, his clothes are wrinkled. He's lifeless, drab, and sour looking, and . . ."

Wendy giggled and interrupted his critique. "Honey, that's not a painting. *That* is a mirror!"

Father, it is so easy to be blind to the realities of our own lives and to criticize others. We need your Word to be our mirror so we can see what needs to be changed in our lives. Thank you for loving us anyway, Father. Amen.

The Reluctant Giver

You must each decide in your heart how much to give.
And don't give reluctantly or in response to pressure.
"For God loves a person who gives cheerfully."

2 CORINTHIANS 9:7

At the height of the Civil War, President Abraham Lincoln met a prominent society woman from Alexandria, Virginia. She had come to request that the president allow a certain church building, which had been captured by Union forces, to be released for use as a hospital in which wounded soldiers could be treated and allowed to recover.

Seeing that she was a woman of wealth, Lincoln responded by asking her why she did not simply donate the money to build a hospital. She replied, with an exaggerated look of sadness, that her wealth was being temporarily hampered by the war effort, and she could not afford to take on such a project at that time.

At her response, Lincoln could not resist a small chuckle. Then he gave this reply:

> *You, as a representative of your class in Alexandria, remind me of the story of the young man who had an aged father and mother owning considerable property.*
>
> *The young man, being an only son, impatient for good fortune, and sincerely believing that his old parents had outlived their usefulness, assassinated them both. He was accused, tried, and convicted of the murders.*
>
> *When the judge came to pass sentence upon him and called upon him to give any reason he might have why the sentence of death should not be passed, the young man stood up and promptly replied that he hoped the court would have mercy upon him because he was a poor orphan!*

Dear Lord, thank you for the amazing blessings you lavish on us every day. May we learn to adopt your generous spirit and share our many blessings with others happily and willingly. We want to be more like you, Lord, in our giving. Amen.

Green-Eyed Monster

God created great sea creatures and every living thing that scurries and swarms.

GENESIS 1:21

Spring had sprung, and everything was blooming, creeping out, and emerging from its long winter's rest. We had been out to dinner at one of our neighborhood restaurants. After arriving home, I went upstairs to prepare for bed.

Opening the door to my walk-in closet, I flipped on the light—and froze as I stared into the bulging eyes of a green-eyed monster perched on top of my clothes. It looked like a giant-sized Geico Gecko but without the smile! I gasped and stumbled backward out of the closet. Then I peered cautiously around the door frame, hoping I had just imagined the long-tailed creature. But, no, he was a glistening, green reality.

I turned and ran for the stairs, yelling at my sister as I went, "Charlotte, help! There's a Gila monster in my closet!" It wasn't really a Gila monster, but that's all I could think of at that panicky moment. It was some kind of large lizard—about fifteen inches long and five inches tall at the head. But it looked like a small dinosaur to me!

Now, I don't *do* lizards, no matter what size they are. So I called my neighbor Jeff, who used to own a fish and reptile store. He came over immediately, took one look at the lizard, grinned, and asked me for a pillowcase. He put his hand down inside the pillowcase, calmly reached out, and picked up the lizard, turning the pillowcase inside out and capturing the lizard inside. He later released it miles away by a creek.

Sometimes I wonder, *God, are Gila monsters really necessary in this world? Or did you create them just for a few grins?* But I guess that's why he's God and why I'm good for a few laughs.

Thank you, God, for all your creatures, even when I don't understand why they're needed. I know that each one, even those I don't like, has a special purpose in your mind and reflects your infinite creativity. Amen.

What's in a Name?

You will be given a new name
by the LORD's own mouth.

ISAIAH 62:2

Several years ago I traveled to China. The trip was an opportunity for thirty-four American Christians to enlarge their understanding of the worldwide church and to provide Chinese Christians with Chinese-language Bibles.

A powerful part of this trip was the thirty-six-hour train ride from Beijing to Hong Kong, which gave us plenty of time to socialize with fellow passengers. We were eager to share the gospel with anyone who would listen, while also being careful not to draw the attention of the police on the train.

We had one Chinese-speaking man in our group. Though we overwhelmed him with requests for translation help, he was gracious enough to serve as translator without ever taking the role of evangelist away from the Americans trying to participate in these spiritual conversations.

One of these conversations resulted in a man deciding to become a Christian. It is common practice in China for a new convert to choose a new, Christian name to signify his new life. Our translator asked this new convert what Christian name he might choose.

The man wasn't sure. He mentioned he would be the first Christian in his family and in his village. So the translator suggested *Peter* as his Christian name, Peter being one of Christ's first followers.

The man agreed, and he was christened Peter. It was only then that we learned he had a very common surname in China: Pan. So somewhere in China today is a church leader named Peter Pan!

—Melanie Jongsma

Lord, I praise you for loving us and redeeming us and writing our names in your Book of Life. I ask you for new opportunities every day to share your name with others. Amen.

Stretching the Truth

Stop telling lies. Let us tell our neighbors the truth.

EPHESIANS 4:25

Hawaii! An island paradise. Vacation heaven. Kissed by the sun and blessed with fresh fruit, glorious beaches, swaying palm trees, and warm, delightful weather. People flock there from around the world to enjoy the many pleasures available on these wonderful islands. Who wouldn't want to go there?

When Abraham Lincoln was president of the United States, it was his job to appoint commissioners of the government to various parts of the world to serve the United States. And, as you might imagine, one of the most eagerly sought-after appointments in all the government was the commissionership of Hawaii, then called the Sandwich Islands.

The story is told that one day a delegation appeared before President Lincoln in Washington, DC, to ask him to appoint a certain gentleman to that position. They said the candidate, in addition to being eminently qualified for the post, was also in poor health. Therefore, he would greatly benefit from the balmy Hawaiian climate.

Lincoln is said to have listened quietly and patiently while the delegation droned on and on about the fellow they were promoting. Finally, when they ran out of expressions of praise, the president smiled politely. Then he said, "Gentlemen, I am sorry to say that there are eight other applicants for the post in Hawaii, and they are all sicker than your man."

Sometimes it's hard in this world ruled by Satan, the father of lies, to determine who is telling the biggest lie, isn't it? Stretching the truth has become a way of life for many people today. As Christians, we need to stick to the truth. And that's all there is to say about that!

O Lord, sometimes it's tempting to embellish the truth or even to tell an outright lie, but please help me always to be truthful, no matter what I think the consequences will be. I would rather be right with you than in good favor with people. Let me be a beacon of your truth in my little corner of the world. Amen.

Fill 'Er Up!

Keep on asking, and you will receive what you ask for. . . . For everyone who asks, receives.

MATTHEW 7:7-8

Several years ago, when I was speaking at Moody Bible Institute, a lady wrote me a note saying, "I didn't worry about getting married. I *did* leave my future to God's will. But every night I hung a pair of men's pants on the bed and knelt down and prayed this prayer: 'Father in heaven, hear my prayer. And grant it if you can. I've hung a pair of trousers here. Please fill them with a man.'" Isn't that a great letter?

I read that letter the next week when I got back to the church I pastored in Fullerton, California. It didn't really fit my sermon; I just rammed it in because I thought it was such a great letter.

The father and older son of a family I knew were in the church service, but the mother was at home with a sick daughter. When I read the woman's note, I watched them. The father just cracked up laughing, but the boy was rather serious.

Interestingly, several weeks later, I got a letter from the mother, who hadn't been in that service. She wrote, "Dear Chuck, I'm wondering if I have something to worry about. I've noticed that our son, when he goes to bed at night, has this bikini hanging over the foot of his bed."

It's amazing how people today are often afraid to ask God for the desires of their hearts when he has plainly said, "Keep on asking, and you will receive what you ask for." And while this story may seem frivolous, at least this young man was taking God at his word—something we could all learn to do better.

—*Charles R. Swindoll*

Heavenly Father, hear me now as I pray and ask you for what I need the most. I know you hear me and that you will answer. I need . . . you! Amen.

Always Ask First

Show proper respect to everyone.

1 PETER 2:17 (NIV)

I come from a long line of well-preserved people. My mom is ninety-two, her older sister is ninety-five, and their younger sister is eighty-nine. I have great hand-me-down genes.

The youngest of the three sisters became deaf when she was two or three. Since it was the 1920s and medical treatment was limited, no one knows why it happened. But that never stopped my aunt. She was always the one who played practical jokes and kept things stirred up around their home.

Each fall my aunt rode the train to Austin, Texas, where she attended a school for the deaf. Mom says it was hard to see her leave, but they knew it was the best thing for her. And she came away with an excellent education and skills. Still, being profoundly deaf, my aunt is not always totally aware of things going on around her, nor does she completely understand why some things are happening. So her reactions are often interesting.

About a year ago my aunt had to undergo surgery and was in the hospital for several days. One of her children was typically in the room to interpret for her and the doctors and nurses. But one day her daughter had gone to get some coffee when the doctor made his rounds.

Knowing that my aunt was deaf, and not knowing sign language, the doctor didn't try to communicate with her. Instead, he walked directly to her bed, raised the covers, and lifted her gown to look at her incision. But not understanding exactly what he was up to, and having been reared as a "good girl," my aunt drew back and slapped the doctor with a mighty wallop.

Don't you think he wished he had shown her a little more respect and asked first?

Dear Father, please help us to remember that we should show proper respect to you and always ask before we charge ahead in our lives. We know that life works better when we allow you to take the lead. Help us to live in the light of that knowledge. Amen.

The Tummy Timer

For everything there is a season,
a time for every activity under heaven.

ECCLESIASTES 3:1

My little blond Shih Tzu, Jazz, has an automatic tummy timer. You can literally set your clock by him. At 8:00 a.m. he sticks his nose in my ear to wake me up. He is hungry! Then he runs around in circles growling and woofing in anticipation while I put on my robe.

After breakfast, Jazz spends most of the day in my office, sleeping in a chair until 5:00 p.m. sharp—unless he detects someone at the front door and feels compelled to act as my noisy, furry doorbell.

I do not have to worry about losing track of the time, because at straight-up 5:00, Jazz starts whining and barking for his dinner. If I do not move quite as fast as he wants, he puts his front paws on my leg, nuzzles my arm, and looks at me with his can't-you-see-I'm-dying-of-starvation eyes. So I finally give in and fix his meal. (Jazz knows I will, of course; he has me very well trained, which gives a whole new meaning to the phrase *dog obedience school.*)

Promptly at 9:00 p.m. he wakes up out of a dead sleep, stretches as only a dog can, and starts the whining-and-barking routine again. It is time for treats! It is absolutely uncanny how he knows what time it is, even when he is asleep.

Most people worry about their electricity going off in the middle of the night and their alarm clocks not working. I never have to worry about that—I have Jazz and his ever-accurate tummy timer!

On this earth, we have only a limited time to live and enjoy God's world. Like Jazz, we should concentrate on the best parts of life.

Thank you, Lord, for the time we have to spend with you. Help me to use it well to study your Word, sing your praises, and share the good news about you with others. Amen.

One, Two, Three

[Jesus said,] "If you love me, obey my commandments."

JOHN 14:15

I drive a red convertible. And yes, I'd love to "put the pedal to the metal" and see how fast it would go. But I don't. I'm a law-abiding driver.

One day I came to a four-way-stop intersection. Before I got there, I noticed there were no other cars in sight. So I stopped, glanced around, noticed a police car parked a block away, and then went on.

Thirty seconds later, the police car appeared behind me with its bubble-gum machine flashing. I had no idea why a policeman would be stopping me, but I pulled over immediately.

The young police*woman* came to the passenger door, and I rolled down the window. She looked inside, I suppose to be sure I was alone and unarmed, then stepped up to the window.

"Hello, ma'am" (a term of respect in the South). "Did you realize you didn't stop long enough at the stop sign back there?"

Surprised, I said politely, "Well, no, ma'am. I certainly thought I stopped correctly."

"Well, ma'am, I didn't feel that you stopped *long enough*."

"Long enough?"

"Yes. When you stop, you should always count to three before you go on."

Because she was obviously young and dead serious, I repressed a giggle. And I thought, *Count to three? What law is that? And is it one . . . two . . . three or one-two-three?* Instead, I said, "Really? I've been driving fifty years" (thinking, *thirty years longer than you've been alive!*), "and I've never heard that before. But I'll try to remember."

"That's good," she said. "I'm not going to give you a ticket. Just be careful."

"Yes, ma'am. Thank you, ma'am."

Now, every time I come to that intersection, I stop and say aloud, "Onetwothree!"

It's a good reminder to be careful. And it makes me smile.

Lord, thank you for your reminders about how to have a happy life. Help me always count to three when I am facing a choice to violate your laws. Amen.

I Go Home Now

Husbands, love your wives and never treat them harshly.

COLOSSIANS 3:19

During World War II, I was uprooted from my home in Texas and sent to North Carolina, where I worked for a government-run manufacturing plant that made a variety of items needed for the war. My job was to supervise a huge crew of people, mostly women, who made everything from parachutes to knapsacks for the soldiers.

Most days in the plant went along without incident. I think most of the workers in the plant actually liked me, except when I had to correct someone. Then I was the bad guy. Still, we got along quite well for the most part.

One of the interesting people in the plant was an older German fellow named Rupert, who still had a distinct German accent underlying his English. I enjoyed Rupert's company. We often ate our lunches together on the back porch of the plant, which looked out over a wide river lined with trees.

I always looked forward to going home to my sweet wife, Thelma, at the end of the day. I knew she would have a nice dinner prepared, and I could spend time playing with my little son, Frank.

One day, just before closing time, I had made my rounds to be sure all the machines and lights were turned off. I was getting ready to lock the front door after the final few workers left, when Rupert ambled toward the exit.

"Good night, buddy," I said, patting him on the back. "See you tomorrow."

Rupert said, "I go home now. If my wife doesn't have dinner ready, I'm going to raise Cain . . . and if she does, I'm not going to eat!" Then he winked at me and left.

I went home thinking, *It will be interesting to see what she puts in his lunch tomorrow!*

—*Clyde Shrode*

Dear Father, thank you for treating me with kindness and gentleness. I need your love and compassion today. And may I extend that same love and compassion to others. Amen.

Running for Life

Don't you realize that in a race everyone runs, but only one person gets the prize? So run to win!

1 CORINTHIANS 9:24

During the great rivalry game between Alabama and Auburn one year, the first-string quarterback for the Alabama team had been injured, so the team was left with the second-string quarterback. Alabama was on the opposing team's twenty-yard line and was ahead by five points. There were two minutes left in the game, and it was a first down for Alabama.

Coach Bear Bryant yelled into the ear hole in the helmet of the second-string quarterback, "Whatever you do, do not pass! Run the ball all four plays. And then, if we have to hold them, our defense will get us through, and we will win."

The second-string quarterback ran onto the field full of zeal and determination. First down, Alabama was smeared. Second down, Auburn held them. Third down, Alabama gained only a yard. Fourth down came. The handoff was somehow muffled, and the quarterback wound up with the ball. Running around the backfield, he looked into the end zone and saw his split end ready to catch the ball, so he passed it. What he failed to see was that the fastest man on the field, Auburn's safety, also saw the pass coming. He came in front of the receiver, intercepted the ball, and started racing down the field. The quarterback, not very fast himself as a rule, raced down the field, caught up with the man and tackled him, and Alabama won the game.

Coach Dye, of the Auburn team, said later to Bear Bryant, "I read the scouting reports, and that second-string quarterback is supposed to be slow. How is it he caught up with the fastest man on the field?"

Bear Bryant replied, "It's very simple. Your man was running for the goal line and a touchdown. My man was running for his life!"

O Lord, thank you for the life race you have given me to run. I love you, Lord, and I want to run my race with joy and with my eyes always focused on you, because I know that I, too, am running for my life. Amen.

March of the Ducks

Be happy. . . . Be very glad! For a great reward awaits you in heaven.

MATTHEW 5:12

In August each year I attend a large convention for a company with which I work part time. The convention is held in different cities, so I also get to enjoy the sights of a new place, different hotels, various restaurants, and unique people. Occasionally, the convention is held in Orlando, Florida—home of the famous Peabody hotel.

The Peabody is truly a class act, with fountains in the lobby, marble floors, brilliant lighting, and other amenities. But one of the most endearing features of the Peabody is its one-of-a-kind parade of ducks twice a day. Yes, ducks! And the parade of waddlers draws an admiring crowd every time because it's so cute.

The hotel plays John Philip Sousa's patriotic march "The Stars and Stripes Forever," and suddenly ducks gather around the big fountain. A long red carpet is then unrolled from the fountain to the opening of a beautiful curtain. And without missing a beat or making a single quack, the ducks line up and march along the carpet through the opening in the curtain, to the utter delight and applause of the watching audience.

Perhaps you're wondering why typically undisciplined ducks would consent to this parade twice a day every day. I wondered that too. So one morning, I nonchalantly wandered over to the opening in the curtain and took a peek inside. *Voilà!* The answer was clear—there was duck food everywhere! And the formal military atmosphere was lost as the ducks quacked, flapped, and competed for the food.

It wasn't, after all, the parade to which the ducks were dedicated. It was the reward at the *end* of the parade.

Dear God, you have laid out a beautiful red carpet for us to travel in this life, stained by the blood of your precious Son, and I know that it leads to a great reward in heaven. I commit myself to staying on the carpet, and I thank you for saving me. Amen.

March 31

Expect the Unexpected

"My thoughts are nothing like your
thoughts," says the LORD.
"And my ways are far beyond
anything you could imagine."

ISAIAH 55:8

I hugged my daughter, Natalie, and kissed my three-month-old grandson, Kameron.

Natalie asked, "When can you come back to Chicago?"

"Not for a while. I have to save for the flight."

"We already miss you."

My husband, John, hugged everyone good-bye, and we left for O'Hare International Airport. Dark clouds overhead mirrored the somberness I felt as we drove through pools of water. Upon check-in we were told the storm would delay our flight one hour. At nine thirty that night, a small break in the weather allowed us to board. It was a full flight, and I had not arranged for advanced seat assignments, which forced us to sit five rows apart.

The plane backed from the gate and stood in line for takeoff. Lightning flashed. I clutched the armrest and wished my husband were near me. Anxious and frightened, I prayed, *Lord, please don't let the plane get struck by lightning.* Instantly, a bolt flashed so bright that it illuminated the plane.

Then the captain spoke. "Folks, our tail wing's been hit by lightning. As a precaution, the fire trucks are arriving to spray the plane."

I heard sirens and chuckled at the irony of my anxious prayer and God's answer.

My seatmate asked, "You find this funny?"

I smiled. "I just prayed and asked God *not* to let the plane get hit."

He laughed. "I bet God had a reason."

When we disembarked, we were told the next flight to Denver was two days away. We opted to fly to Colorado Springs, drive to Denver's airport, find our luggage, drop off the rental, and drive home.

For our inconvenience the airline awarded us two free tickets. I didn't need to save after all! And I offered a thankful prayer as I booked our next trip.

—Genevra Bonati

Lord, help us to remember that your plan is always better than anything we can conceive of. Amen.

Serpent in the Basement

"You won't die!" the serpent [said] to the woman.

GENESIS 3:4

When we moved to an old farmhouse with a dank, dark basement, we were warned that snakes could get in through loose-fitting windows.

Shortly after move-in day, my husband took a job driving an overnight drop-off and pick-up delivery route to a nearby town. After the drop-offs he would get a few hours of sleep there, make return deliveries, and arrive home as our daughter was preparing for school. He would eat breakfast, then fall into bed for a few more hours of sleep.

One morning I ventured downstairs to do laundry, checking for any snakes that might be lurking. I threw clothes in the washer and hurried back upstairs just as my husband came in the back door.

Meeting my husband at the top of the stairs, I gasped, "Snake! Snake!" My hands shook as I pointed down the stairs. "There's a snake down there. I think it went behind the washer. Find it. You have to find it."

Instead of jumping to the rescue, he gave me the please-let-me-eat-and-go-to-bed look.

"No! No!" I cried. "It's laundry day. I can't finish the laundry with a snake on the loose. You have to find it."

Giving in, he trudged downstairs. After some crashing and banging, he returned. No snake. I pleaded my case again, and down he went. The third time he came up totally wiped out, promising there was no snake anywhere. I smiled brightly, then laughed. "April Fool's!"

If looks could kill . . .

Today my husband laughs with me when the story is retold. He forgave my deception, just as God, my heavenly Father, forgives me when my words or actions have misled another.

—Marilyn Eudaly

Lord, help me to realize that my actions and words, although in jest, may lead others down a wrong path. Make me a vessel for your good words, not a vessel for the serpent's deception. Amen.

Ho Hums or Hallelujahs?

Be happy with those who are happy,
and weep with those who weep.

ROMANS 12:15

Jack became a Christian on Sunday. On Wednesday, his wife, Carol, gave birth to a baby girl. Jack, a big, burly guy with a gruff voice and boisterous manner, was thrilled, and he could not wait to tell somebody . . . anybody. So he came to the Wednesday night Bible class at the church, bounded in, and announced to the entire congregation, "It's a girl!"

There were a few muffled giggles, but everyone basically reacted happily. Then Jack bounced past the minister and carefully hoisted himself up to sit on the Communion table, bringing gasps from the conservative group in the back. But Jack, oblivious to anything beyond his exuberance, proceeded to give a blow-by-blow account of the day's events.

Meanwhile, our highly dignified, white-shirt, navy-suit minister was turning ashen, not knowing how to stop Jack politely.

Jack hopped off the "holy" table and hurried down the aisles, handing out cigars to the men and candy to the women. The first cigar went to the minister, whose face instantly flushed from ash to scarlet. I collapsed in laughter on the second pew.

Then, as suddenly as he had burst into the room, Jack was gone—back to Carol and Super Baby. He did not stay for Bible study.

When the guffaws and gasps died down, the minister was left with Bible in one hand and cigar in the other. He could not figure out what to say. Finally, with obvious fluster and fumbling, he stuck the cigar in his pocket and mumbled, "I'll just put this away so no one will smoke it."

With that, I escaped to the ladies' room, where I went into hysterics. I'm sure the Lord was laughing too.

Hallelujah happenings do not deserve ho-hum responses. Way to go, Jack! Thanks for loosening our spiritual neckties a bit.

O Father, thank you for the hallelujahs you send us. Help us not to give ho-hum praise in return but to celebrate your joy with you. Amen.

Never Too Stuck

I love the LORD because he hears my voice
and my prayer for mercy.

PSALM 116:1

Superglue in hand, I applied adhesive to the jagged edges and waited before pressing the broken piece in place. The ringing phone drew my attention. Placing the item on the counter, I picked up the receiver.

After my conversation, I hung the phone back in place . . . with my hand firmly attached. Stuck tightly, laughing hysterically, and a touch embarrassed, I used my convenient mode of communication to call for help. Fortunately, my hand and the phone were separated with a product dear to my heart: superglue remover.

Weeks later our young son, distraught over a broken toy, found me in the kitchen. Donning my Supermom cape, I grabbed the glue to fix his plastic submachine gun.

He touched my arm. "Are you sure you should do this?"

"No problem; this is easy."

He gulped. "But you're using superglue."

Yes, there had been several incidents with the product, but I had always fixed what was broken and eventually gotten unstuck.

I gave him a pat, saying, "I'll be careful."

After a few squirts in proper places to reattach the broken item, I waited several minutes. My son's friends gathered around. Convinced the operation had been a success, I tried to set it on the counter. Arrgh! I was not just stuck; the glue had melted and melded my skin to the plastic. And I was out of remover.

Twenty minutes of sweating and begging prayer later, I handed back the toy. With gasps of appreciation and words like *awesome* and *cool*, the boys stared at my handiwork. Thanks to my fingerprints, complete with the top layer of epidermis permanently embedded, my son now held the coolest toy on the block.

—Lisa Buffaloe

Thank you, Father, for always hearing our cries for help and answering, no matter how stuck we are in life. Amen.

When Will It Be Fixed?

Restore us, O LORD, and bring us back to you again!

LAMENTATIONS 5:21

With three kids ages five and under, our life was an adventure. My husband was a busy pastor, and I did my best to keep everyone happy, fed, and, well . . . alive. Sometimes my biggest accomplishment was surviving the day!

At that time, we lived in the Texas Hill Country. It was beautiful, but when your days are a whirlwind of changing diapers, refereeing squabbles, and picking up toys, you do not want scenery. You want your mommy. So I was thrilled when my mom called to say she was coming to visit on spring break! When she arrived, I gave her a tour of our community. As we passed the dance studio where the girls took lessons, my three-year-old daughter, J. J., wailed from the backseat, "Oh no! We forgot to go to dance today!"

"There's no class today," I reminded her. "It's spring break."

I continued chatting with Mom as I showed her our church and the kids' preschool. As we headed home, J. J. piped up: "When will it be fixed?"

"What?" I looked at Mom quizzically, and she shrugged.

Apparently J. J. thought I was hard of hearing. So she repeated her question, a few decibels louder. "I said, when will it be *fixed*?"

I still didn't get it. "When will *what* be fixed, honey?"

Exasperated, she said, "Spring! When will *spring* be fixed? I want to go to dance class!"

As realization hit, I could not control my laughter. I have no idea how I managed to drive home through those gales of giggles.

Spring is not broken, of course, but it is a chance for us to fix the things that are. Spring is a great time for fresh starts, restored relationships, and a renewed faith in the only one who can truly fix what is broken.

—Jennifer Stair

Father, thank you for spring, both on the earth and in my heart. I'm grateful for new beginnings, and I know that you are the God of new beginnings. Amen.

The Language of Music

Speak to each other with psalms, hymns,
and spiritual songs, singing and making
music in your hearts to the Lord.

EPHESIANS 5:19 (NCV)

Music is an amazing language all its own. It is universal. While spoken dialects and languages are confusing to communication around the world, music is a unifying force we all understand.

As a singer myself, I have experienced the "magic" and power of music and how it affects people in a variety of situations and countries. I love all kinds of music, especially a cappella (without instruments) and standard jazz.

When I lived in Kansas in the 1980s, a group from our church often went to the local nursing homes to sing for the folks who lived there. They loved to see us, and they loved to sing along with us. We mostly sang Christian songs and hymns the older people had known all their lives, and that brought back fond memories for them.

In one of the homes was an older woman named Polly who had suffered a major stroke, which left her unable to speak. She could say two words: *yes* and *no.* Her mind was just as sharp as ever, and she loved to try to converse with us. She just could not use words.

When it came time for the singing, though, Polly really came to life. For some unknown reason, even though she could not say words in regular conversation, she could sing every word of every song. And she did so with great delight, laughing and clapping her hands after each song. The longer we sang, the happier Polly was, because it was her only way of speaking.

Polly truly carried out the Lord's request that we *speak* to each other in song. And she did it with great joy, moving me to tears.

Dear Lord, thank you for creating music and for allowing its power to lift our spirits and touch our hearts. Thank you for giving us the opportunity to praise your name in song. Amen.

Stuck

We were filled with laughter,
and we sang for joy.

PSALM 126:2

As I pulled the car key out of the ignition, I realized I was locked out of the house. A thorough search of my purse, pockets, and car yielded nothing. My housemate would not be home for an hour, and I didn't want to drive all the way to a friend's house to get the spare key.

I'll try the doggy door, I thought. *Maybe I can reach the locks and open the back door to get in.*

With determination born out of desperation, I went to the back door and surveyed my options. I sat down on the top step and maneuvered my head and left arm through. Great, I could reach only the bottom lock. Then I wiggled until I got my right arm and upper torso inside the door.

My face being a foot off the ground delighted my dog. She licked my nose, whined, wriggled, and licked some more. When she finally calmed down, I was able to look and see that there was no way I could reach the top lock. I decided to slide the rest of the way in. Nope. Okay, slide back out. Nope.

I was stuck in the doggy door! I did not have my phone, but whom would I have called in that particular situation anyway? I lay there for a few minutes, half in, half out, and decided to force my way back out. I wriggled and scooted until I was free.

My dignity dented, I knew God was laughing with me. Then I patiently waited for my housemate to get home with the key.

—Stevie Stevens

Father, thank you for the ability to laugh at myself even in the midst of an awkward moment. Laughter truly is a most amazing gift. How would we survive this life without the joy and laughter you give to us? We love you, Father. Amen.

Blew Our Family Away

God has given each of you a gift from his great variety of spiritual gifts. Use them well to serve one another.

1 PETER 4:10

The huge box arrived on our doorstep just in time for Christmas. My husband, Mark, and I had decided to give this practical gift to each other since we needed it anyway. I tagged it "To the Hemingway Family. From Santa Claus" and stuck it under the tree.

Brainstorming among themselves, our six children speculated that the large mystery package must be a Shaggy Bag—a round beanbag-type chair, only softer. The kids had pleaded for one after they had seen one at the mall. Mark and I would smile at each other when they said things like "We know it's a Shaggy Bag. What else could it be?" and "We can hardly wait to open the Shaggy Bag you got us." When alone, we laughed at how sure they were that the box contained a Bag.

They didn't know I dislike those things. To me, they look sloppy, take up too much space, and create clutter. Our gift was much better.

On Christmas Day we saved the big box for last. Excited to finally get to open "the Shaggy Bag," the kids wondered about the color and expressed hope for the gigantic grandpa size. Mark and I kept smiling.

As they ripped off the lid and peered down into the box, they exclaimed, "What? A leaf blower? Are you kidding?" They were mad at us for most of the day.

Mark and I explained that we had never said it was a Shaggy Bag. They complained that a leaf blower was not for the whole family, just for Mark and me.

We said, "No, wait and see; it's for *everyone*!"

—*Paula Hemingway*

Father, help me accept the gifts you think are best for me to use in serving others, instead of what I want for myself. Amen.

April 8

The Best Mistake I Ever Made

Your Father knows exactly what you
need even before you ask him!

MATTHEW 6:8

Tax time is always entertaining. Trying to wade through the myriad forms, deductions, nondeductions, and new laws could burn out a huge computer, much less my brain. So every year I postpone tackling the task as long as possible, hoping that the longer I wait the less money I will owe. *Not!*

For several years, I had a CPA who prepared my taxes. Then I became tired of paying him so much money, and my bookkeeper and I began doing them instead. That was not the wisest course of action.

We worked through my taxes for the current tax year, using the previous year's forms prepared by the CPA as a guide so we would not forget anything. In the process, we entered my deduction for health insurance premiums—100 percent deductible for self-employed people. But when I looked at the previous year's form, no amount had been entered for health insurance premiums. *Strange*, I thought. Barbara did not know why either. It was obviously a mistake.

So I pulled out my records from the previous year and eventually found that I had paid more than $6,000 in premiums, which the CPA had failed to claim. (See me smiling?) We downloaded a form to file an amendment to the previous year's taxes, filled it out, and discovered the IRS owed me $1,978. *Woo hoo!*

Then we continued the current year's filing, holding our breaths as the final "taxes due" number was calculated. Having had very little work for more than a year, I had no idea how I would be able to pay it, no matter how much it was. When Barbara hit "total," it came out to $1,976. I started laughing with glee. And I think I heard God laughing in the background too.

Sweet Father, thank you for always anticipating what I will need and providing it even before I know to ask. What a great Father you are! Amen.

Headless Superheroes

"I know the plans I have for you," says the LORD.
"They are plans for good and not for disaster,
to give you a future and a hope."

JEREMIAH 29:11

My three-year-old grandson, Sam, was very attached to a crocheted red blanket. It had survived two of his older brothers but was ripped and unraveling. He needed a new blanket, but he did not want one. My daughter-in-law talked him into letting me make him a new one, so armed with my scissors, thread, and sewing machine, I headed to the rescue.

The next plan of action was to pick out fabric. I had made the older boys fleece blankets. A large Batman adorned the front of one and Spider-Man the other. Sam envisioned his own with a large action figure on the front—preferably Iron Man, but he would settle for the Incredible Hulk. A Batman-patterned fleece was the only action-figured fabric I found. Sam knew what he wanted, and that was not it. I thought as soon as I pulled out my fancy machine and started to sew, he would be okay. Instead, as I trimmed the fabric to square the edges, Sam started to cry.

"Sam, what's the matter?"

"You cut the Batmans' heads off."

Each Batman was about six inches tall and printed haphazardly all across the fabric. I had to look to see what he was talking about, but periodically heads were missing all the way around the edges of the fabric. I tried to proclaim my innocence, explaining that the saleslady had cut those heads off, but Sam did not care who had hurt Batman—the heads were missing.

Maybe if I start sewing, he will be okay, I thought. But when I sewed the first seam, Sam cried even more.

"Sam, now what's the matter?"

"Now you're sticking that needle into Batman."

Sigh.

—*Pam Whitley*

Father, help me to recognize that your plans are always good for me, even when they don't match my expectations. Amen.

Skuzzy

When I was a child, I spoke and thought and reasoned as a child. But when I grew up, I put away childish things.

1 CORINTHIANS 13:11

My computer, not my phone, rang. Surprised, I turned to look at the screen. A moment earlier my daughter Kari, who lives far away, and I had said, "Love you," before we closed our video chat. Now she was calling again. After I clicked the "Accept" button, she and my two-year-old granddaughter came into view.

"Did Abigail want to say ''bye' to Nana?" I smiled, remembering the first time Abigail had cried because she had missed saying good-bye to me.

"Not exactly," Kari explained. Evidently Abigail's knees went limp like a noodle when she noticed Kari and I had ended the video chat. She had collapsed on the floor in despair. Kari had asked, "Did you want to tell Nana ''bye'?"

With a contorted face Abigail had whined, "No. Want ''bye, Skuzzy.' Want ''bye, Skuzzy.'"

Listening to Kari's quick explanation and seeing the longing in Abigail's eyes, I dove my hand into Skuzzy, a well-worn, purple puppet, and immediately directed kisses toward my webcam.

Abigail grinned with delight, not caring that Skuzzy's Velcro-attached, fuzzy facial features were askew. He instantly cured her cloudy mood and made her toddler world sunny. And I realized, after saying good-bye, that my day was brighter too.

As I put my thrift-store purchase away, I considered the following truth: *Abigail chose Skuzzy over me.* I was not disappointed. After all, I had introduced them and developed Skuzzy's character into who *he* was because of who *she* was.

One day Abigail will not need Skuzzy to hold her attention to the computer during Abigail-and-Nana chats. Then I will put Skuzzy away for good and acknowledge that Abigail is growing up—a bittersweet realization.

—*Sue Ferguson*

Father, thank you for your patience as you help me to mature in my relationship with you. Help me to put away childish ways and learn to choose you over the toys that distract me in this world. Amen.

The Other Half

Tell them to use their money to do good. They should be rich in good works and generous to those in need, always being ready to share with others.

1 TIMOTHY 6:18

In the midseventies, my husband and I ministered at a church in Pittsburgh, Pennsylvania. While there, we became familiar with the famous Carnegie family. In the South we pronounce it "CAR-nuh-gee," but in the Northeast, it's pronounced "car-NAY-gee."

In his book *The Gospel of Wealth*, financier Andrew Carnegie declared his belief that wealthy people have an added responsibility to help and endow social charities and public needs. And he lived up to that declaration by funding many educational and social projects, such as Carnegie libraries around the country and Carnegie Mellon University in Pittsburgh.

Fund-raising people often called on Mr. Carnegie, requesting his generous support. One year a man came to the Carnegie mansion to ask for sixty thousand dollars for a music project. Carnegie started to write out a check, but then he paused.

"I've changed my mind," Carnegie said. "Surely there are other people who like music enough to help with this project by donating their own money." Then he offered a challenge grant, saying if the man could raise the first thirty thousand dollars, Carnegie would donate the other half of the needed funds. The man thanked Carnegie and left.

The next day, the fund-raiser returned to the Carnegie home, announcing that he had already managed to raise the challenge amount. Carnegie congratulated the man and promptly wrote out his own check for the remaining thirty thousand dollars as promised and handed it to him.

The man thanked Carnegie profusely and was about to leave when Carnegie asked, "Would you mind telling me who gave you the other half?"

"Not at all," the man said with a mischievous smile. "It was Mrs. Carnegie."

Dear Father, thank you for your generosity toward us. You lavish your marvelous gifts on us every day, and our lives are so richly blessed. Help us to show our gratitude by sharing our blessings with others. Amen.

Clean Sandwich

Not that I was ever in need, for I have learned how to be content with whatever I have.

PHILIPPIANS 4:11

After her first day of kindergarten, I asked my daughter how school was. She proceeded to tell me about her teacher, her friends, and the things they did. She paused for a minute and told me that at lunch a little boy in her class had a "clean sandwich." I was puzzled by the comment but did not question it. Later that week, as I was preparing her lunch, she started talking about the clean sandwich again. She explained how good it looked and how some days she just wanted to snatch it and take a bite out of it!

Tickled, I replied, "It sounds like a really good sandwich."

A few weeks passed, and one day I forgot to buy bread for the children's lunch. I asked my husband to pick up a loaf on his way home. Later that night, my husband walked in with a loaf of white bread instead of our normal wheat bread. When my daughter saw it, she was very excited and exclaimed, "Mom! Are you going to make me a clean sandwich?"

"Yes," I laughed.

The next day I prepared her lunch, and my daughter was so excited about her sandwich she could not think about anything else. After school I asked her how the sandwich was.

She said, "It was okay."

I asked, "Wasn't it good?"

"It wasn't as good as I thought it would be; it tasted almost like the other bread."

I asked, "Do you understand why we eat wheat instead of white bread?"

She sighed with resignation and said, "Yes, because it's good for us."

—*Felicia Washington*

Father, thank you for giving me what I need for a happy life. Please help me to be content with what you have already provided, because you know what's best for me, even when it may not be my favorite idea. Amen.

Gettin' Thar

I press on to reach the end of the race
and receive the heavenly prize for which God,
through Christ Jesus, is calling us.

PHILIPPIANS 3:14

Hiram and Mary lived in the Great Smoky Mountains, but their homes were about four miles apart. They had, nevertheless, been sweethearts their entire lives. Hiram often walked the four long miles through the mountains to call on Mary at her log cabin, where she lived with her mother.

One fall day, Hiram came to see Mary, and because Mary's mother was taking her typical afternoon nap, they decided to go for a walk so they would not wake her up. They finally returned to the front porch, where they sat quietly for a long time on a rickety, old wooden bench. There they watched the sun slowly set and the big, golden harvest moon rise. Soon the old devil moon worked its magic, and Hiram slid a little closer to Mary.

He patted her hand and said, "Mary, y'know I got a clearin' over thar and a team an' a wagon an' some hawgs an' cows, and I allow as how I'm gonna build me a house this fall an' . . ."

About that time, Mary's mother, who had just awakened from her nap, interrupted Hiram and asked, "Mary, is that young man thar yet?"

Mary responded with a giggle, "No, Maw, but he's agettin' thar!"

Sometimes, when I think of heaven, I just wonder if I will ever get there. It seems so ethereal and far away at times. And yet, I know I am on my way, and some sweet day I will pass through that golden gate and be gathered into the arms of the Lover of my soul for all eternity. I'm agettin' thar!

Dear Lord, sometimes life seems long and hard, but I know that someday I will be at home and at peace with you. Thank you for adopting me into your family and for loving me so. Amen.

Exuberant Worship

True worshipers will worship the Father in spirit and in truth. The Father is looking for those who will worship him that way.

JOHN 4:23

I was a pastor in a small country church in South Africa. We had spent two hours in a praise-and-worship service one Sunday evening, so when Monday morning came, I felt spiritually drained and a little grumpy.

That morning as I was having my daily devotions out in the garden, the Lord and I enjoyed an interesting conversation.

"Morning, Lord," I commenced. "Since last night's service I've been wondering about this eternity business. People often ask, 'What will we do in eternity?' I usually reply with the stock answer, 'We will spend our time praising and worshiping God.' But, Lord, after last night's session, I'm seriously wondering whether I could even spend a single day praising and worshiping. All this hand raising and clapping stuff! Lord, is that what it's really going to be about?"

I half expected a stiff clout around the ear from the Lord. Instead, his reply was so gracious and gentle. "I understand that you must be a bit worn out, son! But tell me, what would you like to do for eternity?"

I thought about that for a while and then replied, "Well, Lord, you know how much I love gardening. If there is one thing that would give me real pleasure, it would be to work in your glorious heavenly garden. Then I could look forward to discovering your marvelous purposes for every living thing. I mean, Lord, why did you create snails, mosquitoes, and ticks?"

I sensed the Lord chuckle as he replied, "And what will you do, son, when I show you that I even have a good purpose for snails, mosquitoes, and ticks?"

"Why, Lord, I would just jump in the air and shout for joy, 'Hallelujah! Isn't God great!'"

There was a poignant silence. I sensed the Lord smile. "I call that worship, my son!"

—Gerald McCann

Lord, teach us to worship you as we enjoy the majesty of your creation all around us. Amen.

Where the Treasure Is

Wherever your treasure is, there the desires of your heart will also be.

MATTHEW 6:21

Today is income tax day—a day when we are, perhaps, more focused on our money than any other day of the year. Most of us are filling out the complicated IRS forms and grudgingly paying "our fair share" to the government, wishing our *fair* share was just a little more *fair*.

In our consumeristic society, we are often overly focused on our money, or lack of it—what it will buy, what we cannot buy without it, the seeming prestige it gives the ones who have it, the lack of respect it sadly gives to those who do not have it. And yet, as my preacher daddy used to say, "The Lord must love poor people, because he made so many of us."

Abraham Lincoln himself came from a poor upbringing, yet he rose to the highest office in our land and became one of the most respected presidents the United States has ever known. His down-home wisdom and natural wit won him an enormous following and endeared him to our nation for all time.

Once Hugh McCulloch, then secretary of the treasury, brought a delegation of New York bankers to meet President Lincoln. As they came into the room, McCulloch whispered to him, "These gentlemen from New York have come to see about our new loan. As bankers, they are obliged to hold our national securities. I can vouch for their patriotism and loyalty, for, as the Good Book says, 'Where the treasure is, there will the heart be also.'"

Lincoln nodded knowingly and said quietly, "There is another text, Mr. McCulloch, I recall, that might equally apply: 'Where the carcass is, there will the eagles be gathered together.'"

O God, please help me today to focus on what I have, rather than on what I do not have. I am so richly blessed in so many ways, and I am thankful to you for providing for me so well. Amen.

Roar of the Dandelions

Stay alert! Watch out for your great enemy,
the devil. He prowls around like a roaring
lion, looking for someone to devour.

1 PETER 5:8

My husband and I have never been known for our gardening skills. In fact, our friends have called our yard the "Garden of Weeden." So, when we landscaped our new home, we called in an expert to help us start with a good foundation.

Thanks to him, no weeds sprouted among the tender shrubs and flowers. We were overjoyed, until we noticed that the weeds had merely packed their bags and moved to our lawn.

Instead of consulting the expert again, my husband took control of the situation himself. A trip to the hardware store netted weed killer and a sprayer.

He was almost finished dousing the invaders when I looked at the empty weed-killer bottle for the first time. I could not believe what I read: "Weed and Grass Killer"!

A month later, our lush lawn was marred by large brown splotches of dirt—missing pieces of a sod puzzle.

For three long years we watched Bermuda runners creep into the dirt patches, multiplying, spreading, and filling in the gaps. Neighbors surely deemed our lawn an eyesore, but we survived the open wounds caused by our inept efforts.

Now, years later, neighbors drive by and see a lush front lawn again. It is well maintained and virtually weed free.

We have learned that it's a mistake not to stay in contact with the expert.

—*Catrina Bradley*

Father, thank you for your Word. May I never neglect to consult you for wisdom when I am under attack and to trust you to keep me safe from the enemy as he prowls around. Thank you for rescuing me when I insist on taking control and then falter and stumble. I know I can't win the battles on my own; I need your strength, your firm foundation. Amen.

An 8-Track Girl in an iPod World

May the words of my mouth
and the meditation of my heart
be pleasing to you,
O Lord, my rock and my redeemer.

PSALM 19:14

There I was, playing on the floor with my two-year-old niece, when suddenly she decided to watch the Care Bears movie. As I slowly got up, feeling my age, she picked up a remote control, pushed the buttons, opened the DVD player, put in her movie, and started the television. She turned around, gave me the biggest smile, and sat down in her chair, with her thumb in her mouth and her baby doll in her arms.

As I sat there with a deer-in-the-headlights look, I realized I was stuck in the past. You know, back when Bluetooth happened when you were eating cotton candy at the festival, when SPAM was on your plate at lunchtime, and when you actually had to get off the couch to change the channel. I never did learn how to program my VCR. I knew I was technology challenged, but did I have to be shown up by a two-year-old?

As I watched my niece, so happy that her movie was coming on, I could not help but think of how poor my attitude was toward modern technology. It was time to stop complaining. Is that not what the Israelites did as they wandered around in the desert for forty years? I am already middle aged. I do not have forty years to waste, so I need to change. Besides, what woman these days can wear only one pair of shoes that long?

In Exodus we read that, when the Israelites left Egypt and wandered in the desert, God was displeased with their murmuring. How often do we complain and have a negative attitude that we do not even recognize? Maybe it is time to give ourselves spiritual checkups and check our vital signs for malfunctioning attitudes. We just might find a diagnosis to text to ourselves.

—Lisa M. Garvey

Lord, please help us to keep our attitudes positive and our mouths full of thanksgiving. Amen.

Taking Charge

Husbands, . . . love your wives, just as Christ loved the church.

EPHESIANS 5:25

Through the years I have edited dozens of books on marriage and family relationships. Some of them I thought offered excellent godly advice, while others were not as strong. Somehow, the books written primarily for men all tended to come back to this verse in Ephesians 5:25, instructing husbands to love their wives as Christ loved the church. And I often thought, *Right, but what mere man could ever actually do that?*

It reminds me of the story about one man who was seriously trying to live up to his husbandly role. He went to the local Christian bookstore and bought one of those marriage books that encourage men to stand up and be the heads of their homes. He took it home; read it; and made notes in the margins, underlined statements that seemed important to him, highlighted others. Finally, he finished the book late one night after his wife had already fallen asleep.

The next morning he woke up, looked at his wife, and decided to take charge of his home and family. So he informed her, without stuttering about it, that from that moment on, he was going to be in charge and she would need to obey his every command and meet his every request.

"You're going to start dressing up before I come home from work. Then you'll cook a real dinner, not something microwaved, and there will be a homemade dessert. When I'm finished eating, you will draw my bath, with bubbles, so I can relax. And beyond that, guess who's going to shave me, dress me, and comb my hair in the mornings?"

His wife looked him straight in the eye and said, "The funeral director."

Somehow, I think he missed the point.

Heavenly Father, please teach us how to treat those we love the most with dignity, courtesy, and kindness. Help us not to take each other for granted. Amen.

Animal Antics

God made all sorts of wild animals.

GENESIS 1:25

Our cats drape themselves across the furniture like decor. Jazzy, the striped gray kitten, sleeps with her leg hanging off the back of the couch, copying my teenagers. Biscuit poses as a furry replica of the sphinx. Sunny sleeps curled up in a coil like a cushion. Their naturally decorative shapes elicit my daily admiration.

About two o'clock one morning a jarring scream interrupted our peaceful night's sleep. It was the familiar story. "Wake up, wake up!" I pleaded, while I shook my husband. "One of our cats got a rabbit."

I did not want to see the result. I followed my husband to the hallway. There, the cat held a bunny in its mouth. The poor thing was chattering in fear. (For the uninitiated, a baby rabbit can scream just as a person does.) Though icky enough, at least this episode did not require us to chase a live bunny under and around our bedroom paraphernalia in the middle of the night.

Our cats use a swing-out door on the side of the house. Consequently, in the morning disturbing, partial gifts occasionally await my inspection on the dining-room rug.

In addition to revealing examples of nature's food chain, our cats teach us the fine art of relationship. My boys would prefer to stuff cats under covers, haul them around like potato sacks, and use them as pillows. They have learned that these actions typically result in invisible cats.

Each cat makes known its individual preference. One likes a pat on the head. Another enjoys a tummy scratch. The third must be lightly scratched from head to midback. If the kids wish cat love in return, they must figure out exactly how to please. After all, as cats make us aware by their aristocratic attitudes, we *are* their servants.

—*Diane E. Kay*

God, the wonder of pets reveals your joyous creativity. Thank you so much for the delightful animals you have given us. Amen.

May I Present . . .

The Lord *[said], "I will indeed do what you have asked, for I look favorably on you, and I know you by name."*

EXODUS 33:17

One of the most important skills of a successful politician is remembering people's names. Unfortunately, President Taft didn't possess that skill to a great degree. So, over time, he became quite adept at avoiding the name issue altogether, often having an aide ask for the person's name and then presenting him or her to Taft.

At one White House gathering, when Taft was serving as secretary of war, he was standing in a receiving line greeting visitors. His aide, Captain Butt, asked one man for his name in order to present him to Taft, but the man refused, saying that he and Taft were old friends and that he would need no introduction.

The line of people progressed toward Taft, who soon found himself facing a stranger. Looking pleadingly at Captain Butt, he received only a shrug of Butt's shoulders. Taft, seeing he was in trouble, dramatically swept his hand high and sent it firmly into the stranger's hand. At the same time, he turned to his wife and said, "Dear, you remember our dear old friend here," and before Mrs. Taft could say anything, Taft had moved the man past him and was greeting the next person in line.

After the man moved on, Mrs. Taft asked her husband who the man was. Taft replied, "My darling, I have not the faintest idea who he is, but I saw he was an intimate friend by the way he stood poised on one foot waiting to be recognized."

Later, the stranger found Captain Butt and said with pride, "I told you there was no need to present me!"

Father, I am so grateful that you know my name and that I will not need to be introduced to you when I get to heaven. Thank you for knowing me and loving me, Lord. Amen.

Another Day, Another Door

Go and make disciples of all the nations,
baptizing them in the name of the Father
and the Son and the Holy Spirit.

MATTHEW 28:19

Once I traveled to Wellington, New Zealand, to work on a short-term mission with Campaign for Christ. Lots of crazy things happened to us while knocking on doors to set up Bible studies. A seventy-year-old farmer from Kansas named Harold had some of the most eye-opening experiences.

One day, shy, reserved Harold was knocking on doors with Rob—a crazy, never-met-a-stranger Kiwi (native New Zealander). Rob said that he and Harold walked up the steps of a large house in a wealthy neighborhood, and Rob rang the doorbell. Soon the wooden door opened.

An attractive young woman pushed the door wide open and smiled at them brightly. She was topless! Not befuddled by her brashness, Rob—keeping his eyes locked on her *face*—calmly talked to her about the Lord. As he said later, she obviously needed to know Christ badly. Rob said old Harold's jaw dropped all the way to his knees, where it stayed until the conversation ended and he stumbled off the porch.

The next day, Harold and I were working together. We climbed some rickety wooden stairs at the side of a house and stood on a small porch. It was Harold's turn to talk, so he knocked on the door.

When the two occupants came to the door, it was obviously—at least to me—a gay couple, one of whom was in a dress and had long hair. Harold, to his credit, held a very calm, competent conversation with the two men. They were not interested in the Lord, so we left our tract, wished them well, and walked down the stairs.

Heading for the next house, I discovered why Harold had been so talkative with the gay couple. He said, "That sure was a homely woman, wasn't it?"

It was a long week for Harold.

Thank you, Lord, for opportunities to tell other people about you wherever we go in life. Amen.

Now That Tastes Good!

Taste and see that the LORD is good.
Oh, the joys of those who take refuge in him!

PSALM 34:8

On two different occasions, my husband and I visited Houston to see my granddaughter, Kelena. On each visit, we took her to church with us. It was a little hard for Kelena to wake up that first Sunday—waking up early on Sundays was not a part of her routine. At any rate, by the time we arrived at church, she was fine. Kelena enjoyed the singing and worshiping, and she excitedly clapped her little hands, mimicking Greg and me.

It was a Communion Sunday, and as the baskets were being passed around, she asked, "Maw-maw, what is that in those baskets?"

"Honey, that is Communion."

With a puzzled look on her face, she asked, "What's a Communion? Can I have one when the basket comes by?"

I told her no, thinking, *If her mom and dad went to church, this child would not be puzzled about Communion. Okay, Lord, how do I explain this one?*

"Kelena, Jesus died for the sins of mankind, and that included you, me, and anyone who accepts Jesus and his dying for us. To share in his dying for us, we drink the juice and eat the wafer symbolizing our being one with him in body." I was hoping she was able to understand a little.

On our way home from church, Kelena asked us to call her parents so she could talk with them. She was excited to tell her mommy about her day in church. "I was singing and clapping with Maw-maw and Paw-paw."

The next words out of her mouth would have found me proverbially spitting out anything in my mouth had there been something there. "Mommy, guess what happened today in church? Maw-maw and Paw-paw ate God."

All I could do was look at her and smile.

—Elaine W. Cavalier

Dear God, help me to remember that whatever I do is a reflection of you. Let the sweetness of your Word be like honey in my mouth. In Jesus' name, amen.

I Domino!

All the people will [say], "Amen."

DEUTERONOMY 27:15

When I was a young man, we lived on a working farm in East Texas. And when I say "we," I am talking about my four brothers, my dad, and my bachelor uncle. My mom had died when I was about twelve years old and I had no sisters, so all the men and boys did what we called "batching" together.

In the summertime, while we worked hard in the fields by day, we also went to church meetings a lot at night. In those days, traveling preachers would come through the country and hold two- or three-week gospel meetings. We would build a brush arbor, carry the pews from inside the church building outside where it was cooler, and listen to the preacher every night.

During the week, old Brother Harvey and some of the other older men in the small community would spend a lot of time at the general store, where they would sit around drinking sodas, slapping flies, telling stories, and playing dominoes.

One night they asked Brother Harvey to lead the opening prayer. I was happy, because he was known for his long prayers and I could close my tired eyes and get in a little catnap before he said amen. True to form, Brother Harvey prayed on and on, praising the Lord for most things under the sun and asking him for everything else.

That particular night, Brother Harvey's prayer went on so long I got my nap over with and woke up. Something funny was going on. Brother Harvey was stuttering around and could not seem to find the words he needed. Everyone in the old arbor was starting to squirm and whisper.

Finally, in total frustration, unable to think of the word *amen,* Brother Harvey blurted out, "I domino!"

—Clyde Shrode

Dear Lord, thank you for hearing our prayers, even when we don't always express them very well. We know your Spirit hears our hearts and translates our longings into the words you want to hear. Amen.

Distracted

I want you to do whatever will help you serve the Lord best, with as few distractions as possible.

1 CORINTHIANS 7:35

My younger son is always telling me to get off Facebook. But I am a multitasker, and one evening I was cooking for seven people and playing on Facebook at the same time. Before dinner I was chatting on Facebook, while the food was cooking I was chatting, and after dinner I was chatting.

While I was doing the dishes, I put a wet pot on a hot burner to dry—a trick for drying pots and pans my mother-in-law had taught me. This particular night I forgot to turn off the burner. My mind was on Facebook and getting back to interacting with my friends.

Several minutes passed, and when I realized the burner was still on, I immediately turned it off. I moved the pot, but I did not place it on a cool burner. Rather, I set it directly on the glass of the countertop range and went back to my computer. *Boom!* A shotgun-type sound exploded in the kitchen!

The family ran in to see what had happened. The heat from the burner and the pot had spiked the temperature in the glass to explosive levels. Some of the glass flew across the room. No one was hurt, thankfully, but a thirty-seven-year-old woman who is proficient in the kitchen had managed to blow up a stovetop.

I received many disparaging looks and comments from my children and husband. All I could do was smile sweetly and explain that I was chatting. It was an expensive chat. The stove still works, but there is no glass.

My younger son is always telling me to get off Facebook. Imagine!

—Heather Lawley

Father, please keep us close to what is important in our personal lives and help us not to be distracted by things that can hinder us. Amen.

Confetti

[Jesus] said, "Give to Caesar what belongs to Caesar, and give to God what belongs to God."

MATTHEW 22:21

Before my husband and I married, he ran his own business in Belle Plaine, Kansas—a small town about forty minutes south of Wichita. It was a successful business that generated a lot of bookkeeping and tax paperwork, which he kept well organized.

Eventually, he decided to close his business and enter the ministry. So he packed all his records and moved them to his parents' farm for safekeeping. Since there was no room in the house, he carefully packed his accounting records and tax returns into a large wooden barrel and stored it in the barn. Then he went off to Texas for a year's internship to become a personal evangelist.

A year or so later, he received a letter from the IRS saying they wanted to audit his tax return. Knowing his records were in order, he set an appointment with the IRS and made the trip from Texas for the meeting. When he arrived at his parents' home, he went to the barn to get the necessary paperwork and found a barrel full of . . . confetti! Rats had gnawed through the wooden barrel and devoured the tasty paperwork from top to bottom, leaving nothing but a barrel full of paper shreds, as useless as turkey giblets.

Oh no! Now what do I do? he wondered. The IRS agent was due at the farm in less than an hour. Sadly, there was just nothing he could do but face the music.

When the IRS agent arrived, my husband explained the situation and took the agent to the barn to show him the rats' leftovers, thinking he was in legal trouble. The agent took one look in the barrel, closed his portfolio, and said, "Congratulations, Mr. Hollingsworth. You have passed the audit! When no records exist, no audit can be performed." And he left. *Whew!*

Dear heavenly Father, sometimes, in spite of our best efforts, things just don't go right in this life. Thank you for your forgiveness when they go wrong. Amen.

E-Mail from Heaven

The day you die is better than the day you are born. . . .
After all, everyone dies—
so the living should take this to heart.

ECCLESIASTES 7:1-2

It seems there was a couple from Minneapolis, Minnesota, who decided to go to Florida for a few days to thaw out during one particularly cold winter. Because both of them worked, they had some difficulty coordinating travel schedules. They finally decided that the husband would leave for Florida on a certain day, and the wife would follow him the day after. The man made it to Florida as planned and went directly to his hotel.

Once in his room, he decided to open his laptop and send his wife, who was still in Minnesota, an e-mail. However, he accidentally left off one letter in typing his wife's e-mail address and sent the e-mail without realizing his error.

Meanwhile, in another part of the country, a widow had just returned from the funeral of her husband, a Lutheran pastor of many years, who had been "called home to glory" a few days earlier. Although distraught over the loss of her beloved husband, she decided to check her e-mail because she was expecting to hear from some of his many relatives and friends around the world. But upon reading the first e-mail message, she let out a loud scream, fainted, and fell to the floor.

The woman's son rushed into the room and found his mother lying on the floor. While trying to revive her, he glanced up at the computer screen and saw the following e-mail:

To: *My loving wife*
Subject: *I've arrived!*

I've just checked in. Everything has been prepared for your arrival here tomorrow. Looking forward to seeing you then!

Your devoted husband

Father, I pray that I will be ready to go when you come to take me home to glory. I rest in your saving grace and your wonderful promises, and I look forward with joy and anticipation to being in your presence. Amen.

New Ideas

The one sitting on the throne said,
"Look, I am making everything new!"

REVELATION 21:5

The elderly priest, speaking to the younger priest, said, "It was a good idea to replace the first four pews with plush theater seats. It worked. The front of the church fills first."

The young priest nodded, and the old one continued, "And you told me a little more beat to the music would bring young people back to church, so I supported you when you brought in that rock 'n' roll gospel choir. We are packed to the balcony."

"Thank you, Father," answered the young priest, "I am pleased you are open to the new ideas of youth."

"However," said the elderly priest, "I'm afraid you've gone too far with the drive-through confessional."

"But, Father," protested the young priest, "my confessions have nearly doubled since I began that!"

"I know, son," replied the old man, "but that flashing neon sign, 'Toot 'n' Tell or Go to Hell,' is just not staying on the church roof."

It is fascinating that God did not define certain things in the Bible. By leaving more general terms and commands in his Word, he has allowed his church to stay "new every morning" (see Lamentations 3:23) and ever fresh, connecting with each new generation.

The rest of us? Not so much. For the most part, younger people like newness and change, and older people like sameness, familiarity, and comfort. And yet, God is not the God of comfort. He is the God of action, challenge, and tackling difficulties. So, before we complain about all the changes happening in the church, perhaps it would be good to seek his wisdom, his mission for the church, and his love of the lost.

"Now," as my dad would say, "you've quit preaching and gone to meddlin'."

—J. John and Mark Stibbe

O Lord, thank you for making your church ever new and able to touch the hearts and lives of people in every age. Please help me to be part of the solutions needed and not part of the problems. Amen.

Yuck-cumbers and Omelets

*Three things will last forever—faith, hope,
and love—and the greatest of these is love.*

1 CORINTHIANS 13:13

I think I'll cook us an omelet," my husband, Larry, announced one Saturday morning. He tossed off the covers and headed downstairs.

What a treat for me! I am ordinarily the cook, so it was a luxury to have someone else fixing the meal. I love a nice omelet, chock-full of fresh veggies like onions and green peppers and maybe some cheddar cheese.

With anticipation, my son and I pulled up our chairs to the table.

"Boy, this looks delicious," I said with gusto. "What did you put in it?"

My husband replied, "Why don't you try it and see?"

Uh-oh. That particular comment might be a bad sign. He tended toward weird cooking ideas. Lovingly, yet truthfully, I acknowledged Larry's breakfast effort might challenge my wifely wisdom.

My son and I looked at each other across the table with concern as we brought our forks to our mouths. Both of us wanted to thank the cook for cooking. Both of us, however, are honest.

Unbelievable! Yuck. Cooked cucumbers! It was worse than I had imagined. My son was trying to keep that nice, I-love-omelets look, but I could see the tension in his face.

Aha. I'll redeem the moment. I began with a twist of discretion: "Did you put cucumbers in it?" I added a dot of truth with my less-than-thrilled tone.

Next, I tossed in a hint of humor—a smile for my son—followed by a dash of love: "Honey, thank you for making breakfast." And, finally, another dollop of truth finished it—a lot of omelet remained on our plates. I realized with satisfaction that I had managed successful love navigation.

To spare us further torture, I mentally planned a future "*yuck*-cumber" discussion.

—Diane E. Kay

Lord, remind me to be a blessing, even when it is not my first inclination. May your love direct the moments of my days. Amen.

Showers of Blessings

The godly are showered with blessings.

PROVERBS 10:6

For weeks I had been buried in work and deadlines, and I was so tired. Finally, I just had to take a break. So my friend Charlotte and I decided to take a weekend road trip. We headed south from Fort Worth toward one of our favorite shopping towns—Salado—a quaint little community with numerous curio shops, rare bookstores, and our favorite home decor store, called Horsefeathers.

En route I complained to Charlotte about all the projects and deadlines I had been juggling. She listened patiently, as always, and tried to soothe my frustration. In the midst of my tirade, we came up behind an older RV that had obviously spent lots of time on the road. A bumper sticker simply said, "Count Your Blessings."

That made me pause for a moment, and I realized how richly blessed with work and income I had been over the past few months. I stopped complaining and turned up the music in the car. For the next two hours, we talked about other things, including the beautiful Texas wildflowers that were blooming along the roadside: bluebonnets (my favorites), Indian paintbrush, and crimson clover.

We had a pleasant evening in Salado with dinner at an outdoor restaurant, followed by a movie, then rest at a delightful bed-and-breakfast. The next morning, we dressed, had breakfast, and drove into town for shopping. On the way, I started ranting again about my hectic work schedule and all the accompanying irritations. Charlotte listened patiently. (Are you seeing a pattern here?) As we pulled into town, an older RV turned the corner in front of us. You guessed it: The same RV, and the bumper sticker still said, "Count Your Blessings." I stopped and smiled.

Then I said aloud, "Thanks, Lord. I think I've got the message now." And the rest of the trip was fun and free of complaints.

Dear Father, thank you for the many blessings you give to me every day. There are just too many to count. Amen.

Slapping on the Plaster

A cheerful heart is good medicine.

PROVERBS 17:22

As a preacher for some fifty years, I learned that people paid better attention if I told a funny story now and then to help make my points. That kept them awake long enough to pull them through the more serious Bible teaching I needed to do. As my old African American preacher friend Marshall Keeble used to say, "If you want to teach my people something important, first you've got to get them laughing. Then you can slap the plaster on, and it'll stick every time."

One of my favorite stories is about two soldiers in a combat zone. Bullets were flying, and each of these soldiers took a running dive into a nearby foxhole, ending up in the foxhole together. While they were ducking the incoming fire from the enemy, they had the following conversation:

"Hey, there, my name's Henry. What's yours?"

"Well, that's funny, because my name is Henry too!"

"No kidding. Where are you from?"

"I'm from Memphis, Tennessee. How about you?"

"No! Really? Well, I'm from Memphis too! Say, what part of town do you live in?"

"I live over in the Rock Creek area. You?"

"I don't *believe* this! I live in the Rock Creek area."

"Well, I'll be. What street do you live on?"

"I live on Presley Avenue—you know, named for Elvis. How about you?"

"Well, now, you're just not going to believe this, but I live on Presley Avenue too! Say, what's your house number?"

"My house is at 4703 Presley. Do we live close together?"

"Uh, I'd say so, because my house number is 4703 too."

"No! Hey, wait a minute. What's your wife's name?"

"My wife's name is Georgia."

"Now, doesn't that just beat all—my wife's name is Georgia too. You know what? I think we must be husbands-in-law!"

—*Clyde Shrode*

Thank you, Lord, for laughter. It is such a soul-refreshing treat. Amen.

Floored

Wise choices will watch over you.

PROVERBS 2:11

Our plane taxied into the Gulfport-Biloxi International Airport with thirty people from my church aboard. We were there to serve the people of First Baptist Church of Gulfport. Before nightfall, we sat in our barracks in sight of the church. The beautiful old building faced the Gulf Coast, and when Katrina had come ashore, a twenty-five-foot water surge had smashed through it.

Our prayer-and-planning room consisted of a handful of plastic chairs circled under a tree, and our sleeping quarters were two bunk bed–filled FEMA trailers. Our bath area was in a separate trailer, lined with curtained shower stalls and divided in half—a men's side and a women's side, each with its own door.

Night approached, and a couple of women took their pajamas, towels, and toothbrushes and traipsed to the showers. They returned shortly, saying the floors were wet and there was no place to lay their clean clothes.

I had a solution. I hurried outside and grabbed a plastic chair from our meeting area. We had been told to back into the shower area to give people privacy, so I darted up the ramp and backed into the room. One lady was already in the shower, or so I thought. I walked to her door and said loudly, "Here's your chair."

A man cleared his throat and mumbled something. Immediately, I knew I had chosen the wrong door.

Returning to the barracks, I laughed with embarrassment until tears spilled down my face. The ladies insisted that I share what was so funny. I hesitated, but they promised not to tell anyone.

The next morning as we assembled under the tree for devotions, one woman said, "I think there's a chair missing." The others giggled and agreed—while I struggled to look innocent.

—*Pam Whitley*

Lord, help me to slow down long enough to be alert to my surroundings and my choices. And keep me from stumbling into places and situations I need to avoid. Amen.

Silly Goose

Be honest in your evaluation of yourselves.

ROMANS 12:3

No Christian is a misfit. We all have one or more gifts to complement the functions of our local Christian community. When we identify and practice our gifts, we have the deep satisfaction of seeing God our Father using us as he planned, and we become aware of miracles happening around and through us. That does not allow us to crow with a sense of superiority, but it does illustrate that God's ways are higher than our ways and that he longs for us to walk in his highway.

For example, we have a gaggle of noisy geese that parade around the farmyard, every now and then setting off in a screeching run/fly at some imagined threat. They are at their most peaceful in the duck pond.

Some of our neighbors asked us to take their home-reared goose to give it a chance to live in harmony with its fellows and enjoy swimming in the pond. When Flower arrived, though, it quickly became clear that she did not see herself as a goose at all and that she longed to return to living in a house with loving children. She stood to one side of the flock and honked loudly for the humans she loved.

She seemed to say, "What am I doing in the company of these uncouth birds? I'm superior."

When a person appeared, Flower rushed up and demanded their undivided attention. I think she saw herself as a human too. In the end, her former owners took her back into their home and the family circle she loved. We hope she will live there happily ever after. Now, if only she could lay golden eggs . . .

—*John McCutcheon*

Father, thank you that you have a divine purpose for me and have given me the ability to live it out. Help me today to hear your voice and to do your will so that your glorious purposes will be fulfilled in and through me. Amen.

A Clean Sweep

My child, pay attention to what I say.
Listen carefully to my words.

PROVERBS 4:20

When my nephew, Andrew, was about six years old, he was out jumping on his trampoline. Ignoring calls from his mother and grandmother Mimi that it was time for him to come into the house, he kept jumping. Eventually the two women made their way out to the trampoline, and for the next few minutes they cajoled, promised, bribed, and threatened Andrew, trying to get him to come inside. Nothing worked.

As long as Andrew could stay in the middle of the huge trampoline, he was virtually untouchable. He knew that neither one of the women would climb the stepladder to grab him. So he kept right on jumping, laughing at them, sticking out his tongue, and just generally being a stinker.

A few minutes into the standoff, Andrew's mother realized Mimi was gone. Sighing, she turned back to the task of getting Andrew down.

As he was jumping to the far side of the trampoline to stay out of reach, Mom saw something out of the corner of her eye and turned to see Mimi with a broom. Sure enough, she swept it under Andrew's feet and brought him down to where he could be grabbed and forced off the trampoline. The determined expression on Mimi's face, mixed with the shock on Andrew's face, made it difficult for his mom to keep from laughing as she told him he was headed for time-out.

Her mission accomplished, Mimi led the way to the house, the broom on her shoulder, like a soldier coming home from battle in triumph.

A clean sweep is good for the soul.

—*Stevie Stevens*

Father, I thank you for the times in my life when you are quiet, a whisper in the wind. Thank you, also, that you gain my attention by knocking me off my feet when I need it. Amen.

Flip-Flops and Mountain Streams

Many waters cannot quench love,
nor can rivers drown it.

SONG OF SONGS 8:7

An African proverb says, "Let your love be like the misty rain, coming softly but flooding the river." My falling in love, however, was more like a baptism.

As a blossoming young woman, I noticed that the boy I had climbed trees with as a child had matured into a strapping, handsome young man.

I invited Noel to join some friends and me for a picnic at a popular spot. It was to be the perfect day, until my friends could no longer come. But Noel was still keen to keep our date.

I had not visited this spot, surrounded by flowing waterfalls, for years. By the time we got there, we had soft rain instead of sunny skies. The trees and waterfalls had grown since my last visit, leaving little dry ground.

We took a shortcut around a rocky ledge that bordered an icy mountain pool. Afraid I would fall, I clutched a borrowed camera and my flip-flops tightly to my chest with my right hand, while navigating the slippery edge with my left.

Noel reached back to me and said, "Let me help you."

"It's okay. I can manage," I said.

Seconds later, my foot slipped. As I sank beneath the icy water, my right hand shot up to keep the camera out of the water. When my head broke the water's surface, I looked up to see my perfectly dry flip-flops silhouetted against the sky. The camera, secured around my neck, hung beneath the water.

This time I eagerly accepted Noel's extended hand to pull me out.

One fuzzy photo and an exorbitant repair bill were not all I got from the cold experience. Eighteen months later, Noel and I married. Our love is still strong after twenty-seven years.

But isn't it exciting that God's unquenchable love is far greater than the deepest earthly love?

—Marion C. Ueckermann

O Lord, how priceless is your unfailing care! Engulf us with a sense of your divine love, we pray. Amen.

Gun-Packing Granny

Even when I walk
through the darkest valley,
I will not be afraid,
for you are close beside me.

PSALM 23:4

A woman in her eighties was determined to continue driving. Her family, however, was worried about her slower reflexes. She would go out at night alone, so they were concerned about her safety. They told her about muggings, kidnappings, and carjackings, thinking the scary stories would keep her at home. But they didn't.

Instead, she went out and bought a gun—a .38 Special. She did not know a thing about handling a gun, but she loaded it and shoved it into her purse. She decided she would use it if someone gave her problems.

As she was walking out of a large department store with her packages during the Christmas season, she saw three guys getting in her car and closing the doors.

This is my moment, she thought. Carefully setting her packages on the trunk of a nearby car, she pulled out her gun, walked up to the car window, and said, "Get away from my car! Get out from behind that steering wheel! You guys, move it or lose it!"

The three surprised guys clambered out of the car and took off running in three different directions.

By that time, a crowd of people had gathered around, and they were staring at her and smiling. She was feeling pretty proud of herself. *No carjacker's going to take my car!*

Putting the gun back into her purse, she picked up her packages. Then she got her car keys out of her jacket pocket and walked to her car. When she tried to insert the key into the ignition, she found that it did not fit. It was then she realized that the car she had "protected" was not hers.

Father, thank you for protecting us from our fears and worries, even when they are false. We know you are our Protector and our Provider, and we can rest in that truth. Amen.

Seeking Wisdom

Getting wisdom is the wisest thing you can do!
And whatever else you do, develop good judgment.

PROVERBS 4:7

You may remember the Bible story of Solomon. He had a dream in which God promised to give him anything he requested. Solomon could have asked for great wealth or fame or good fortune. He could have had anything in the world he wanted. Instead, Solomon asked God to make him wise so he could rule God's people well.

God was so pleased with Solomon's request that he made Solomon the wisest man who ever lived. It is no surprise that Solomon wrote the words above about getting wisdom. It reminds me of this story:

One day three men were hiking and unexpectedly came upon a large, raging river. They needed to get to the other side, but they had no idea how to do it.

The first man prayed to God, saying, "Please, God, give me the strength to cross this river."

Poof! God gave him big arms and strong legs, and he was able to swim across the river in about two hours, after almost drowning a couple of times.

Seeing this, the second man prayed to God, saying, "Please, God, give me the strength and the tools to cross this river."

Poof! God provided a rowboat, and the man was able to row across the river in about an hour, after almost capsizing a couple of times.

The third man had seen how this worked out for the other two men, so he also prayed to God, saying, "Please, God, give me the strength and the tools and the wisdom to cross this river."

And *poof*! God turned him into a woman. She looked at the map, hiked upstream a hundred yards, and then walked across the bridge.

O Lord, I pray that you will give me a double portion of your wisdom so that I will always live according to your precepts and guidelines. Amen.

I Proved It!

The eyes of the LORD search the whole earth in order to strengthen those whose hearts are fully committed to him.

2 CHRONICLES 16:9

I didn't mean to raise my children with lies. It just kind of happened that way. Here are some of the accidental lies I told. You may be familiar with some of these from your childhood as well.

"If you don't clean your ears better, potatoes will grow in them."

"If you're not careful, your face will freeze like that."

"The thunder is the sound of angels bowling. The lightning means they got a strike."

"If you go to sleep, the car sprouts wings and flies."

"If you eat all that candy, your teeth will fall out."

"If you swallow one of those seeds, a watermelon will grow in your stomach."

"If you tell a lie, your tongue will turn purple and your nose will grow."

And the ever-famous, "I see everything. I have eyes in the back of my head."

I'm afraid I feed the lies to my granddaughter, too. One day Gracee rushed into my office, saying, "Grandma, Grandma. I need to show you something."

"Not right now. I'm busy."

"Please, Grandma. Just turn around real quick."

"I can't turn around right now; I have to finish this."

"But just look."

"I will in just a minute."

Moment of silence.

"Ha!" she exclaimed. "I just proved it!"

I sighed. Finally I turned around.

"You just proved what?"

"I just proved that you *don't* have eyes in the back of your head!"

—Sandra Heska King

Dear God, I know that you alone see everything that goes on in the world and in our lives. And I know that you are never too busy for me. Please help me to be more committed to you every day, and give me strength to live for you. Amen.

May 8

Feeding Sheep from a Piñata

After breakfast Jesus asked Simon Peter, "Simon son of John, do you love me more than these?" "Yes, Lord," Peter replied, "you know I love you." "Then feed my lambs," Jesus told him.

JOHN 21:15

My plan for the party was simple. I stuffed the *second* piñata with sweet, hard candies and chocolates. But I filled the *first* one with raw potatoes, celery, onions, and carrots.

I would let the kids think they were going to get the usual sweets after the papier-mâché star burst open. Then, after their initial shock of not seeing their favorite candies flying through the air, I would give a minisermon about how the piñata represented sin—something that can look good but still be misleading and have unexpected, dire consequences in life.

Next, I would bring out the goodies-filled piñata, and the party would resume with joy and excitement.

The star was in place, and several blindfolded kids took turns swinging the plastic baseball bat at the piñata. With each missed attempt, both their anticipation and mine grew. Finally it was time for the surprise. A solid hit, and the veggies flew. The kids stopped short after rushing forward a few steps, and the disappointed looks on their faces were priceless.

Up to that point everything had gone according to my well-thought-out plan, but then I learned an unexpected lesson when I heard one mother exclaim, "Great! Dinner tonight!"

God has stuffed our lives full of everything we need for life and godliness, including sweet goodies and unexpected surprises, if we are just patient enough to wait for them.

—*Al Speegle Jr.*

Father God, it is hard to reach people with the Bread of Life when they are starving physically. Remind us to help feed those who are hungry. We are thankful that, one day, your children will not have to beg for bread. Amen.

A Missionary's Mission

The LORD God placed the man in the Garden of Eden to tend and watch over it.

GENESIS 2:15

I heard about a couple, Mark and Kim, who decided to move to South Africa as missionaries. The decision to leave their beautiful home in Texas was not an easy one, but the couple went out of love for the Lord.

One of the other missionaries had purchased a small farm for Mark and Kim before their arrival, so they were excited to get moved in and settled. But they were dismayed by their first look at the dilapidated farm.

The old farmhouse was shabby. The fields were full of boulders, fallen trees, and head-high weeds. Old, rusted-out farm tools and machinery lay scattered about. The whole place was a mess.

Looking at each other with sighs of resignation, followed by smiles of determination, Mark and Kim went to work. During their spare time they began hauling away all the old junk and machinery. They repaired the barn and made it livable for their horse and two cows. They fixed the chicken house, repaired the fence around the corral, and stacked the hay in the barn loft.

Next, they refurbished the house with new doors, new windows, a new roof, and a paint job. Then Kim planted a garden and built a walkway from the house to the garden. As the final touch, Mark repaired and painted the sign that hung over the entrance to their little farm.

Just as Mark completed his work on the sign, a neighbor across the road, who had been watching their progress, walked over and said, "Well, Mark, it looks like you and the Lord have done a pretty fine job on your farm."

Mark looked up at the neighbor, smiled, and said, "Yes, I guess so, but do you remember how it looked when the Lord had it all to himself?"

Dear God, thank you for giving us meaningful work to do and for allowing us to help you take care of the earth. We love your world, Father. Amen.

Standing Room Only

When [Jesus] saw the crowds, he had compassion on them.

MATTHEW 9:36

On a cool fall day, Mark Twain—the famous American humorist and popular speaker—arrived in a small town in mid-America where he was scheduled to lecture that evening. Since he had several hours before his speech, he decided to have his mustache trimmed and get a shave and a haircut at the local barbershop.

Dropping into the shop rather unassumingly, he sat down in one of the available chairs and patiently waited his turn.

The barber, who was a bit preoccupied with his work and other clients, did not recognize his customer as the famous Mark Twain. So, as he began to trim Twain's hair, he said to him, "You're new here, aren't you?"

"Yes," Twain responded. "Guess I am."

"Well, you've come to visit our city at a good time," said the barber.

"Oh, how's that?" asked Twain.

"Mark Twain is speaking here tonight."

The humorist responded, "That's what I hear."

The barber asked, "Have you bought your ticket yet?"

And Twain said, "Well, nope. Not yet."

The barber then said, "Well, that's too bad, because it's all sold out. So you'll have to stand to hear him speak."

"Just my luck," said Twain. "I always have to stand when that fella lectures!"

In a similar way, huge crowds of people followed Jesus because they wanted to hear him speak. Even when he was weary from his long days and stressful ministry, he had great compassion on the people who traipsed around after him like hapless sheep who needed the Shepherd. And he fed them with gentle words of love and hope.

One time the crowds were so large that Jesus had to climb into a boat and push off from the shore to speak to them. Like Mark Twain, when Jesus spoke, it was standing room only.

O Lord, we stand in awe of your majesty and glory. We are your sheep. We know your sweet voice, and we will follow you wherever you lead. Amen.

Attitude Is Everything

You must have the same attitude that Christ Jesus had.

PHILIPPIANS 2:5

Attitude makes all the difference in the world when it comes to how happy and contented you are in life. What matters most is not so much what actually happens to you, whether good or bad, but how you *respond* to what happens to you. People with negative, self-absorbed attitudes are often the losers in life. But people with positive, outreaching attitudes are overcomers and winners, as the following story shows.

A woman woke up one morning, looked in the mirror, and noticed she had only three hairs on her head. And while that might have caused great consternation for most of us, this woman had an interesting response.

"Well," she said, "I think I'll braid my hair today." So she did, and she had a wonderful day.

The next day she woke up, looked in the mirror, and saw that she had only two hairs on her head.

"Hmmm," she said, "I think I'll part my hair down the middle today." So she did, and she had a grand day.

The next day she woke up, looked in the mirror, and noticed that she had only one hair left on her head.

"Well," she said, "today I'm going to wear my hair in a ponytail." So she did, and she had a fun, fun day.

The next day she woke up, looked in the mirror, and noticed that there was not a single hair left on her head.

"Yay!" she exclaimed. "I don't have to fix my hair today!"

Attitude is everything!

O God, please help me to have the same attitude that your Son had while he was on earth. I want to show the people around me that my faith and confidence in you are strong by responding to life's bumps and bruises with a conquering, positive attitude. Amen.

Tickled to Death

Laughter can conceal a heavy heart,
but when the laughter ends, the grief remains.

PROVERBS 14:13

My mother's death was not funny, but that day we laughed. Watching cancer rob my parents of active, vibrant lives during their fifties, while I was in my twenties, produced plenty of tears. The laughter came unexpectedly—emotional relief for our sorrowful hearts.

My husband, my sister-in-law, and I stood in the mortuary vestibule with a solemn, well-dressed gentleman. He had the job of helping us make necessary arrangements. His too-soothing voice, accompanied by the too-peaceful music, in the too-meticulous setting knocked us silly.

Months of caring for Mother while she wore a hospital gown, struggled through surgeries, and lost her hair made choosing the color of the silk-lined casket seem pointless.

"Would your mother prefer blue or pink?" the suit-wearing guy asked. "Do you like pine, maple, mahogany, or oak?"

He walked away to give us some decision-making time. I looked at my husband and sister-in-law and whispered, "Blue or pink? Are you kidding me? I'm pretty sure Mother doesn't care." We burst into laughter. While considering the displayed caskets, each feature struck us like the punch line of a joke. The politely provided personal time was filled with laughter.

Out of control, we acted like children in church with an inappropriate eruption of giggles. We did not want to appear uncaring or disrespectful; after all, my mother had just died.

Certainly the padded wooden box where Mother's body would be laid to rest would not provide her, or us, any comfort; but we were surprised by our unexpected outburst. No matter how hard we tried to respect the gravity of the moment, we could not stop laughing. I'm sure Mom was laughing too.

—Sue Ferguson

Thank you, Lord, for laughter that lightened the magnitude of our terrible loss. Amen.

The Whole Truth

You will know the truth, and the truth will set you free.

JOHN 8:32

If you ever have to go to court and give testimony here in the United States, you will be asked to swear that what you will testify to is true. The statement you will be asked to swear to goes like this: "I swear to tell the truth, the whole truth, and nothing but the truth, so help me God."

In court, it seems like a perfectly legitimate thing to do. But in life outside the courtroom, telling the whole truth is not always quite so easy. At least that's what George found out.

When people asked George about his broken arm, he could not give a convincing explanation about how it happened. He kept muttering some story about accidentally sticking his arm through his car window, which he thought was down.

That's the public version. In private George confessed that it happened when his wife, Donna, brought some potted plants inside that had been out on the patio all day. A garter snake had hidden in one of the pots and later slithered out across the floor where Donna spotted it.

"I was in the bathtub when I heard her scream," George related. "I thought Donna was being murdered, so I jumped out to go help her. I was in such a hurry that I failed to even grab a towel.

"When I ran into the living room, she yelled that a snake was under the couch. I got down on my hands and knees to look for it, and my dog came up behind me and cold-nosed me. I guess I thought it was the snake, and I fainted.

"Donna thought I'd had a heart attack and called for an ambulance. I was still groggy when the ambulance arrived, so the medics lifted me onto a stretcher. When they were carrying me out, the snake came out from under the couch and frightened one of the medics so badly that he dropped his end of the stretcher.

"That's when I broke my arm."

Dear Father, it is not always easy to tell the whole truth, but please give me the courage to do it anyway. For I know that the truth will, ultimately, set me free. Amen.

I See That Finger

It is good to give thanks to the Lord,
to sing praises to the Most High.
It is good to proclaim your unfailing
love in the morning,
your faithfulness in the evening.

PSALM 92:1-2

I grew up in a large family, where we usually ate together around the dinner table. We also observed certain traditions. One of these was to pray before eating. Sometimes, for fun, my dad held up his index finger. As each of us noticed this, we quickly held up ours, because the last one to do so had to pray.

Many pastors, missionaries, and other Christian workers stayed with us over the years. My dad often used the finger method when they were at the table. I remember when one man had begun eating his roll without thinking. My dad's finger went into the air, with all of ours following like lightning. When informed of what this meant in our family, the man bowed his head and prayed, "Bless the Lord, O my soul: and all that is within me, bless his holy name" (Psalm 103:1, KJV). I never forgot it.

Toward the end of his life, my father valiantly battled Parkinson's disease, which caused him to fall frequently. When he took his final spill, it happened that I was on my way there to visit. When I arrived at the house, it was empty, and a note had been left on the table for me. I rushed to the hospital to find him in the emergency room with a small monitor on his finger. As he lay in the bed, his hand was elevated. The first thing I saw was his index finger pointing toward the ceiling. I laughed and said, "What are you doing, trying to get someone to pray for you? I've been doing that already."

—Max Elliot Anderson

Father, thank you for giving us prayer so we can communicate directly with you, the almighty God of this universe. Amen.

Pretending

Don't be concerned about the outward beauty of fancy hairstyles, expensive jewelry, or beautiful clothes. You should clothe yourselves instead with the beauty that comes from within.

1 PETER 3:3-4

Flushed with excitement, I raced to the mall and blew into the clothing store.

Two employees hurried to my side. "May we help you?"

Relieved, I took a breath. "Yes!" Twirling so they would get the full effect of my desperate condition, I tossed over my shoulder, "I'm going to be a diplomat. I'm flying to the capital."

Gasping in unison, they launched into action. One led me to a dressing room, the other gathered outfits—barking staccato orders on style and accessories. An hour and a half later, I exited with a wardrobe fit for a queen.

After hauling my load to the car, I fumbled for the keys and noticed my hands. Because I had kids and a menagerie of farm animals to care for, my hands and nails were rough. I tossed the garment bags into the backseat, spun around, and raced back to the mall. I knew what I was looking for—I had seen the commercial. I found them in the drugstore on aisle five.

When my big day arrived, sunlight reflected off my manicured nails as I reached for the door handle and heard the satisfying little clicks of long nails against glass. Smiling, confident, I entered the government building and hurried into my classroom. The instructor noticed me and crooked his finger. "Type something on this computer so everyone can see our program."

"Sure." As my fingers tap-danced across the keyboard, I noticed small objects arcing skyward. One hit the instructor in the chest. Someone gasped. A press-on fingernail hung from the instructor's lapel. I glanced down and saw that all mine were gone.

—Colleen Luntzel

Forgive me, Father, for being so concerned with outward beauty and for pretending to be something I'm not. I want to look my best, but please remind me that you care more about what's on the inside. Amen.

Back to Basics

You have been believers so long now that you ought to be teaching others. Instead, you need someone to teach you again the basic things about God's word.

HEBREWS 5:12

Legendary football coach Vince Lombardi never knew the word *can't.* He refused to make the game of football complicated when it could really be boiled down to just a few basics—passing, receiving, blocking, tackling, running. But these basic skills had to be done with unfettered abandon in order to win the game.

Lombardi often said, "You do all those things right, you win. It's a matter of the basics. You have to concentrate on the basics."

As he faced a ragtag bunch of discouraged rookies and tired has-beens, his flashing eyes danced from face to face of his Green Bay Packers. His lips were drawn tight across his teeth. His words were clipped and forceful. He did not fool around. He was as tough as a mountain man in a Colorado blizzard. And his job was simple—take that bunch of "losers" and turn them into a championship team. No small chore, but one he was determined to do.

In the locker room Lombardi stood before "tons" of massive men hanging on his every word. And he did not pull any punches. Instead, he picked up a pigskin and held it high over his head. Then he shouted, "Okay, gentlemen. Today we go back to the basics. You guys, look at this. *This* is a football!"

Sometimes when we seem to be losing at life, we might imagine that Jesus would like to hold the Bible high over his head and say to us, "Okay, Christians. Today we go back to the basics. You guys, look at this. *This* is God's Word!"

Father, forgive me for not spending as much time as I need to in your Word. I know the answers to life's problems are there, if I will just study it. Amen.

Fairy Faith

Jesus was filled with the joy of the Holy Spirit, and he said, "O Father, Lord of heaven and earth, thank you for hiding these things from those who think themselves wise and clever, and for revealing them to the childlike."

LUKE 10:21

My own children are almost grown. Barb brought her little four-year-old granddaughter to Bible study. The little angel played in the room next to the living room where we were meeting. Every half hour the little beauty skipped in and whispered in her mommy's ear.

Isn't this little girl the prettiest girl in town? I wondered. Her hair was loosely plaited. Her eyes were friendly. Her skin was so young and clear. Her skip was as light as a fairy's.

After study, we all went out to lunch. In the restaurant I sat next to the small fairy.

"Where did you get your beautiful sweater?" I asked her. "It's so pretty. I really like the flowers on the front." And I really did. It looked handmade.

She looked up at me and smiled a big smile. I leaned over to confide, in a girlish shared interest in fashion, "I wish I had a sweater just like yours."

Then the magic happened. The fairy princess with her magic smile granted my wish: "My grandmother will get you one, too, for your birthday!"

This pronouncement was made with perfect faith in her loving and able grandmother. We hardly knew each other. Yet, with all the love in the world, she granted my wish.

And with all the love in the world, Jesus Christ has granted us his amazing grace, his astonishing kindness, and his eternal salvation, all of which we can receive by faith in his ability, as the Son of the living God, to do so.

—Diane E. Kay

Father, let my faith in you be like the unwavering trust of a child. May I understand the pure, limitless depths of your love. Amen.

Oozing Joy

Dear brothers and sisters, when troubles come your way, consider it an opportunity for great joy.

JAMES 1:2

In a tumbling roll, Zach-man bounced into the enchanting threes. However, he entered that age pressed down and overflowing with mischief. It did not take long to realize that his personality matched the clown decor of his room perfectly. But that was not always a good thing.

At times his antics bordered on frightening. The worst was the month his lightning-fast hands resulted in our having to call poison control—three different times. It was critical that he learn self-control. A corner was cleared, and often he found himself in it.

This made his older siblings, Jesse and Mykah, anxious. Neither seemed to remember that corner time was the way they had learned how to manage their impulses. All they saw was that time-out meant an interruption in their play.

One morning at the breakfast table, Zach was too rambunctious, and I ordered him to the corner. Before he left, Jesse snapped, "You're too hard on him. He's always in time-out."

Right then Zach spun into motion. It was as if he was the lead in our breakfast play and had heard his cue. He picked up his bowl of oatmeal, and in an aerial feat, firmly planted it upside down on his brother's head. Gooey oats dribbled down his big brother's startled face.

Jesse turned his piercing hazel eyes on his brother's dancing blue ones and squinted. In a low growl he said, "Never mind. Send him to the corner."

Like a bubbling volcano, laughter erupted from deep inside me. One by one everyone joined in, including oatmeal-faced big brother, as well as the little troublemaker, now facing the corner.

—Sandy Lackey Wright

Father, as time passes, let the trials we face be memories of joy. For we know that what seem like such huge problems now will be but faded recollections in years to come. Amen.

A Kneaded Diagnosis

Can you solve the mysteries of God?
Can you discover everything about the Almighty?

JOB 11:7

I don't know about you, but I am always astounded at how God comes into our lives. It is not often with a shout and a thundering roar. Rather, he comes as a gentle breeze, a whisper, or a butterfly on gossamer wings. He kisses us on the cheek with his soft breath, showing us his faithful love and tender care. It is a mystery we do not often grasp or see.

Don't get me wrong, I know he can thunder and scare the daylights out of us when he needs to, but somehow I think he saves that for occasions when we're really hardheaded and have refused to listen and hear. Most of the time, I think, his approach is quiet and comforting or surprising and unexpected, as it was with my friend Nancy.

At a church care-group dinner one night, several women were sitting around the table talking about women's issues—husbands, grandkids, menopause, and breast cancer.

Nancy said she had discovered her breast cancer in an unusual way. She was lying on her back on the sofa when her cat hopped onto the sofa at her feet and proceeded to walk up her body. When the cat stepped on Nancy's breast, Nancy screamed with pain. A visit to the doctor resulted in a diagnosis of cancer, the treatment for which ultimately saved Nancy's life.

Several women commented about the surprising way Nancy had found the deadly disease and discussed how blessed she was to have found it in time.

"It was a miracle!" Nancy said with finality.

"What miracle?" I asked. "It was just a simple *cat scan*!"

Father, thank you for the marvelous ways you touch our lives and actively lead us. Help us never to forget that you are there for us every day and every hour. Amen.

Rub-a-Dub-Dub

Pride leads to disgrace,
but with humility comes wisdom.

PROVERBS 11:2

Have you ever known people who think they *know it all*? No matter what the topic of conversation, they jump in with both feet, relating their superior or limited information. Sometimes they are right on target and the information they relate is helpful, but often their comments are completely off base and everyone else knows it. That's when eyes roll and people yawn from sheer boredom.

Buddy was sure he knew it all and wanted everyone around him to enjoy the wealth of his infinite knowledge on whatever subject came up. He was the guy who, no matter what the subject, knew just enough to talk about it but not enough to know what he was really talking about.

That practice finally caught up with Buddy during medical school, when a requirement for one of Buddy's classes was to observe people who had been institutionalized. At a visit to a mental hospital, Buddy, already "showing out," as my mother would say, actually asked the director of the asylum what the criteria were that defined whether or not a patient should be institutionalized.

"Well," said the director, "we fill up a bathtub; then we offer a teaspoon, a teacup, and a bucket to the patient and ask him or her to empty the bathtub."

"Oh, I understand," said Buddy, with great confidence. "A normal person would use the bucket because it's bigger than the spoon or the teacup."

"No," said the director, "a *normal* person would pull the plug. Do you want to be by the wall or near the window?"

The bad news, I'm afraid, is that sometimes we all have a little Buddy in us.

—Tanya Magnus

Lord, forgive my foolish pride. Help me not to allow pride to be my downfall. Teach me to be humble and to see that all my worth is in you. It is your wisdom I seek. Amen.

Get Down!

Their command is a lamp
and their instruction a light;
their corrective discipline
is the way to life.

PROVERBS 6:23

As commander in chief of the nation during the Civil War, Abraham Lincoln felt it was his duty to visit the front to see for himself how the struggle was progressing. Although that may not have been the wisest idea since he was such a recognizable figure, he was determined to make the trip.

During the Confederate attack on Fort Stevens, near Washington, DC, Lincoln traveled to the front lines. Young Oliver Wendell Holmes, a general's aide, was given the wonderful privilege and serious responsibility of showing President Lincoln around the camps and battle lines.

At one point during the tour, Holmes pointed out to Lincoln the Confederate troops advancing toward them. Lincoln, well over six feet tall and wearing his distinctive black suit and stovepipe hat, stood up to get a better look, and he immediately drew musket fire from the Confederates.

"Get down, you fool!" cried Holmes, grabbing the president by the arm and pulling him down under cover. Once he had the president safe, Holmes suddenly realized what he had said. *I called President Lincoln a fool!* he thought in horror. Knowing the potentially harsh punishment for such an impulsive action, he waited in dread of the impending disciplinary response he expected would surely come.

President Lincoln kept Holmes waiting all afternoon as the tour continued. Finally, as he was making preparations to leave the front and head back to Washington, Lincoln turned to Holmes with a wink and said, "Good-bye, Captain Holmes. I'm glad you know how to talk to a civilian."

Father, thank you for loving and disciplining me in the ways you know I most need it. Otherwise, my life would surely drift off course and away from you. I am so grateful for your grace and mercy. And please help me to stop and think before I speak! Amen.

How Can You Tell?

They were bewildered to hear their own languages being spoken by the believers.

ACTS 2:6

My travels have taken me to many major cities in the United States and abroad, including Chicago, New York, Los Angeles, London, Hong Kong, Auckland, Munich, and Bangkok. The biggest challenge, of course, is navigating the languages that change from place to place.

My Texas accent is often a point of fascination to people in other places. And although my more colloquial words and phrases sound perfectly normal to me, other people stumble over them.

For instance, when I lived in Pittsburgh, Pennsylvania, I worked for United States Steel Corporation. One day an Italian engineer who worked in the office with us came to my desk to ask a question. In answering, I referred to something as being "yay long." Now in Texas, when you say an object is "yay long," you also have to show with your hands how long you really mean, because "yay long" does not have just one set definition. It can be whatever length you are describing at the moment.

He looked at me curiously and asked, "*How* long did you say?"

I said, holding up my hands again, "About *this* long."

He grinned and said, "No, that's *not* what you said."

Because *yay long* was such a normal descriptive term for me, I could not recall exactly what I had said. Then it dawned on me. "Oh, you mean *yay long*."

He laughed and said, "Yes, that's it! What does that mean?"

Holding up my hands once again, I laughed and said, "About *this* long."

My Italian friend nodded and asked, "Say, when you went to school in Texas, what was your major, anyway?"

I smiled and joked with an exaggerated drawl, "Speech. Cain't you tay-ul?"

Heavenly Father, we are honored and humbled that you always take the time to speak to us in ways that we can understand. We want to hear your voice, Lord, and we know that you hear and understand us when we speak to you. Amen.

Found Money

Never speak harshly to an older man, but appeal to him respectfully as you would to your own father.

1 TIMOTHY 5:1

A couple who had been childhood sweethearts married and settled down in their old neighborhood. On their fiftieth wedding anniversary, they walked down the street to their old school. There, they held hands as they found the old desk they had shared and where he had carved "I love you, Sally."

On their way home, a bag of money fell out of an armored car practically at their feet. The woman quickly picked it up, but they did not know what to do with it, so they took it home. There she counted the money and found that it totaled fifty thousand dollars!

The husband said, "We've got to give it back."

She said, "Finders keepers." Then she put the money back in the bag and hid it up in their attic.

The next day, two FBI agents were going door to door in the neighborhood looking for the money and showed up at their home.

The agents asked, "Pardon me, but did either of you find any money that fell out of an armored car yesterday?"

She said, "No."

The husband said, "She is lying. She hid it up in the attic."

She said, "Don't believe him; he's getting senile."

But the agents sat the man down and began to question him.

One said, "Tell us the story from the beginning."

The old man said, "Well, when Sally and I were walking home from school yesterday . . ."

Whereupon she rolled her eyes and said, "See what I mean?"

The FBI guy looked at his partner and said, "Let's get out of here."

Dear Lord, thank you for the older people in our lives. They bring us such joy and love. We pray that we will always treat them with the dignity and respect their years deserve. Amen.

Give It to Him!

Keep on asking, and you will receive what you ask for. Keep on seeking, and you will find. Keep on knocking, and the door will be opened to you.

MATTHEW 7:7

Do you ever wonder why you do not have some of the things you need or want? I think about that sometimes, and I wonder if it is because I just do not ask God for it. After all, Jesus said in Mark 11:24 that we can pray for anything, and if we believe that we have already received it, it will be ours. So sometimes I have to conclude that I have not received something simply because I did not ask for it. Perhaps I am not properly taking advantage of that promise from God.

And that reminds me of the story my friend Marvin Phillips once told as he was getting older.

"When I turned sixty-five, I got an AARP card, a Medicare card, and senior discount cards by the dozen. I can deal them like a poker player—pick a card, any card! I went to the movies in Australia, and they let me in on pensioner rates.

"I remember when I was fifty-eight. We were having breakfast with a few friends. It occurred to me that Denny's gives senior discounts early, so I asked the cashier, 'At what age do you give senior discounts?'

"'I don't know; I'll ask,' she said. Then she yelled at the top of her voice, 'Larry, at what age do we give senior discounts?'

"A million eyes peered at me. Larry stuck his head out of the kitchen and looked me over. 'Give it to him!' he said."

O Father, help me to remember that you have promised to give us what we ask for in your Son's name. So please give me the wisdom to grow old gracefully and to accept aging as a blessing from you, not a curse. In Jesus' name, amen.

The Endorsement

It was at Antioch that the believers were first called Christians.

ACTS 11:26

In the Christian publishing business, where I have served for about twenty-five years, we often help new authors promote their books by asking more seasoned authors or people with important credentials to read and endorse the new author's book. They typically write a short paragraph praising the author and the book, and we place it in the front of the new book. Those endorsements help to give the new author and his or her book credibility in the eyes of potential buyers and readers.

In the same way, God puts his stamp of approval—his endorsement—on us as his beloved children. As Christians, we wear his Son's name, and he smiles with pleasure when we go about his business in the world.

Endorsements are sometimes tricky things to get, though, depending on whom you approach to request them.

A young bride walked into a bank to cash a check. She was somewhat taken aback when the clerk informed her that she would need to endorse the check before it could be cashed.

"But it's a good check. My husband sent it to me. He's away on business."

"Yes, madam, it's perfectly all right. But please just sign it on the back so that your husband will know that *you* actually got the money."

The bride walked to the writing desk, seemed to be lost in deep contemplation for a moment, signed the check, and then returned to the teller's window and handed the check to him.

The teller was surprised when he saw, scrawled across the back of the check, "Your loving wife, Ethel."

Dear Father in heaven, please accept my humble gratitude for adopting me into your spiritual family and for putting your stamp of approval and endorsement on me through your Son. I wear his sweet name with honor and great joy. Amen.

Weighing In

Don't you realize that your body is the temple of the Holy Spirit, who lives in you and was given to you by God?... You must honor God with your body.

1 CORINTHIANS 6:19-20

During my lifetime, I have probably lost close to seven hundred pounds. It has happened like this: I lose ten and put on fifteen. Then I lose fifteen and put on twenty. You may know the drill. So I finally decided I had to get serious about taking the weight off and keeping it off.

At the time I wrote this, I had been going to Weight Watchers (WW) for more than a year, and I had done well with the program. I enjoyed the meetings because our WW coach was upbeat, funny, and knowledgeable. We always had a great time and learned a lot while we were there.

The coach was a real inspiration to us. She had lost 110 pounds on the program and had been a WW coach for many years. A couple of years earlier, she found out she was pregnant with twins. Although she was thrilled about the babies, she had to watch herself gain 85 of the 110 pounds she had lost. What a bummer!

But by the time her boys were a year old, our coach had lost almost all the 85 pounds she had gained. She looked svelte again and felt great. So we were all as proud of her as she was of us—we had a mutual admiration society!

Her story makes me think of the woman who went to a WW meeting and said she was still trying to lose the "baby fat" she had gained from the birth of her son. That seemed a bit odd, because she did not really look the age of most women who are having babies. She seemed quite a bit older than that.

Someone in the class asked her, "How old is your son?"

And she replied, "Forty-four!"

Dear Father, I want to honor you with my body, but you know it's not easy for me. When it comes to food, please help me to stay focused on what I need rather than what I want. Amen.

What Can You Do?

There are different kinds of spiritual gifts, but the same Spirit is the source of them all. . . . A spiritual gift is given to each of us so we can help each other.

1 CORINTHIANS 12:4, 7

The Bible plainly teaches that every believer has been blessed with at least one special gift to use in service to God and to other people. Sometimes, though, identifying that particular gift and exactly how it can best be put to work is a challenge. It reminds me of this story:

A married couple returning to America from Europe by ship became interested in an attractive red-cheeked Finnish girl traveling in economy class. They spent quite a bit of time getting to know her, and they found that she was coming to America to look for work. After a few days together on the ship, they came to like the girl a lot, so they decided to offer her employment in their home.

Calling her to their first-class cabin one day, they tried to discover exactly how they could work together.

"Can you cook?" they asked.

"No," said the girl, "I can't cook. My mother always did the cooking."

"Well," they said, "then you can do the housework."

"No," she said, "I don't know how. My oldest sister always did the housework."

"Well, then, we could let you take care of the children."

"No, I couldn't do that. My youngest sister always took care of the children."

"Well, can you sew?"

"No," said the girl, "my aunt always did the sewing."

"Well, then, what *can* you do?" cried the despairing couple.

The girl was quite bright and cheerful as she volunteered, "I can milk reindeer!"

O Father, I know that you have blessed me with special gifts and abilities. I am very thankful to you for blessing me so. Please help me to find the exact place in your church and in my life to use those gifts to honor and glorify you. Amen.

Salute!

You have been weighed on the balances
and have not measured up.

DANIEL 5:27

When I was commanding a field artillery battalion in Germany in the early eighties, we were undergoing a general inspection by the VII Corps Inspector General (IG). A portion of the inspection was to evaluate the level of training of our soldiers in basic skills. These are skills all soldiers should possess, regardless of their specialties. An example of a basic skill, for instance, is how to administer first aid.

The IG selected a random number of soldiers to evaluate. One of the soldiers was a newly assigned cook. The IG asked him to explain the acronym S.A.L.U.T.E.

Expecting to hear the definition of an intelligence spot report a soldier might make from a battlefield observation, the IG awaited the soldier's response. His answer should have included, in order, six elements that begin with the letters in the word *salute*—size, activity, location, unit, time, and equipment.

The soldier thought for a moment as the IG waited patiently, and then the light came on. The soldier proudly responded, "Sir! It is when one cooks something in oil in a shallow pan over high heat."

The young cook had just defined how to *sauté* something.

This lighthearted story reminds me that someday we, too, will be inspected to see if we measure up in the eyes of God. We will be "weighed on the balances," so to speak. Fortunately, although our sins and shortcomings may weigh heavily on one side of the balance, God's grace through Jesus will be balancing the scale on our behalf on the other side, and we will "measure up" and be welcomed into the arms of our patient, loving God.

—*John H. Kelly, Col. US Army Ret.*

Thank you, God, for your saving grace and for giving us the incomparable blessing of being with you for all eternity. Without your mercy, we would surely be found wanting. Amen.

Who Is Your Chief?

Those who accept my commandments and obey them are the ones who love me. And because they love me, my Father will love them.

JOHN 14:21

During the American Revolution, the Colonial soldiers sometimes had great difficulty getting enough horses to sustain their war efforts. So on one occasion, General George Washington sent a young officer to make the rounds of the Virginia countryside and confiscate all the horses he could find.

This was not, as you can imagine, a very popular thing to do, and the Virginians, although supportive of the war effort, highly resented having their prize horses taken from them. So the young officer was often met with stern faces and stubborn resistance.

After several days the officer finally came to a fine old mansion and, seeing a sturdy, matching team of plow horses out in the field, rang the bell at the front door of the mansion and asked to see the mistress of the house.

He was invited into the house and was asked to wait in the drawing room.

In due time, a refined voice asked, "Yes? How may I help you?"

"Madam," he said to the dignified elderly woman who received him, "I have come to claim your horses in the name of the government."

"Sir," was the answer, "you cannot have them. I need them for the spring plowing."

"I am sorry, Madam. Those are the orders of my chief."

"And just who *is* your chief?" she demanded to know.

"General George Washington, commander in chief of the American army."

"Well, young man," replied the woman, a smile softening her previously stern features, "you go back and tell General George Washington, commander in chief of the American army, that his mother says he cannot have her horses."

O Master, we know that you are the Lord of Heaven's Armies—the commander in chief of the universe—and we want to show that we honor and respect you by obeying your commands. Help us to be obedient and honorable soldiers in your army. Amen.

Upside Down

When troubles come your way, consider it an opportunity for great joy.

JAMES 1:2

In Las Vegas for a family wedding, we were fascinated by the roller coaster that was part of the New York–New York Hotel. My sister and I asked our mother, not the amusement-park type, if she would mind sitting with our purses while we rode.

The look on her face surprised us, so I asked, "Mom, do you want to go with us?"

To our amazement, she exclaimed, "Sure!"

Mom was fine with the roll bar clanking into place in our laps, but her puzzled expression showed she did not understand the point of the shoulder harnesses.

I asked, "Mom, did you know this thing goes upside down?"

Eyes wide, she protested, "What!"

And we were off!

Julie and I loved it, but Mom's mouth was tightly pursed, and her eyes were narrowed as she kept her gaze locked on her feet. She was *not* having a good time. In fact, she was downright miserable.

The three of us were experiencing the exact same event, but our responses were worlds apart. The difference was our attitudes. Isn't that like life? Sometimes we find ourselves locked into a roller coaster that is upside down, and we do not *like* being upside down. It is terrifying, and we have no control. We were expecting something lovely and smooth, but that is not what we encountered.

Near the end of the ride, a camera snapped a picture of us. Mom was absolutely not interested in buying it, but we did anyway. And the picture, now an heirloom since Mom is gone, is a priceless illustration of the difference attitude makes.

—*Sue Bohlin*

Lord, help me to invite you into my attitudes. Help me release them into your hands. Transform them so I will not be miserable when the roller coasters go upside down and your goal is to show me that, whatever my circumstances, I am safe in your love. Amen.

Tradition!

You skillfully sidestep God's law in order to hold on to your own tradition.

MARK 7:9

During rehearsals of Verdi's great opera *Otello* by an American opera company, the tenor, who was preparing for the chief role, was perplexed by certain instructions from the stage director. The director insisted that, at a certain moment near a climax in the action, while the chorus was singing and during a rest of only a few bars in the tenor role, the tenor should walk to the back of the stage and return again toward the footlights to resume singing. Doing so required impeccable timing and seemed utterly senseless from the point of view of dramatic action.

The tenor protested, but the stage director would not yield, saying, "It is the tradition of the part."

"Why?" asked the tenor.

"I don't know," came the reply. "It is the tradition. You must do it."

"Who created this role?"

"Tamagno."

Unable to do anything but accede to the director's wishes, the tenor carried the incident in his memory. A year or so later, being in Italy, the American sought out the great, aged tenor Francesco Tamagno. When he was granted an interview, he asked, "Maestro, I wish to ask you about a certain piece of business in the role of Otello."

The old man heard him out and was obviously puzzled. In an effort to recollect his motive, he peered for a time at the pages of the operatic score.

"Yes, yes," he said at last, "it is very simple. Note that in the final passage Otello must sing a high B-flat. So, while the chorus was singing, I went upstage to spit."

Father, we are often frozen in time by our long-held traditions, unable to move past them to more-effective or more-useful ways of doing things. Help us, Lord, to be willing to look into your Word to compare honestly our human traditions with your holy commands and freedoms. Help us not to worship our traditions over your truth. Amen.

My Other Daddy

You have not received a spirit that makes you fearful slaves. Instead, you received God's Spirit when he adopted you as his own children. Now we call him, "Abba, Father."

ROMANS 8:15

During the scary days of the Bay of Pigs incident, my brother-in-law, Loren, a Green Beret in the United States Marine Corps, was on high alert, expecting to be called up for duty at any moment. When the call came, he did exactly what he had always done in preparation for a mission—he packed his military gear, pressed his uniforms, and got a military haircut. The morning he was scheduled to leave on the mission, he got up, showered, and shaved off his beard and mustache.

Not realizing the effect this would have on his baby daughter, Julie, he was surprised when she wouldn't have anything to do with him that morning. She didn't recognize him without his beard and mustache. And she kept asking her mother, "Where's my daddy?"

"Boy, that will take the wind right out of your sails," said Loren when telling me the story a few years later.

Loren left on the mission and was gone for a few weeks. When he returned home, even though my sister-in-law, Penny, had been trying to help their little girl through the hairless-dad issue, Julie did not recognize him and would not have much to do with him for a long time.

One day he took her into the backyard and was pushing her in her swing. They were laughing and playing, having a wonderful time. Suddenly, little Julie looked at Loren seriously and said, "You're nice . . . but you're not like my other daddy."

Whoever said freedom is free did not know some of the costs involved.

Abba, Father, thank you for being the same yesterday, today, and forever. We know you are our only real Father, and we love you so. Amen.

Sooty and Shielded

We put our hope in the LORD.
He is our help and our shield.

PSALM 33:20

The Civil War raged, and Mrs. Walden had been warned bushwhackers were coming. Praying, she gathered their meager possessions and guns and placed them under the feather bed. She dusted her daughter's face with flour, circled her eyes with soot, and laid the tiny, frail girl in bed, instructing her, "Whatever happens, don't move."

Mrs. Walden hurried to the front porch, sat in the rocking chair, placed a shawl on her lap, and opened the family Bible. Four men rode their horses into the yard, one circling to the back. Before they could dismount, she stood. Holding the Bible to her breast, she beckoned to the leader. "Thank you, Doctor, for coming. Oh, thank you for coming all this way!"

The men drew their guns and, with wary eyes, scanned the house and yard. Slowly, they approached the porch.

Grabbing the leader's arm, she pulled him onward. "Oh, hurry, sir. It could be the dreaded fever that has taken so many of our neighbors."

The men stopped and glanced through the screen door. She pushed them through and then ordered them to wait while she soaked rags in coal oil for protection against the bad air. The leader backed up, bumping into those behind him. Continuing to beg for help, Mrs. Walden prodded them forward until they stood in the bedroom. Breathless, they stared at the young girl, her face white as snow, black circles around closed eyes.

The girl's eyes flew wide open and a scream of quivering terror filled the room. The lead man wrenched his arm from Mrs. Walden's grasp. Stumbling and cursing, with feet flying, the men jammed through the doorway, leaped over the front steps, mounted their horses, and disappeared in a cloud of dust.

—*Lisa Buffaloe*

Thank you, heavenly Father, for being our hope and our shield. Thank you for protecting Mrs. Walden from those men and for protecting us from harm. Amen.

June 3

Why Parents Have Gray Hair

Children, always obey your parents,
for this pleases the Lord.

COLOSSIANS 3:20

The boss of a big company needed to call one of his employees about an urgent problem with one of the main computers. He dialed the employee's home phone number and was greeted with a child's whispered, "Hello?"

Feeling put out at the inconvenience of having to talk to a youngster, the boss asked, "Is your daddy home?"

"Yes," whispered the small voice.

"May I speak with him?" the man asked.

To the surprise of the boss, the small voice whispered, "No."

Wanting to talk with an adult, the boss asked, "Is your mommy there?"

"Yes," came the answer.

"May I talk with her?"

Again the small voice whispered, "No."

Knowing it was not likely that a young child would be left home alone, the boss decided to just leave a message with the person who should be there watching over the child. "Is there anyone else there in your house?" the boss asked.

"Yes," whispered the child, "a policeman."

Wondering what a cop would be doing at his employee's home, the boss asked, "May I speak with the policeman?"

"No, he's busy," whispered the child.

"Busy doing what?" asked the boss.

"Talking to Daddy and Mommy and the fireman," whispered the child.

Growing concerned, the boss asked, "What is that noise?"

"A hello-copper," answered the whispering child.

"What is going on there?" asked the boss, now alarmed.

In an awed, hushed voice the child answered, "The search team just landed the hello-copper."

More than a little frustrated, the boss asked, "What are they searching for?"

Still whispering, the young voice replied, along with a muffled giggle, "Me."

Dear Father, thank you for caring enough to find me when I was lost and for bringing me back home to you. Amen.

The Warrior and the Mice

When Ahab got home, he told Jezebel everything Elijah had done, including the way he had killed all the prophets of Baal. So Jezebel sent this message to Elijah: "May the gods strike me and even kill me if by this time tomorrow I have not killed you just as you killed them." Elijah was afraid and fled for his life.

1 KINGS 19:1-3

It was a sparkling, sunny day, with a deep-blue sky and cool, crisp air. My husband, Bill, decided it was a perfect day to cut the chest-high grass in the vacant lot next to our house. We had been seeing signs of mice—it was definitely time to get rid of their habitat.

I could see Bill from the kitchen window, going back and forth through the high grass. I thought about the mice and shuddered, but Bill was not afraid of a few mice; they would not slow him down. I listened to the putter of the mower and heard it stop and then start again. Looking out, I noticed Bill was gone, but I could still hear the mower running.

Where is Bill, and why is the mower running? I wondered.

I went outside and found him passed out on the ground. Our neighbor noticed what was happening and came over, stopped the mower, and helped me get Bill up. Bill's hand was bleeding, but fortunately he was not hurt badly. When the mower had stopped earlier, Bill had banged his knuckles on the mower trying to get it started again.

Yes, my big, six-foot-three, mice-killing he-man had passed out at the sight of his own blood. Bill was prepared to chase the mice, but he was not prepared to see his own blood.

—Marty Prudhomme

Dear Lord, prepare me for the battles of your choosing. Let me be ready at all times to walk in the fear of the Lord and to not be afraid of anything else. Amen.

June 5

Breaking It Gently

Even when I walk
through the darkest valley,
I will not be afraid,
for you are close beside me.

PSALM 23:4

Facing death is never easy, whether it is your own or someone else's close to you. Death is inevitable for each of us, but as human beings, getting the news of someone's death is usually difficult. It reminds me of a story Mark Twain once told:

> *Once a simple man named Higgins hauled rock for old Maltby. When the lamented Judge Bagley tripped and fell down the courthouse stairs and broke his neck, the great question was how to break the news to poor Mrs. Bagley. Finally the body was put into Higgins's wagon, and he was instructed to take it to Mrs. Bagley. But he was cautioned to be very guarded and discreet in his language and not break the news to her all at once—to do it gradually and gently.*
>
> *When Higgins got to the Bagley house with his sad freight, he shouted till Mrs. Bagley came to the door. Then he said, "Does the widow Bagley live here?"*
>
> *"The* widow *Bagley? No, sir!"*
>
> *"I'll bet she does. But have it your own way. Well, does* Judge *Bagley live here?"*
>
> *"Yes, Judge Bagley lives here."*
>
> *"I'll bet he don't. But never mind—it ain't for me to contradict. Is the judge in?"*
>
> *"No, not at present."*
>
> *"I just expected as much, because, you know—now take hold o' suthin, mum, for I'm a-going to make a little communication, and I reckon maybe it'll jar you some. There's been an accident, mum. I've got the old judge curled up out here in the wagon—and when you see him, you'll acknowledge, yourself, that an inquest is about the only thing that could be a comfort to him!"*

Dear Lord, thank you for being with us throughout our lives and for holding our hands as we walk through death's door. With you by our sides, we can face anything. Amen.

Fired Twice

Let us run with endurance the race
God has set before us.

HEBREWS 12:1

Thomas Edison, the great inventor of the lightbulb, the phonograph, and many other important scientific developments, had an unusual and interesting life. Today we celebrate the many inventions of Thomas Edison. In fact, we cannot imagine how we would get along without them. I am astounded when I think of how electric lighting and recorded sound have morphed into such a multitude of useful and entertaining products.

Mr. Edison failed many more times than he succeeded in his work, but the key to his ultimate great success was his perseverance and endurance in pursuing his dream and his personal goals. That eventually led to his establishing a permanent place for himself and his work in the annals of world history.

Edison once commented about his having been fired from two different jobs: "The first time was when I was a telegraph operator. It was my fault, all right, but I got so interested in the dinged machine and its workings that I began to see how I could improve it. But I forgot all about the messages that were coming over the wire, and I left a lot of messages unsent and undelivered. Of course, they discharged me, and I didn't blame them.

"Then," he laughed, "I got a job in an office, and there were a fearful lot of rats; terribly old office, you know. I came up with a thing that killed them like flies—the same with cockroaches. The floor used to be covered with dead roaches, and they fired me for that!"

He could not win! Ironically, it was inventions such as the two for which he was fired that make his name a household word today.

Father in heaven, we know that you are the Master of the universe and the greatest Inventor-Creator in all of history. Thank you for gifting people like Thomas Edison with special abilities to make our lives better. We are truly blessed. Amen.

The Tale of Two Books

I have learned how to be content with whatever I have.

PHILIPPIANS 4:11

One of the most famous opening lines for a book is from *A Tale of Two Cities*: "It was the best of times, it was the worst of times." And I am sure that line has been used and abused as much as any quotable lines in history.

I have certainly had my ups and downs in the publishing business. Mostly, I have been greatly blessed and have loved the crazy ride, but sometimes the downhill slide has been like a runaway sled on an icy mountain slope.

One day a few years ago, I retrieved my mail from the mailbox and found two royalty statements from different publishers—one for an older book that was going out of print, the other for a new book that had just been released.

The royalty check for the new book, starring Barney the Dinosaur, was for ninety-eight thousand dollars. (The big purple guy should have been green!) I nearly fainted from the shock. I felt as if I had won the lottery.

I eagerly opened the second envelope and pulled out the final royalty payment for the older book, and reality hit full force: It totaled thirty-eight cents. (Can you hear the air gushing out of my tires?)

That is when I started to laugh. The Lord really knows how to tell a joke, doesn't he? And he surely knows how to keep us humble.

As a constant reminder that I should be content, no matter what my circumstances, I created a framed document titled *The Tale of Two Books*. At the top is a photocopy of the ninety-eight-thousand-dollar check with the caption "It was the best of times." And at the bottom is a photocopy of the thirty-eight-cent check with the caption "It was the worst of times."

Father, I am so grateful for your great generosity, especially when I don't deserve it. Please help me to be content in all circumstances. Amen.

Well Prepared?

In his grace, God has given us different gifts for doing certain things well.

ROMANS 12:6

The night before our wedding, I lay in bed thinking about the changes in my life soon to take place. In less than twenty-four hours I would have a new name, a new address, and a new role. I would be a wife, a homemaker, and someday, I hoped, a mother. I was prepared, or so I thought.

After two full months of bridal showers and teas, I could have opened my own department store. Our prenuptial festivities made the inauguration look spur of the moment.

At linen showers I received sheets to fit any size bed, towels to wrap around any shape body, and enough blankets to warm the entire population of Iceland.

But it was kitchen showers that really pushed my domestic button. I was ready to set up house. If I wasn't given every kitchen gadget ever invented, Martha Stewart can't cook. And dishes—I had enough dishes to host a buffet dinner for the state of Tennessee. No matter if I had forty-two place settings, I kept them all.

Although I started married life with top-of-the-line paraphernalia, it never dawned on me that I did not have the first hint about homemaking. Maybe it was when I dumped an entire cart of groceries in the parking lot beside my car. (No one told me I was supposed to wait for the next available sacker to take them out.) Or maybe it was the multicolored specks in a dip I whipped up. (The hand-painted cutting board should have included instructions to chop on the back side.) But I think it was when I used a rectal thermometer to see if my roast was done that Bill knew homemaking was probably not my strong suit.

—*Kathy Peel*

O Father, thank you for the many gifts you give me every day. Help me to identify my special gifts and to use them wisely and humbly. And help me not to be frustrated by the gifts I don't have. Amen.

June 9

Squeaking Sheets

I cried out to [God] for help,
praising him as I spoke.

PSALM 66:17

Several years ago, I was a counselor at a church camp. The dorm I was assigned, along with other counselors, held about twenty-five girls, all between nine and eleven years old.

On Wednesday I was awakened by one of the girls around three o'clock in the morning.

"Help me! My sheets are squeaking!" She was rocking from side to side in her bunk.

"My sheets are squeaking!" And by that time so was the bed.

After stumbling around in the dark and stubbing my toe on a footlocker, I arrived by her bed at the same time as her counselor.

"What is it, honey?"

"My sheets are squeaking."

"Sweetie, we don't hear anything. Try to go back to sleep."

Her voice rose in frustration. "Help me! My sheets are squeaking!" Her counselor took her hand.

"It's okay. We'll take care of it."

"My sheets are squeaking. My sheets are squeaking." She was grabbing at them, trying to make them stop. The bed was really rocking, and the camper in the top bunk was waking up. We had no idea what she was hearing, but the other campers were stirring, so we had to do something.

We got her out of bed, took everything off, shook it all, and remade the bed for her. She lay back down and was asleep before we could straighten up. Together we got the squeak out.

And while getting up in the middle of the night is not my favorite idea, the little girl had it right—when your life is squeaking, cry out for help! God will hear, and he will help you get the squeak out.

—Stevie Stevens

Dear Father, I am so glad you help me with the squeaks in my life. Help me to stay close to you in squeaky times. Amen.

A Grave-Opening Night

As for me, God will redeem my life.
He will snatch me from the power of the grave.

PSALM 49:15

Maury H. B. Paul was a young society editor in New York City in years gone by. One of his first big assignments as an editor was to cover the season opening of the Metropolitan Opera House—a prestigious responsibility. He rented a tuxedo, hired a limousine, and went to the popular event with pad and pen in hand.

Maury was new to New York, so he was not familiar with enough of the wealthy patrons to identify the occupants of the lavish boxes in the theater. Not intending to fail at his first big assignment, he resorted to slipping around the corridor behind the boxes during the acts of the opera. He noticed that outside the door to each box was a brass plate with names of important people on them. He surmised that the brass plates identified the occupants and went about copying the names onto his pad.

When the event was over, Maury returned to his desk at the office and wrote his editorial about the opening, mentioning the names of the people he had listed from the brass plates. Then he turned his story in by his appointed deadline to make the morning edition and went home.

The following day, Maury was summoned to the office of his employer, Frank Munsey.

"I have just had a telephone call from Mrs. Stuyvesant Fish," said Munsey. "She has read your account of the Metropolitan premiere. She thought you might be interested to know that you have succeeded in opening half the graves in Woodlawn Cemetery."

Thus it was that Maury learned—albeit the hard way—that the name of the original box owner is usually left on the door, no matter who may subsequently occupy it.

O Lord, we know that someday you will rescue us from the grave and take us to live with you for all eternity. Thank you for making the thought of death one of joy and not fear. Amen.

I Love to Tell the Story

I will proclaim your name to my brothers and sisters.
I will praise you among your assembled people.

PSALM 22:22

My three-year-old son loves to make up elaborate stories. He often entertains his sisters and friends with tall tales featuring monsters, superheroes, and various cartoon characters.

On the way to his preschool the other day, he told me a story that went something like this:

"Once upon a time, there was a big castle. And on the top floor lived a prince who had a blue room and a Lightning McQueen bed. One day, the prince said, 'Today, I'll invite my friend Landry to go bowling with me!' So he went down the elevator and got his dinosaur.

"But on his way to Landry's house, he ran into a big monster! It was green with yellow spots all over it. The prince said, 'Get out of here, you yucky monster!' And the monster got scared and ran away.

"Then the prince got to his friend's house. Landry rode back to the castle with the prince, where they went bowling. And they won! So they had a big party and invited all their friends and danced and ate lots of ice cream. The end."

I have to admit, my son's fanciful tales are some of the wackiest things I have ever heard. And he loves to tell them—over and over.

But the most far-fetched tale of all has the ring of truth to it. It is an old, old story we never get tired of hearing. And it is a story we love to tell—over and over.

I love to tell the story, 'twill be my theme in glory,
To tell the old, old story of Jesus and his love.

—*Jennifer Stair*

God, I never get tired of hearing your story of grace and redemption. Help me to share your good news of salvation with those who need to hear it. Amen.

Making Lemonade

Always be full of joy in the Lord. I say it again—rejoice!

PHILIPPIANS 4:4

The ocean was breathtaking as my dear friend Gail and I traveled down the Oregon coast in Gail's aging motor home. We thrilled to see the waves wildly pounding the rocky seashore, sending salty spray hundreds of feet into the air. Only God could create such majesty.

While driving, I noticed the large side mirror was violently shaking. We pulled over and secured it with duct tape. Then the picnic awning began to flap. The brace was broken, so we stopped again and secured it with lots more duct tape. People did stare, but the scenery was glorious, and we determined nothing would stop us. I made up a little duct tape song called "Quack, Quack." Gail giggled with delight.

On the third day, we parked the motor home at the hotel where Gail was the speaker for a women's retreat. That night I came back to the motor home alone, and as I entered the small shower enclosure, I noticed the stars were very bright. This seemed odd since the sky had not been visible on previous nights. We had parked at campgrounds where the trees obviously had blocked the starlight.

Then it clicked. *Where was the ceiling? Oh no! It must have blown off along the road.* I was soon on the floor laughing in hysterics when a sudden wave of guilt came over me. Poor Gail, her motor home was falling apart piece by piece. How awful!

When Gail returned, she smiled at me and chuckled, "Oh, don't feel bad; the top on the shower was gone before we left home." We cackled till our sides hurt, then we cried with joy.

Gail's attitude was an example of the joy of the Lord during trying times. She taught me that when life gives you lemons, make lemonade . . . and trust God.

—*Marty Prudhomme*

Lord, please help me to always have a heart full of gratitude and your wonderful sense of humor. Amen.

The Fun in Funny

A cheerful heart is good medicine.

PROVERBS 17:22

It had been a stressful day. Len dropped into his easy chair and retreated behind the newspaper. After unwinding with the funnies and the sports, he would be ready to enjoy the family at dinner.

Sara had a different idea. In eager anticipation, our five-year-old niece asked her uncle to take her for a "horsey ride."

Len kindly requested that she wait until after dinner. She willingly accepted postponed gratification and began rocking her teddy bear for a few minutes. Soon Sara approached him with increasing fervor. "Uncle Len, *p l e e e a s e* take me for a horsey ride."

"Let me rest a little longer." So she rocked Teddy a few more times.

The third time she approached him, Sara pulled down the newspaper. In an authoritative voice, she insisted, "Uncle Len, you *have* to have fun whether you like it or not!"

So he got down on his hands and knees and took her for a bumpy ride. (Why bumpy? Have you ever tried crawling on your hands and knees while laughing?)

As I laughed from the kitchen, biblical illustrations came to mind. I thought of the story in Luke 11:5-13, in which the neighbor demanded that his tired friend give him some bread.

A cheerful heart had transformed a tired uncle into a willing and energetic stallion. I wonder how many of my childish requests my Father finds humorous. I do know he answers prayers and enjoys blessing his children.

—Barbara Ferguson

Father, thank you for teaching me so many things about my relationship with you through experiences of children. Thank you for your patience and your encouragement to share my concerns with you, especially when I become impatient. Thank you for your many blessings, including the blessing of humor to neutralize stress. I love you, Father, and enjoy being with you, even in my childish way. Amen.

Well-Groomed Diplomacy

Don't think you are better than you really are.
Be honest in your evaluation of yourselves, measuring
yourselves by the faith God has given us.

ROMANS 12:3

Through the years, I have sung at close to two hundred weddings. From the varied experiences at those events, I have concluded that there are few things in life more stressful than weddings. Parents are nervous, brides are nervous, grooms are practically hysterical, and the entire wedding party is typically on edge.

I remember one wedding where the groom was so nervous that he fainted three different times during the wedding. Each time, the minister revived him, helped him to his feet, and continued the ceremony. They finally managed to get through the I-dos, but it was no small chore.

Another time, we began singing the bride's entrance song, but she did not come in. We sang through the song three or four times, but still no bride. Finally, the minister came down off the podium, walked out the back door of the church, and personally escorted the bride down the aisle. She was just not paying attention and had not realized it was time for her to enter. Duh!

One groom actually managed to retain his diplomacy, though, in the midst of all the hurry and tension of the ceremony and the departure for the honeymoon.

Finally seated in the car that was to take them to the train station, the bride asked if he had remembered the tickets. He reached into his pocket and pulled out . . . *one* ticket. Remembering his flustered state of mind when he had gone to purchase the tickets, he hurriedly gathered his thoughts and said, "Dear me. Look, only one ticket. You see, darling, I was so focused on you that I forgot all about myself."

Nice catch!

My Father, I want to be humble in your sight, not proud and arrogant. Help me to stay focused on you, and that will surely remind me to forget about myself. Amen.

My Turkey's Cooked . . . or Not

Don't worry about anything; instead, pray about everything. Tell God what you need, and thank him for all he has done.

PHILIPPIANS 4:6

You don't understand." I was losing patience with the fast-food clerk. "I ordered this turkey two weeks ago for our Thanksgiving office party. Twenty people are supposed to be eating it"—I pointed to my watch—"in thirty minutes. It was advertised as 'cooked.'" I tapped the frozen bird. "It's hard as a bowling ball."

"Sir, it *is* cooked. You need to thaw it and warm it for about two hours."

I was fouled and frying. "You sell cooked, ready-to-eat chicken, not frozen. I expected the turkey to be cooked!"

"Sir, it is cooked. If you don't want it . . ." she said, reaching for it as if it were a long-lost relative.

I grabbed it and left. Then I said a quick prayer in my car. *What am I going to do, Lord?* I did not really expect an answer short of a heavenly zapped microwave beam, which was possible but not probable.

Driving to work I saw a barbeque restaurant I have frequented, and I thought, *Maybe they have a way to quickly heat it?*

Willie smiled as I explained what had happened. "I might be able to have it warmed in an hour, but not any sooner."

I leaned against the wall, closed my eyes, and uttered another short prayer: *"What must I do to be saved?"*

I opened my eyes to see Willie slicing a loaf of meat. "What's that?"

"Turkey breast."

My answer appeared. "How many of those would I need to feed twenty people?"

"Most people can eat five, maybe eight ounces. Six loaves should feed them."

"Give me seven loaves to go. That should tide them over." I handed him the subzero turkey, saying, "I'll be back in an hour."

And it worked, providing me another reason for Thanksgiving.

—*Al Speegle Jr.*

Father, thank you for knowing our needs and meeting them with an answer beyond our expectations. Amen.

Like Little Children

[Jesus] said, "I tell you the truth, unless you . . . become like little children, you will never get into the Kingdom of Heaven."

MATTHEW 18:3

At his home Rob goes to Sunday school—he's in the Frog class, a roomful of jump-happy, make-a-joyful-noise, three-year-olds. But on his first solo weekend visiting us, we decided to stick together. There we were, Nana, Granddad, and a squirmy Rob, sandwiched tightly in the middle of the pew in the middle of the crowded sanctuary. I prayed for lots of singing and a short sermon.

Our pastor is a wonderful shepherd, but not a dynamic speaker. No forceful voice or fancy words. He makes his point by repetition. Simple words repeated often.

That day the sermon came from Romans 8:14. Pastor David read it twice: "For all who are led by the Spirit of God are children of God." Then, leaning out over the pulpit, he asked, "Are you a child of God?"

Rob stopped fiddling with Granddad's tie clasp, turned to the pulpit, and thrust his hand into the air.

During the course of his sermon, Pastor David sent those words out into the congregation again and again: "Are you a child of God?" Each time, Rob stretched his hand high above Granddad's shoulder and smiled his one-dimple grin. People behind us were chuckling, then the giggles spread across the aisle. Every time Rob answered the pastor's question by raising his hand, the laughter grew louder.

With his flock now grinning from aisle to aisle, Pastor David finally saw the reason. Pointing his finger and smiling at Rob, he said, "Now *that* child of God gets the idea!"

"Become like little children." It is harder than it sounds. It does not take a big voice or fancy words. It takes courage to raise our hands for the Lord for everyone to see.

—Kathleen Brown

Help us become like little children, Lord, loving you joyfully, trusting you completely, serving you faithfully. Amen.

This Old House

Though our bodies are dying, our spirits are being renewed every day.

2 CORINTHIANS 4:16

There's a wonderful gospel song called "This Ole House." It's been a favorite of Southern gospel music fans for decades, especially those who love bass leads.

On the surface, the lyrics of "This Ole House" describe a rickety old house that is decaying and beginning to fall down. The roof is leaking, the shutters are falling off, the windows are broken, and it shows other deteriorating features. The composer's conclusion is "I ain't a-gonna need this house no longer."

The underlying message of the song is that, like the Scripture passage above, our bodies (houses) are slowly decaying or dying, but we are getting ready to meet the saints of heaven so we are not going to need these old "houses" anyway.

When former president John Quincy Adams grew very old, he was slowly and feebly walking down a street in Boston one day when an old friend met him. Greeting him and shaking Adams's trembling hand, he asked, "And how is John Quincy Adams today?"

"Thank you," said the ex-president. "John Quincy Adams is well, quite well. I thank you. But the house in which he lives at present is becoming quite dilapidated. It is tottering upon its foundations. Time and the seasons have nearly destroyed it. Its roof is pretty well worn out. Its walls are much shattered, and it trembles with every wind. The old tenement is becoming almost uninhabitable, and I think John Quincy Adams will have to move out of it soon. But he himself is quite well, quite well."

In contrast to these old houses in which we live, God has promised to give us glorious mansions in heaven when we arrive there. So giving up this old house of mine will be like trading a worthless piece of real estate for a palace. Who doesn't want to do that?

Dear God, I look forward to moving into my mansion in heaven someday and being with you for all eternity. Amen.

How's Your Light?

You are the light of the world—like a city on a hilltop that cannot be hidden.

MATTHEW 5:14

Grandma Marge and Grandpa Leejay were getting the house spruced up. Grandpa's sister, Aunt Althea, was coming into the city for a visit. Aunt Althea was the second oldest child, and Grandpa Leejay was the youngest of ten children. This was Althea's first visit to the house. She lived out in a rural country area about eighty miles away.

I loved to visit my grandparents' big white house trimmed in red, especially when company was coming. Grandma was sure to have food for days.

"Here, Lee," my grandpa called out to my uncle—one of my mom's two younger brothers. "Take this soap and water and make this porch sparkle." Grandpa had not seen Aunt Althea in about ten years, as she did not like to travel.

It was about noon when the automobile pulled up to the house. Everyone hugged and kissed. I was only five years old, and this was my first time meeting my great-aunt Althea. Grandpa blessed the table and everyone; about twenty-five family members were there as we broke bread together.

About five o'clock that evening, Aunt Althea went in to take a nice soak. After finishing, she sat and talked a little, then announced that she was off to bed. Grandma had already turned the bed down and placed a glass of water on the lamp table. My uncle Lee passed the room about fifteen minutes after Aunt Althea had gone into the room. She was standing over the lamp. He thought perhaps she was praying. About thirty minutes later, he saw the light was still on.

"Aunt Althea, is everything all right?"

She was still over the lamp, making a blowing sound. "Lee, I can't seem to blow this candle out."

Lee smiled and said, "No, Auntie, this is an electric lamp; we just turn it off."

—Elaine W. Cavalier

Heavenly Father, help me to keep my light shining for you so that others will see their way to you. Amen.

Birthday Bloopers

Thank you for making me so wonderfully complex!
Your workmanship is marvelous—how well I know it.

PSALM 139:14

When it comes to celebrating my husband's birthday, I have made some bloopers.

Noel and I had been married only a few months. I was going to cook a special, romantic birthday dinner. I found an interesting recipe, but it required translating. With instructions I could understand, I set about making "Tom Selleck's Chicken in White Wine," wondering why the recipe spoke of wine when none was listed.

One medium onion. One cup Marsala.

I checked the recipe: A cup of curry seemed rather excessive. Perhaps I had misread. No, the recipe clearly stated one cup. But I thought I needed masala curry, unbeknownst to me one of the hottest curries. I did not know that Marsala was a sweet Italian wine.

It took only two bites to realize our taste buds would not survive the meal.

My second blooper ended on a cooler note several years later.

Noel loved Carvel ice cream. I secretly ordered an ice cream cake with "Happy Birthday, Noel" written in a blue Jell-O–type icing.

The afternoon of Noel's birthday, I jumped into the car with Ryan, our four-year-old son. We had guests coming for dinner, and I had to pick up the cake secretly.

"'Bye, Daddy. We're going to fetch your ice cream birthday cake."

Groan.

So much for a surprise! But I was the one in for a surprise. What looked like a dinner plate–size cake in the catalogue turned out to be side plate size. To make matters worse, I did not refreeze it once home, so when cake time came, we had a cake larger than a dinner plate. The problem was it was barely an inch high.

We now eat out on birthdays.

Thankfully, God does not make birthday bloopers. He wove us together in our mothers' wombs, journaling every day of our lives before we were born. That is how special we are to him.

—Marion C. Ueckermann

Father, every day of my life is noteworthy to you. From the moment I was conceived, you had a unique plan for me. Help me to follow your will. Amen.

Simplicity

For everything there is a season,
a time for every activity under heaven.

ECCLESIASTES 3:1

A man at the Los Angeles International Airport was worried about missing his plane. He had no wristwatch and could not locate a clock, so he hurried up to a total stranger and said, "Excuse me, could you give me the time, please?"

The stranger smiled and said, "Sure." He set down the two large suitcases he was carrying and looked at the watch on his wrist. "It is exactly 5:09. The temperature outside is 73 degrees, and it is supposed to rain tonight. In London the sky is clear and the temperature is 38 degrees Celsius. The barometer reading is 29.14 and falling. And, let's see, in Singapore the sun is shining brightly. Oh, by the way, the moon should be full tonight here in Los Angeles, and . . ."

"Your watch tells you all that?" the man interrupted.

"Oh, yes, and much more. You see, I invented this watch, and I can assure you there's no other timepiece like it in the world."

"I want to buy that watch! I'll pay you two thousand dollars for it right now."

"No, it's not for sale," said the stranger as he reached down to pick up his suitcases.

"Wait! *Four* thousand. I'll pay you four thousand dollars, cash," offered the man, reaching for his wallet.

"No, I can't sell it. You see, I plan to give it to my son for his twenty-first birthday. I invented it for him to enjoy."

"Okay, listen—I'll give you *ten* thousand dollars."

The stranger paused. "Ten thousand? Okay. It's yours for ten thousand even."

The man was elated. He paid the stranger, took the watch, snapped it onto his wrist with glee, and said, "Thanks," as he turned to leave.

"Wait," said the stranger. With a big smile he handed the two heavy suitcases to the man and added, "Don't forget the batteries."

—*Charles R. Swindoll*

Father God, we know that time is really important only to us as human beings. Please help us to think beyond clocks and schedules to eternity, where time will disappear in the joy of your presence. Amen.

Going Broke?

The love of money is the root of all kinds of evil.

1 TIMOTHY 6:10

In 1971 I began working as a writer on the personal staff of oil billionaire H. L. Hunt in Dallas. It was the first real paid writing job I had ever had, and I was excited. I wrote political-comment columns that bore Mr. Hunt's name—the series was called Hunt for Truth.

Frankly, being raised in a small town and going to a conservative Christian college, I had no clue who H. L. Hunt really was when I first went to work. When the president of my college had asked me if I would like to work for Mr. Hunt, I asked, "Does he make ketchup?" Little did I know that, at the time, he was considered the richest man in the world.

One of Mr. Hunt's sons, Lamar, was a world leader in the sports arena. He founded World Championship Tennis, owned racehorses around the world, and had recently purchased the Dallas Texans football team. He moved the team to Kansas, where it became the Kansas City Chiefs.

Reporters were always trying to catch Mr. Hunt saying something that would make him look foolish, but he usually managed to turn the tables on them, even though he was elderly.

One day a reporter came to interview Mr. Hunt. One of the questions he asked was, "Mr. Hunt, your son Lamar purchased a football team about two years ago. And he has lost a million dollars a year on that team. Now, just what do you think of that?"

Mr. Hunt ran his hand through his wispy white hair, thought for a minute, then said with a twinkle in his eye, "Well, I figure if Lamar loses a million dollars a year, he'll be broke in about four hundred and fifty years."

O Lord, you are the source of all blessings, including our money. May we learn to concentrate on you rather than on money, knowing that you will provide everything we need in this life. Amen.

While You're in There

Why worry about a speck in your friend's eye
when you have a log in your own?
. . . First get rid of the log in your own eye;
then you will see well enough to deal
with the speck in your friend's eye.

MATTHEW 7:3, 5

While traveling together to see an old friend in a distant city, Ethel and Louise, two elderly sisters, decided to stop at a shopping mall for a break from the drive. After window shopping for a while and having lunch in the food court, they made a few purchases. Then they left the mall and started on down the road to their destination.

When checking out at the last shop, Louise had inadvertently left her wallet on the counter, but she did not miss it until they had been driving for quite some time. When she discovered she had left the wallet behind, she called the shop on her cell phone to inquire if they had found it. The clerk said they had it and would keep it for her until she could return for it.

Ethel, who was driving, was frustrated by having to go all the way back to the mall to get the wallet. Even worse, they had to drive several more miles along the freeway before finding a turnaround.

On the way back to the mall, Ethel griped and complained about her sister being so absentminded. She criticized and scolded Louise during the entire return drive. The more she chided Louise, the more agitated she became. Ethel just would not stop for a moment.

To Louise's great relief, they finally arrived at the mall. Ethel was going to wait in the car while Louise went in to get her wallet. Then, just as Louise got out of the car to hurry inside, Ethel called after her, "Well, while you're in there, get my sunglasses and checkbook!"

Father, please forgive me for being critical of other people. Help me, instead, to look into the mirror of your Word and work on myself. Amen.

June 23

God Won't Tell

You may be sure that your sin will find you out.

NUMBERS 32:23

I remember that we went to visit some relatives when I was about five years old. While there, my cousin and I found my uncle's cigarettes and decided to give them a try. We each took one, along with his lighter, went outside, and hid behind their Jeep in the driveway. Then we lit the cigarettes, took a drag, and nearly choked. They were horrible! And that was the last time I tried them. In fifty-eight years I have not wanted to relive that bitter taste.

I suppose everyone tries things that are tempting or interesting as they grow up. That's just part of the maturing process. And we often hope we can hide those experiences from others. Sometimes it seems as if we have succeeded, at least for the moment. Other times our sins find us out quickly and with appropriate results.

My experience with the cigarettes is likely similar to that of other curious kids. It reminds me of a teacher of a sixth-grade class who was discussing with twelve-year-old John about John's experience trying out cigarettes with two other boys the night before.

"Tell me what happened, John," said the teacher.

"I got really sick on them," said John.

The teacher asked, "What did you think of the whole experience?"

John replied with a grimace, "I won't ever try it again, but don't tell the principal."

The teacher looked puzzled and said, "But God knows what you did. What's the difference between God's knowing and the principal's knowing?"

John explained in a whisper, "God won't tell my parents!"

Dear Father, forgive me for trying to hide my sins from you. I know you are fully aware of every mistake and act of sin in my life, whether I admit them to you or not. Help me to live my life fully aware of your presence. Amen.

The Way

Jesus [said], "I am the way, the truth, and the life.
No one can come to the Father except through me."

JOHN 14:6

Atlanta's traffic was heavy. Darkness threatened to overcome daylight. Forty-five minutes from home, I had just dropped off my daughter at a friend's house.

Jill (the name I had given my GPS) had guided me to my unknown destination; I assumed she would lead me back home. But shortly after my daughter Audri joined her friends, Jill malfunctioned. I was lost!

I was new to the Atlanta area, so Jill was more than my best friend; she was my only friend. Her voice had soothed my nerves as she guided me from one adventure to another, until that night.

I phoned my husband, who was away on a business trip. His advice was, "I noticed Wal-Mart had navigational systems on sale when I was there. Buy another one."

Okay, but where was a Wal-Mart? Tears raced down my cheeks.

An hour later I stood in the checkout line, embracing my new best friend, Jill Junior.

The next day Audri exchanged text messages with her older sister:

"Did Mom tell you Jill died?"

"Jill, the car helper?"

"Yes! What other Jill do you know?"

"None, but I wanted to make sure we weren't talking about a soul."

"She was Mom's best friend. Be considerate. They spent a lot of time together."

"True, but replaceable. She can buy another one."

"She already has!"

"Ha ha."

"Jill was dead less than two hours."

"No way! That's hilarious."

"Yep, less than two hours and Mom bought Jill Junior."

"J. J."

"Love it!"

—*Sue Ferguson*

Father, I am thankful you never fail. I trust you, I depend on you, and I delight in your companionship. Thank you for showing me the way. Amen.

June 25

Even Split

[Jesus said,] "That is why I tell you not to worry about everyday life. . . . Look at the birds. . . . Your heavenly Father feeds them. And aren't you far more valuable to him than they are?"

MATTHEW 6:25-26

My Weight Watchers leader loves to point me out as the member who eats out all the time and has still lost lots of weight. The other members are constantly asking me where I eat, what I order, and the like.

I usually say, "It's not about *where* you eat. It's about *what* you eat when you get there."

They just shake their heads as if to say, "You're crazy! I could never do it."

But it works for me.

One day I was in one of my favorite local diners at lunchtime. It's not a fancy place, but the food's good, it's clean, the service is great, and the prices are reasonable. I go there for good vegetables and down-home Southern cooking. And I enjoy the welcoming atmosphere and the fact that everyone knows my name.

The clientele at the diner is varied, including well-dressed business people, blue-collar workers, construction guys, and a delightful cross section of local humanity. The waitstaff treats everyone the same, so everybody feels comfortable and important.

On this particular day, two shabbily dressed guys came in and sat at a table near me at the back. It looked as if they had just jumped off a freight train. They ordered regular lunches and iced tea, ate hungrily, and enjoyed it immensely.

Finally, wiping his mouth with his napkin, one of the guys picked up the check and looked at it. Then he said to his friend with a grin, "Say, Ernie, shall we split the check evenly?"

"Sure, Dutch," said his friend. "That's fine with me."

"Okay, so do you want to wash or dry?"

Dear Lord, thank you for providing for your people—in one way or another. Teach us to help each other along the way. Amen.

Too Busy for Blessings

I will bless my people and their homes around my holy hill. . . . There will be showers of blessing.

EZEKIEL 34:26

In our world of breakneck speed and jammed schedules, we often think we are too busy to stop and receive the blessings God has in store for us. Instead, we blaze through life in a blur, missing the beauties of nature, the comfort of quiet companionship, and the joys found on side trails and unplanned excursions. Then we come to retirement and look back, wondering where it all went.

One day in London, England, a gentleman, rather shabbily dressed, came to the National Gallery carrying a picture under his arm. The man asked to see Sir William Boxall, the governor. He was, however, peremptorily refused an audience, and only after repeated rebuffs was he granted a moment's interview.

The stranger intimated that he had a painting in his possession that he wished to give to the National Gallery, and he began to unbuckle the straps around it to show the painting within.

Sir William, however, brusquely ordered him either to leave it or take it away altogether, saying that he was too busy to look at it.

"But you had better have one glance—I ask for no more," said the stranger.

Again Sir William refused, and he was just on the point of turning away when the covering fell off the picture and there was revealed one of Terborch's masterpieces, which the governor himself, some time previously, had failed to gain, though he had offered six thousand pounds for it.

"My name is Wallace," said the stranger quietly, "Sir William Wallace, and I came to offer this picture to the National Gallery."

"I almost fainted," related Boxall later.

Father of mercies, please help me to slow down and enjoy the blessings you have for me. Nothing is more important than taking the time to share life's joys with you. Amen.

June 27

A Journey to Remember

God places the lonely in families.

PSALM 68:6

A seven-hour drive at night through a severe snowstorm with a man I hardly knew!

My neighbor, Les, had arranged for a young man named Ted to take me to my aunt's home on his way to his mother's. Les had assured Ted I would help keep him awake.

"When Mary and her mom talk, you can't get a word in edgewise."

Nervous and unusually quiet, this eighteen-year-old girl found herself on a dark, lonely road with a twenty-two-year-old man of the world. *What if he tries to take advantage of me?* Eventually, I relaxed and we began discussing all sorts of topics.

Ted made frequent pit stops, unlike my dad, who hated to stop except for gas. At one deserted campground, we trekked through the snow to the outhouses. Ted handed me the flashlight. After I emerged, I shone the beam toward the men's outhouse to help light his way back to the car.

We arrived safely at my aunt's, our fun adventure ended. I thought I would probably never see Ted again.

I sent a note of thanks, signing it, "Love, Mary," as I did all my letters. A couple of weeks later, I got a letter. My heart jumped as I read the signature: "Love, Ted."

We continued corresponding, and then he came to visit. The fourth time we were together, he proposed. Three months later we married. The date happened to be his mom's birthday (which he didn't remember). Thirty-seven years later, that love at first sight has grown to maturity and a wonderful companionship.

—Mary A. Hake

Dear Lord, thank you for placing us in relationships. Please bless and strengthen our marriages and our bonds with our children and others. Amen.

The Plans

"I know the plans I have for you," says the LORD.
"They are plans for good and not for disaster,
to give you a future and a hope."

JEREMIAH 29:11

Some things sound too good to be true, don't they? And, as the old saying goes, "When things sound too good to be true, they usually are." In contrast, though, if we knew the plans the Lord has for us, we would likely be surprised at how wonderful they are.

The Bible is full of passages about God's plan for his people, assuring us that his plan is for our good, not for evil. It also says that his plan cannot be stopped. And yet, we are usually so busy making our *own* paltry plans that we fail to see the bigger, better plan God already has in place for us.

The story is told of a wealthy man who wanted to build a luxurious hunting lodge in the Northwoods of Wisconsin. After having his plans drawn up by a famous architect, he dispatched them to a local carpenter with instructions to go ahead and build the lodge according to the blueprints.

Only a few days had passed when a postcard arrived at the rich man's house from the carpenter, saying, "The plans are all wrong. I can't do anything until you get them straightened out."

In a hurry to get the lodge finished, the rich man sent a letter posthaste, assuring the local workman that the plans were correct and to proceed as ordered.

By return mail came the following postcard: "I don't aim to saw a plank until I get them plans straightened out. Why, if I was to build that lodge the way it's laid out here, you'd have two bathrooms!"

Dear God, we know that you are the great Architect of our lives and that we can count on your blueprints to be right and true. Help us to build our lives based on your plans and not our own. Amen.

Stay Calm, Jenny

Since God chose you to be the holy people he loves, you must clothe yourselves with tenderhearted mercy, kindness, humility, gentleness, and patience.

COLOSSIANS 3:12

It had been an extremely busy, hectic day, and I just wanted to get home to the peace and quiet of my small house. It would be good to fix a nice dinner, sit in my recliner to eat it, and watch a little television. Then I would take a long, hot bath and crawl into bed early for a good night's sleep. Tomorrow was Saturday, and I could sleep late. *Ah.*

On the way home I stopped at a small grocery store near my house to pick up a few things for dinner and the weekend. I liked the store because it had very fresh produce and was rarely crowded. But not today.

As I pushed my grocery cart around the corner and into the dairy aisle, a young mother was trying to comfort her baby, who was screaming at the top of her lungs. The mother said, "Stay calm, Jenny. Just stay calm. This won't take too much longer."

As I continued gathering the few items I needed, the baby continued her caterwauling, like a cat on a back fence at midnight. And the patient mother quietly said again, "Stay calm, Jenny. Just stay calm."

This went on for a full fifteen minutes. Everyone in the store was becoming irritated at the noise level created by the baby. And I was amazed as the mother retained her cool and continued to soothe the baby with, "Stay calm, Jenny. This will be over soon. Just stay calm."

Finally, I had to say something. So I walked up to the young mom and said, "I really admire how patient you're being with little Jenny there."

She looked at me with a wrinkled brow and said, "Lady, *I'm* Jenny."

Father, thank you for being so patient with us as your children. We know we frustrate you sometimes with our immaturity and failures. We love you, Abba, Father. Amen.

The Birthday Gifts

They entered the house and saw the child with his mother, Mary, and they bowed down and worshiped him. Then they opened their treasure chests and gave him gifts of gold, frankincense, and myrrh.

MATTHEW 2:11

Birthdays are always fun, especially for children who anticipate them for a full year. Children love everything about birthdays—games, friends, cake, ice cream. Mostly, though, they like the gifts. Who doesn't?

History indicates that when Jesus was a boy, birthday parties were already being held, including birthday cakes, pony rides, and other fun activities. So they are not new.

A young lady of eight was almost overcome with joy when her birthday netted her the two gifts she had most ardently wanted. She received a wristwatch and a bottle of perfume. She was elated! And she chattered about the new possessions all day long, finally wearying her parents of the subject.

Guests were expected for dinner, and the mother gently admonished the child in advance, saying, "Now, dear, everybody knows about your presents, and everybody is very happy for you. But now we must not go on talking about them all the time."

The little girl held her peace at the table throughout the greater part of the meal. When a lull finally occurred in the conversation, she was unable to restrain herself any longer. So she burst out with, "If anyone hears anything or smells anything, it's me!"

O Lord, thank you for the many gifts you shower on us each day. We are so richly blessed. Amen.

July 1

The Great Pretender

Imitate God, therefore, in everything you do, because you are his dear children.

EPHESIANS 5:1

One year we planned a different kind of vacation Bible school. Instead of regular Bible classes, we decided to dramatize the Bible stories. We moved the kids around from classroom to classroom in groups as if they were the twelve tribes of Israel. There they watched the stories come to life one by one. They loved it!

One of the VBS stories was about Jesus' driving the money changers out of the Temple in Jerusalem. Naturally, the key figure in the drama was Jesus. The man chosen for the role was a big, burly guy who drove a cross-country truck, chewed tobacco, and hit home runs on the church softball team. However, he rarely made it to church services or other spiritual events. His personal relationship with the man he was portraying was definitely limited to a nodding acquaintance.

He did a great job as Jesus, actually enjoying the part where he got to knock over the tables, scatter the money, and chase the bad guys out of the Temple. The children were in awe of this hero.

After VBS concluded, our "Jesus" started showing up for other church activities. Somehow, playing the role had touched him in a way he never expected. What really affected him the most was how the children responded to him after his portrayal. As he walked by them at church functions, ball games, and other activities, they would point at him and whisper, "Look, there's Jesus!"

Soon he stopped just playing the role and started seriously trying to imitate the Lord. Today he's a deacon in the church and a real spiritual leader. In short, he stopped just *acting* like Jesus and began really *living* like Jesus.

O Master, please help me to imitate you with my thoughts, my words, and my actions. I pray that when people see me, they will think, Look, there's Jesus. Amen.

Tiller-Riding Buffaloe

Plans go wrong for lack of advice;
many advisers bring success.

PROVERBS 15:22

Bummed, I sat on the tiny concrete stoop at our back door. I longed for a deck or patio where our family could sit in the cool spring evenings. My husband advised professional help and/or careful planning before taking on such a major project. But, being headstrong and a tad impatient, I decided I could build a patio.

With my husband safely at work, I read books, took notes, purchased materials, made plans, and rented a tiller. A male neighbor provided the manpower to wrestle the industrial-sized machine out of the van and around to the backyard. Once he was gone, I threw a prayer over my shoulder and started up the behemoth contraption.

The engine roared to life and the blades spun and dug into the ground, sending seismic shocks through the neighborhood. I felt like a rodeo rider on a bucking bull. The thing dragged me halfway across the yard before I was able to firmly plant my feet. Unfortunately, once immobile, I taxed every ounce of strength I possessed as I wrestled to keep from digging clear to the earth's core.

Five miles from China, I finally succeeded in shutting off the out-of-control, overpowered monster. Collapsing on the ground, I surveyed the potholes, chunks, trenches, and valleys marring our yard. Quick plans and a tossed-up prayer had led to disaster. Fortunately, after several weeks of hard labor with an understanding, sweet husband by my side, we created a halfway decent patio. I learned my lesson (for the moment), and the neighbors still chuckle about the wild, tiller-riding Buffaloe.

—Lisa Buffaloe

Heavenly Father, please help me to always plan carefully and to listen to the wise advice of others. Thank you for loving us even when we are covered in the mud of hasty mistakes. Amen.

Between Two Thieves

Then were there two thieves crucified with him,
one on the right hand, and another on the left.

MATTHEW 27:38 (KJV)

Some of the most famous paintings and pictures in the world center on the life of Christ—his birth, his ministry, his miracles, his death, his resurrection, and his ascension. Well-known painters such as Rembrandt and Michelangelo spent their careers—indeed their entire lives—preserving Christ's life and times on canvas and in other places, as in Michelangelo's famous work on the ceiling of the Sistine Chapel.

Perhaps the image most often captured on canvas is the crucifixion of Christ. These masterpieces are highly valued around the world and are carefully protected in art museums or in the private collections of wealthy art lovers.

When Thomas Killigrew, the celebrated Master of the Revels to Charles II of England, visited Louis XIV in Paris, the French monarch showed him his great personal gallery of paintings. He finally pointed out to him his most prized painting—a picture of the Crucifixion displayed between two other portraits.

"That portrait on the right," said His Majesty, "is the pope." Then taking Killigrew past the crucifixion painting to the portrait on the left of the crucifixion, he said, "And that one on the left is me."

"I humbly thank you for the information, Your Majesty," replied the English court jester, "for though I have often heard that the Lord was crucified between two thieves, I never knew who they were till now."

Although that story is humorous, today it is being reenacted on a regular basis. Jesus, who has chosen to live among his less-than-perfect people, must often find himself being crucified all over again because of our sins. We are, in effect, thieves on each side of him.

Father in heaven, we are sad that our sins are the cause of your Son's suffering. Please have mercy on us, Father. Forgive us. Save us from ourselves. Amen.

Liberty Sings!

Set this year apart as . . . a time to proclaim freedom throughout the land for all who live there.

LEVITICUS 25:10

For more than seventeen years, I sang with a marvelous choir called the Richland Hills Family Singers. One year we were scheduled to travel to Europe on a mission outreach tour. In preparation, we presented our program called *Liberty Sings!* to the folks at home before we left.

The "star" of the finale was a guy named Keith dressed up as Yankee Doodle Dandy in pants made of blue taffeta, a band director's coat with tails, a white shirt, a red cummerbund, and a wonderful top hat and cane.

About halfway through the six-minute finale, with its choreography, flag-waving, and hoopla, Keith was a little out of sync. His high-stepping march had deteriorated to a small kick-step. And the hand with the cane was hanging on to his electric-blue pants. The elastic in the waist had broken!

Still, the show must go on. So we kept singing and Keith kept dancing, but he was having major problems.

Meanwhile, we were all captivated and terrified by Keith's dilemma. Somehow, though, when the music swelled to its climax at the end, Keith managed to put his hat and cane in one hand, hang on to his pants with the other, balance the dancer on his knee, and sing the final notes of the song. He was amazing.

With the final crash of the cymbals, the curtains came rushing together, the choir broke into gales of laughter, and Keith grabbed his pants and ran off the stage before stage hands could open the curtains to a standing ovation from the audience. It was a hilarious end to a great patriotic show and the beginning of a trip we'll never forget. Keith had saved the show with one hand behind him—hanging on to his patriotic pants!

God, please bless our land today, and help us to always be grateful for the incredible freedom you have given us in Christ. Amen.

Family Ties

If [a widow] has children or grandchildren, their first responsibility is to show godliness at home and repay their parents by taking care of them. This is something that pleases God.

1 TIMOTHY 5:4

Our eight-passenger van stopped at the single blinking red light in the small Oklahoma town where my husband, Mark, was born. It had been a long trip from Texas on that hot day in July. We arrived at the VFW hall ready to climb out of our vehicle and enjoy the family reunion. I was excited to see everyone and find out the latest family news.

Aunt Janice had brought her most recent scrapbook creation. We reminisced about past family happenings as we perused the beautiful pages full of pictures. The younger children played games outside on the playground, apparently having a wonderful time. Before long, everyone came together to view Uncle Fate's slide show of old pictures.

Our son, Daniel, yelled out, "Hey, that's me!" when a photo of his dad as a young boy appeared on the screen.

We consumed a yummy Oklahoma lunch of chicken-fried steak, mashed potatoes, and gravy, all the while chattering about current events, sports, and more family experiences. As the day came to an end, we hugged one another and said our good-byes, thanking God for the family he had given us.

As our six children piled back into the van, six-year-old John seemed annoyed. He asked in an exasperated tone, "Well, who *were* all those people, anyway?"

"John, those were your relatives."

Disgusted, he replied, "Humph! I didn't know a single one of them!"

—Paula Hemingway

Thank you, God, for the families you have given us, and please help us to love and care for them, even the ones we do not know well. Most important, thank you for allowing us to be your children and be part of your family. Amen.

If Only . . .

Christ is also the head of the church, which is his body.

COLOSSIANS 1:18

The idea of the church is a fascinating concept, dreamed up by God. Who else would think of throwing together every kind of sinner and "baddie" in the world and form them into a cohesive family whose members love and support one another through good times and bad? Oh, yes, the church was built specifically for sinners, not for perfect people. And if that is not the case, Christ died for nothing.

Do you ever wonder, then, why we are often so surprised and shocked when we see people—ordinary people—in the church commit sins of all kinds? After all, becoming a Christian does not automatically turn us into perfect people. We are all still sinners; Christians are just *forgiven* sinners who have banded together to try to survive and serve God. So we need to cut one another a lot of slack and work hard on the love and support parts, rather than on the criticism part.

Famous preacher Henry Ward Beecher was once contemplating buying a horse. After Beecher had looked over many of them, the owner of the stables finally burst out in praise of one particularly fine animal.

"Now here's a horse that's really sound. He can go any gait. He stands without hitching, works anyplace you put him, goes when you want him to, and stops the minute you say, 'Whoa.' He is perfectly gentle yet full of spirit. He has no bad traits—doesn't kick, doesn't bite, comes when you call him, and doesn't run off when he sees something strange."

With a wistful look in his eye, Mr. Beecher sighed and said, "If only that horse were a member of my church."

Heavenly Father, I love your church, and I love my brothers and sisters in the church, warts and all. Thank you for loving and supporting me through my spiritual family. I don't know how I would get through life without them. Amen.

Pride Goes before the Fall

Pride goes before destruction,
and haughtiness before a fall.

PROVERBS 16:18

As the kids played in the backyard one hot Texas afternoon, I treated them to one of their summer favorites—Popsicles. I had just one rule: Eat them outside. After all, it is physically impossible for preschoolers to devour brightly colored frozen treats without decorating themselves, the table, the floor, and everything else within sight.

"Here you go!" I said, handing them the treats. "Just be sure to keep these outside."

"But, Mom!" my four-year-old daughter, J. J., protested, "I'll be good this time! I promise I won't drip!"

"I know you'll try, honey," I assured her. "And I appreciate the thought. But go ahead and eat it outside. Then, if you want to come inside later, that's fine."

With a determined flounce, J. J. sat on the patio chair and began to eat her Popsicle, painstakingly slurping the syrup before it dripped on her clothes or the porch. When she got down to the last clump of ice, which was barely clinging to the bottom of the stick, she knocked on the back door, eager to show me her accomplishment through the French-pane windows.

"Look, Mom!" she squealed, showing me her red-tinted stick, dripping syrup dangerously close to her T-shirt. "I didn't spill anything!"

Chuckling at her determination, I said, "That's great, honey. But you're not quite finished yet, so be careful. And remember, pride comes before the fall."

J. J. screwed up her face in thought. And then as understanding struck, she said brightly, "Oh! So pride comes in the summer?"

Well, yes, I suppose it does. And if we are not careful, pride can come in the fall, winter, and springtime, too.

—*Jennifer Stair*

Father, please keep us humble, even when we do something truly amazing, like eating a Popsicle without spilling a drop. Amen.

Theft and Conscience

If you are a thief, quit stealing. Instead, use your hands for good hard work, and then give generously to others in need.

EPHESIANS 4:28

I have seen it stated in print that as a boy I was guilty of stealing peaches, apples, and watermelons. I read a story to this effect very closely not long ago, and I was convinced of one thing, which was that the man who wrote it was of the opinion that it was wrong to steal, and that I had not acted right in doing so. I wish now, however, to make an honest statement. I do not believe, in my entire checkered career, I stole a ton of peaches.

One night I stole—I mean I removed—a watermelon from a wagon while the owner was attending to another customer. I crawled off to a secluded spot, where I found that it was green. It was the greenest melon in the Mississippi Valley.

Then I began to reflect. I began to be sorry. I wondered what George Washington would have done had he been in my place. I thought a long time, and then suddenly felt that strange feeling which comes to a man with a good resolution, and took up that watermelon and took it back to its owner. I handed him the watermelon and told him to reform. He took my lecture much to heart, and, when he gave me a good one in place of the green melon, I forgave him.

I told him that I would still be a customer of his, and that I cherished no ill feeling because of the incident—that would remain *green* in my memory.

—*Mark Twain's Helpful Hints for Good Living*

Dear Lord, I am sorry for the times I have stolen something that was not mine. Please forgive me and teach me to be content with the many blessings and gifts you have already given me. I want to be pure and holy. Amen.

Spell-Check, Please

If we confess our sins to him, he is faithful and just to forgive us our sins and to cleanse us from all wickedness.

1 JOHN 1:9

Have you noticed the increasing number of young people sporting multiple tattoos? Recently my son wanted to pay tribute to his deceased older brother. I watched as he anxiously unwrapped the covering around his forearm, showing me the carefully planned artwork of angel wings and sun rays backlighting the sketch. It struck me right away that his brother's name had been misspelled.

Even into adulthood, *Timmy* was the name everyone affectionately called him. He never grew too tall because of his kidney disease, and he kept his youthful appearance and nickname. His birth name was *Timothy*.

In my son's confusion and anticipation, he had added an extra *m*, spelling out *Timmothy*, and that became a permanent letter on his brother's tattoo memorial.

As I began to chuckle and point out the mistake, I saw my son's shoulder and arm relax. I giggled with mercy, posing the question, "Do they make 'Flesh-Out'?"

We both laughed, understanding how this might have happened, not with intent or disregard, but with maybe a bit of impulsiveness and an emotional attachment to the name with two *m*s. Timmy probably was getting a giggle out of it himself there in heaven.

Although God does not think our mistakes or lack of attention are particularly funny, when we confess to him our blunders, he looks past our stains and sees his creation as a new canvas awaiting the Artist's touch. God sees into a humble heart. He sees our wings and our potential through the gifts he has given us. God's shining light of grace illuminates us. Our correct names are written on the cross in the shed blood of Christ.

—*Coleene VanTilburg*

Thank you, Lord, for the knowledge that our stains are not permanent, that our mistakes are forgiven because of your ultimate sacrifice. Help us to be living memorials to you throughout our lives. Amen.

Job Security

No discipline is enjoyable while it is happening—
it's painful! But afterward there will be
a peaceful harvest of right living for
those who are trained in this way.

HEBREWS 12:11

During times of slow economy, many people lose their jobs, or their work assignments slow to a virtual stop, creating extreme financial and emotional stress. This stress extends into other areas of their lives, such as their relationships, self-confidence, and even physical health.

People go to great lengths to find jobs—traveling to distant cities, reeducating themselves to qualify for better or different positions, and calling in every favor they can from friends and family. Sometimes their efforts pay off quickly; sometimes it takes months to reap a harvest. Once they have, at long last, managed to secure another job, their stress begins to fade, and their lives begin to return to "normal," whatever that is. (I learned a long time ago that "normal" is whatever I think it is, and everything else is *not* normal.)

One butterfingered man, who had been suffering from a long siege of unemployment, finally found a job in a chinaware shop. He had been at work only a few days when he smashed a large, expensive vase. Naturally, he was summoned to the manager's office and told that they would have to deduct ten dollars from his wages every week until the vase was paid for in full.

"How much did the vase cost?" asked the man.

"Three hundred dollars," said the manager, shaking his head sadly.

"Oh, that's wonderful!" said the employee. "I'm so happy!"

The employer was puzzled about the man's glee in having money taken out of his check every week. "I don't understand. Why does this discipline make you happy?"

The man grinned and said, "At last I have a steady job!"

Father, I am grateful that you love me enough to discipline me when it is needed. I know that even though the discipline is not pleasant, I will be better for it in the long run. Amen.

Listen Up!

Everything that is hidden will eventually be brought into the open, and every secret will be brought to light.

MARK 4:22

Raising four children, my parents always looked for ways to save money. I was eight years old the summer they installed an energy monitor that gauged our home's electricity use.

To test the unit, the salesman and my father walked through our house, turned on every light and electric appliance, and then went into the basement. Dad had warned us children to stay out of the way while they worked. But the heat of the day drove me inside for a glass of water. Walking through the kitchen, I was startled to see flames flickering inside the oven. I ran to the basement and shouted, "Dad, did you know there's a fire in the oven?"

"Yeah, it's fine, honey," he responded absently. "Go back outside."

Incredulous but not wanting to be a nuisance, I turned to go just as Dad and the salesman came back upstairs.

One look at the oven, however, told Dad that things were not, in fact, fine. As the salesman ran to his car to grab a fire extinguisher, Dad quickly ushered me outside.

Later, with the fire out and the salesman gone, we laughed as we assessed the damage: The charred remains of a package of cookies and a loaf of bread that Dad had forgotten were stored in the broiler. Grinning sheepishly, he turned to me, sighed, and said, "When you said there was a fire in the oven, I thought you meant, 'Did you know the oven is on?'"

Too often we become upset when God does not seem to listen to us, but how often do *we* really listen to *him*? Remember: He gave us two ears but only one mouth, as a gentle reminder to listen twice as much as we speak!

—*Carrie Bezusko*

Father, quiet my mind, open my heart, and bless me with the ability to hear you as you guide me through life. Amen.

Refugees

Stay alert! Watch out for your great enemy, the devil. He prowls around like a roaring lion, looking for someone to devour.

1 PETER 5:8

During World War II, refugees from occupied France used many varied and devious devices in order to escape from their captured country. One such man threw himself on the mercy of the proprietor of a small traveling menagerie.

"Please, sir, take me with you, I beg of you!" pleaded the refugee.

"I will try to help you, but I'm afraid to disguise you as a simple employee," said the proprietor. "You might be discovered too easily."

"Surely you can think of some way to hide me from the authorities so I can get out of the country," begged the man.

"Well, it happens that our gorilla died a little more than a week ago, and we preserved his hide, thinking that we might recoup the loss by having it stuffed someday. If you want to put it on, you can travel with us in the cage. The authorities will certainly not think to look for you there. If they do, just growl and act like a crazed gorilla."

Faced by his desperate need, the refugee did so. Whenever the menagerie was on exhibition, he put on as good a gorilla show as he could manage, trying to pay his debt of gratitude to the proprietor.

One night when no one was around, he was horror struck to discover that the bars between his own cage and the adjoining one had become loose. One of the bars had fallen completely out, and through the opening came his neighbor—the lion! As the animal slunk toward him, the "gorilla" cringed in the corner and began to cry, "Help! Help!"

"Be quiet, you fool!" growled the lion. "You aren't the only refugee here."

O Lord, our Protector, please protect us from the wiles of the devil, who wants to destroy us. We place ourselves in your hands and pray for your constant care and love. Amen.

July 13

Where's Donn?

Not a single sparrow can fall to the ground without your Father knowing it. . . . So don't be afraid; you are more valuable to God than a whole flock of sparrows.

MATTHEW 10:29, 31

What family with seven children would be crazy enough to travel from one end of the country to the other by camping? Ours was that crazy. This was back in the dark ages of the 1950s, when there were no iPods, laptops, or in-car movies. So our family had to make up our own fun.

We used to play games such as "I spy," where someone called out an object, and the others strained to look out of the car windows, trying to be the first to spot whatever the object was.

Often our travels took us into the night before we would reach the next campsite. One of our favorite tricks was to wait until we had made a stop for gas and then have one of the seven hide on the floorboard. Then we would let Dad drive for a time. Later someone would ask where the hidden child was. My parents usually played along, and all of us thought it was funny until one night I will never forget.

It was late, we had been driving all day, way out west somewhere, and we had just made a stop for gas. In those days, a station had only one or two restrooms. When we pulled up with a carful of people, it took longer than for most families.

After about an hour back on the road, in the middle of the night, in the middle of nowhere, someone called out, "Where's Donn?"

As usual, everyone laughed, except the person who had asked the question.

"No, really. He's not here!"

Panic ensued! Back then, high-tech communication didn't exist. But with the help of the state police and their radios, and with God's help, we were eventually reunited with the missing child.

—*Max Elliot Anderson*

Father, thank you for the knowledge that no matter where I am or what I need, you are never far away. Amen.

Based on the Evidence

Come now, and let us reason together, saith the LORD.

ISAIAH 1:18 (KJV)

Ratiocination is the process of exact thinking or of thinking things through using reason. And although I am a left-brained, logical sort myself, I am not as adept at exact thinking as one man I heard about.

Because the people of France appreciate logical thinking, the works of Sir Arthur Conan Doyle are greatly admired in that country. Sir Arthur once taxied from the train station to his hotel in Paris, and as he left the cab, the driver said, "Mercí, Monsieur Conan Doyle."

"How did you know who I am?" asked Doyle curiously.

The taxi driver explained his logical deduction: "There was a notice in the paper that you were arriving in Paris from the south of France. I knew from your general appearance that you were an Englishman. It is evident that a barber of the south of France last cut your hair. By these indications I knew you. It was really quite simple, don't you see?"

"That is absolutely extraordinary, my good man. You had no other evidence upon which to go?" asked Doyle with fascination.

"Nothing," said the driver with a mischievous grin, "except the fact that your name is on your luggage."

We human beings seem to apply ratiocination to most things in life except politics and religion. When it comes to those topics, we tend to think with our hearts instead of with our heads. And yet God is the author of logic and reason. It is entirely reasonable, for instance, that God created the world with all its intricate workings and wonders rather than our world resulting from some big explosion. In fact, I believe it takes a lot more *faith* to be an atheist than it does to believe in God. God invites us to think logically with him, and that logic will surely lead us to right conclusions and actions.

O God, we know that you are the creator of life and of our world. And although it makes logical sense to me, I also accept it with my heart, Father, because I love you so much. Amen.

Colleen and the Fountain

Tombs opened. The bodies of many godly men and women who had died were raised from the dead. They left the cemetery after Jesus' resurrection . . . and appeared to many people.

MATTHEW 27:52-53

A few years ago, our church choir presented an Easter play about the resurrection of Christ, based on the Scripture verses above. We presented it as theater-in-the-round in the huge atrium of our church, surrounding a massive fountain.

My friend Colleen—a professional dramatist and an altogether delightful lady—played the lead. The finale centered on her character's accepting Christ and being immersed in the fountain. We built wooden steps to help her get down into the water. And so that the water would be deep enough to actually immerse Colleen, we had stopped up the drains to allow the water level to rise.

Toward the end of the play, I suddenly noticed that the water level was much too high. A few more minutes, and we would need to change our play to "Noah and the Flood"!

I panicked, but I could not just walk off the stage. Finally able to make my exit, I ran to tell our stage manager about the water. He turned the water off just before it ran over the top and onto our unsuspecting audience. *Whew.*

Then it was time for the finale. Colleen started down into the fountain, but the extra water had caused the wooden steps to float unsteadily. With help from the man who was helping with the baptism, she finally managed to get her foot on the top step, push the steps down to the fountain floor, and make a wobbly descent. But two extra bodies in the fountain pushed the water level dangerously close to overflowing.

Fortunately, Colleen . . . and all of us . . . were saved as God protected us from dramatic disaster. Colleen's lasting memory of the event is how incredibly cold the water was. She says, "Instead of being washed away, I think my sins were freeze-dried!"

Thank you, Lord, for saving us from our follies! Amen.

The Bug Letter

Do everything without complaining and arguing, so that no one can criticize you.

PHILIPPIANS 2:14-15

Have you ever written a letter of complaint to a big company? My experience with doing that has been less than satisfactory on the whole. I get the impression that companies have a file full of standard complaint responses, and they reply automatically based on the kind of complaint submitted. In other words, complaint number two generates response number two, and so forth. Basically, trying to get a personalized answer to a complaint is often an exercise in futility.

In the publishing business, there's no such thing as a book with no mistakes in it. Imperfect publishing folks simply cannot produce perfect books, no matter how diligently we try. And readers love to point out a typo or a misspelled word they find. To their surprise, rather than become defensive about their complaints, we thank them for helping us make our books the best they can be and promise to fix the mistake as soon as possible.

One complaint case I heard about (not in the publishing business, thank goodness!) concerned a man who was tormented by bedbugs in his sleeping car on the train. He wrote an indignant letter about the matter to the general passenger agent of the railroad.

His friends cautioned him that he would probably not receive so much as a reply, but he was so upset that he decided to try it anyway. To his surprise and great satisfaction, in due course he received an apologetic letter from the railroad assuring him that such a thing could never happen again. He smiled to think that his letter had caused such action on the part of the railroad.

His elation was quashed a moment later, however, by the discovery of an interoffice memo, which had inadvertently been inserted in the envelope with the letter. It said tersely, "Send this jerk the bug letter."

Dear, patient Lord, please forgive us for being such complainers. Help us, rather, to count our many blessings and to praise your wonderful name for everything you do for us. Amen.

A Better Boy

Anyone who becomes as humble as this little child is the greatest in the Kingdom of Heaven.

MATTHEW 18:4

Luke, my firstborn grandchild, was barely three when his sister, Sarah, came along. He had been the happy recipient of all the attention for three years straight, so having a sister was a major adjustment in his little life.

When Sarah was only a month old, she caught a cold, so we stopped by the drugstore on the way home from picking Luke up from the church day care. I was giving baby Sarah more attention than Luke because of her illness and did not want her to become fussy during the long wait at the pharmacy. Luke did not appreciate that one little bit! He proceeded to put on a one-boy show for all those in line with us, while stretching his mother's already paper-thin patience.

Finally, meds in hand and heading to the car, Christy, my daughter, very sternly scolded Luke for his misbehavior. "You were *not* a good boy in the store! I think you need to pray to Jesus that you can be a better boy."

After buckling both children in the backseat, Christy and I settled into the front seats of the car. I glanced back at Luke, ready to assure him of my love and soothe his tiny ego. There he sat, head bowed, eyes closed, hands clasped in prayer, earnestly pleading, "Dear Jesus, *please* make me a better boy."

How sweet, and how touching. Luke melted our hearts, and although we tried to keep from laughing, we couldn't keep from crying. I think sometimes Father God longs to hear such earnest, childlike prayers from his grown-up children too.

—Shari Gunter

Dear God, please help me to be the best me I can be, and let me do it not for me but for your glory and praise. I want to be like you, Lord. Amen.

Powerful Prayer

The earnest prayer of a righteous person has great power and produces wonderful results.

JAMES 5:16

Down through the ages, a great religious debate has raged about how we are supposed to pray. Should we kneel? Should we be prostrate? Should we stand with our hands held toward heaven? Just what is the definitive way to pray?

Three clergymen were talking one day about the power of prayer in general and about the appropriate and effective positions in which to pray. As they were talking, a telephone repairman was working on the phone system in the background.

The Baptist minister said that he felt the key to powerful prayer was in the hands. He always held his hands together and pointed them upward as a symbolic form of worship.

The Catholic priest insisted that real prayer was always conducted on one's knees.

The charismatic preacher, however, suggested that they both had it wrong—the only position worth its salt was to pray while stretched out flat on your face.

By that time the repairman could not stay out of the conversation any longer. He interjected: "I found that the most powerful prayer I ever made was while I was dangling upside down by my heels from a power pole, suspended forty feet above the ground."

Perhaps, when it comes right down to it, what is really important when it comes to prayer is not the position of your body but the position of your heart. Whether you are standing, sitting, lying down, walking, climbing a mountain, or in any other physical position, the real question is this: Is your heart kneeling in humble submission before the great throne of God?

Father in heaven, please accept my humble prayer of praise and gratitude to you. You alone are worthy of my worship, and I bring my heart to you in obedience and honor. In Jesus' precious name, amen.

A Horse Is a Horse?

God showed his great love for us by sending Christ to die for us while we were still sinners.

ROMANS 5:8

Farmer Jones had a beautiful horse, of which he was very proud. One day he rode the horse into town and carefully tied the animal to the hitching post in front of the general store. Two thieves, hurrying through the town, happened to spy the handsome horse and decided to steal it. Realizing the animal was much too fine and valuable to be stolen in the ordinary manner, they decided on a stratagem to carry out their plan.

One of the thieves hurriedly untied the horse and rode swiftly away while the other thief remained by the post.

The farmer finally emerged from the store. Seeing that his horse was not where he had left it, he was just about to shout when the thief walked up to him. In a sad, low tone he said, "Sir, I am your horse. Years ago I sinned, and for my sins I was punished. I was changed into a horse. Today my punishment is over, and I can be released if you will be so kind."

The farmer, amazed and yet touched by the story, sent the man on his way, wishing him good luck in his new life.

Several weeks later Farmer Jones went to a fair in a neighboring town. Great was his surprise to see his own horse for sale there. Gazing long enough at the animal to make sure his eyes had not deceived him, he walked over and whispered in the horse's ear, "So, you've sinned again, eh?"

Jesus came to earth to turn sinners into saints. But, like the horse, we often fall back into our sinful ways. I suspect that sometimes God wants to say, "So, you've sinned again, eh?"

Thank you, Lord, for changing me from a sinner into a saint. I pray that you will continue covering me with your saving grace and forgiveness. I can't make it without you. Amen.

In My View

Worship him who made the heavens, the earth,
the sea, and all the springs of water.

REVELATION 14:7

California is one of my favorite places to travel. The Pacific Ocean is breathtaking, and the vibrant multicolored flowers are astonishing. I love to sit by the ocean and listen to the waves slap . . . slap . . . slap against the shore. You could put me by the ocean with my laptop, and I think I could *become* Book-of-the-Month Club all by myself—it is such an inspirational scene and sound for me. My soul feels centered and calm by the water.

Groucho Marx, who lived in California, once tried his best to avoid a pesky real estate agent who wanted to show him a palatial oceanfront estate that was for sale. Groucho did not want to go, but he finally gave in and agreed to view the property.

The salesman drove the comedian up the mile-long, beautifully landscaped drive and then escorted him through the house, the stables, the gardens, and the kennels. The entire time he was babbling on about the wonders of this dream palace by the sea.

Groucho patiently plodded after him, nodding gravely, apparently much impressed. Finally he was ushered onto the flagstone terrace, and the confident salesman waved proudly toward the broad expanse of the great Pacific.

"Now what do you think?" he challenged.

"I don't care for it," replied Groucho thoughtfully, and he waved in turn at the view. "Take away the ocean, and what have you got?"

I imagine that heaven will be by an ocean. I will sit on the shore for all eternity with my notebook, quiet music playing in the background, writing poems and songs in praise of the glorious Father. My soul will surely be at peace forever.

Heavenly Father, I humbly bow in worship to you for your majesty, your holiness, and your omnipotence. It will be my joy to be in your presence for eternity, and I thank you for making it possible. Amen.

The Bargain

Teach people to live disciplined and successful lives, to help them do what is right, just, and fair.

PROVERBS 1:3

If you travel to a foreign country such as Israel, you will find an interesting tradition that we do not typically observe here in the States. In that culture it is extremely important that merchants make a sale to the first customer who enters their shops in the morning. They believe that if they make those initial sales, business for the rest of the day will go well. If they fail in their first attempts, the rest of the day will not be financially rewarding.

What that means, then, is that merchants hustle first customers really hard. Once my husband bought an expensive brass pitcher for four dollars, because he was the first customer in the shop that day.

Something similar happened on one of those downtown Manhattan streets where salesmen rush out and seize people by the arm.

"Look," said a salesman eagerly to the man he had seized. "A fine suit—the best, nice cut, fine quality materials. To you, fifteen dollars."

"No," said the customer, trying to break free.

"Listen," said the clothier, dragging his victim a little closer to the shop, "this is a very special cut, with cuffs even—the last suit. To you, special, twelve dollars."

"No," said the man, trying to pull away.

"An opportunity that shouldn't be passed up," continued the salesman. "Because it's early, to start the day right, the first sale, eight dollars."

"Nothing doing," snarled the customer.

"Dear me!" wailed the proprietor, throwing his hands up into the air. "Such a person. To make the thing right, to start the day; I start something, I should finish it. I'm giving it to you for nothing."

To which the customer replied, "Not without two pairs of pants!"

Father God, please help me to do what's right, to be just, and to deal fairly with people every day as I live my life. I want to treat others as you do. Amen.

Who'da Thunk It?

"There is hope for your future," says the LORD.

JEREMIAH 31:17

I don't know about you, but I am constantly astounded by the futuristic advancements in technology. If you had told me when I was in high school that I would be using something called a *computer*, I would have thought you had fallen off your rocker. At that time, I was working on an old Royal Standard typewriter. (If you're under forty years old, go ask your mother about those.)

Since then I've progressed with every kind of typewriting equipment imaginable—electric typewriters, Selectric typewriters, computers with one-line screens, computers with five-line screens, computers with full screens—and now I have a MacBook Pro with a twenty-five-inch monitor that does everything but cook lunch.

For years when I traveled, I had to take my Day-Timer, my phone book, my camera, my calculator, my laptop, and my phone. It was like moving. Now I just plop my iPhone into my belt holder and take off. Life is definitely easier for me today because of technology. Somehow, though, I'm still in amazement mode at what might be coming next.

It makes me think of the old mountaineer who was on his way to a nearby town. He decided to use the new highway that had just been completed. Just as he was about to steer his horse onto the road, an automobile whizzed past at sixty miles per hour. The old man had never before seen one of those newfangled machines, so he stopped and, openmouthed, stared after it.

Scarcely a minute had passed when, following in hot pursuit, came a motorcycle cop who flashed by. The old man was amazed!

Muttering aloud, he said, "Well, I'll be! Who'da thunk that thang coulda had a colt?"

God of the universe, thank you for giving people the ability to discover more and more of the wondrous things you have in store for us in the future. We know that all these good gifts come from you. Help us to use them in ways that glorify and please you. Amen.

July 23

Taking Leave of His Senses

You must have the same attitude that Christ Jesus had.

PHILIPPIANS 2:5

An old adage says, "Attitude is everything!" And that's a fact. With the right attitude, mountains of trouble become molehills easily spanned, and hysteria can become hilarity. Being positive and upbeat makes life more enjoyable and less arduous, something to which you can look forward. With the right attitude, relationships are sweeter, work is not drudgery, and duty is handled with a smile.

The apostle Paul challenged us to have the same attitude that Christ Jesus had—one of humility, sacrifice for others, and hope. Can you imagine how good life would be if everyone had that kind of attitude? Think of how that would change the hours and days of your life as you interact with other people.

A certain American soldier, attached to one of the American tank units fighting with the British in the Libyan campaign during World War II, had been carried by the requirements of the service many miles deep into the heart of the desert with his comrades. This outpost at the front had been quiet for several days, so the soldier found himself one afternoon with a few hours' leave, and he became inventive.

It was with some surprise that his commanding officer spotted the man striding purposefully across the desert sand clad only in his green-striped swimming trunks and carrying a cooler and a brightly colored beach towel.

"Murphy!" shouted the officer in some astonishment. "Where in the world do you think you're going?"

"Why, sir," said the soldier, "I just thought while I had a couple of hours off, I'd take a dip in the beautiful surf."

"Are you crazy?" demanded the officer. "The ocean is five hundred miles away from here!"

The soldier responded, "Beautiful big beach, isn't it?"

Lord Jesus, thank you for showing us the kind of attitude we need to have to make our lives better. Help me to develop the same attitude about life and living that you demonstrated when you were here on earth. Amen.

No Need to Worry?

O death, where is your victory?
O death, where is your sting?

1 CORINTHIANS 15:55

For us as normal human beings, the thought of dying is disconcerting, to say the least. It is hard to get past the idea that death is the end of life as we know it. It is doubly hard, as the old hymn says, to "think of a home over there" in heaven. Heaven seems so far away and ethereal that we tend to simply ignore the fact that death is inevitable for each of us at some point.

That denial and avoidance play out in many ways in our lives. For instance, even though we know our lives on earth cannot go on forever, we may not have our wills drawn up, we do not buy enough life insurance, we do not buy mortgage pay-off insurance, and we do not prepurchase funeral plans and burial plots. Somehow, dealing with those end-of-life chores feels as if we are bringing death to ourselves sooner than it would otherwise come.

One old-timer had been sick in bed for several weeks. The local doctors had been unable to help him or to diagnose his problem. The old codger insisted that he did not need anybody's help, but over his continuing protests, his family called in various specialists to see whether any of them could pinpoint what the problem was.

When all the specialists had come and gone, the old man's relatives asked him what the doctors had said about his condition.

"Told you I was all right," he said triumphantly. "Them gentlemen used a lot of big words I couldn't understand, but they finally said, 'Well, no use worrying about it or arguing over it. We will get the answer soon enough from the autopsy.'"

In other words, the patient was standing at death's door, and the doctors were trying to pull him through.

God of life, thank you for the assurance that heaven is on the other side of death's door. Help us to live in the light of that truth. Amen.

What Did You Say?

Anyone with ears to hear should listen and understand!

MATTHEW 11:15

Over time, the well-used hymnals in the old church had worn out. The congregation really needed to purchase a new set of hardcover songbooks for the sanctuary, but it was a small church with limited resources. So purchasing new books out of the church treasury was simply not an option.

After discussing the issue in a business meeting one Sunday afternoon, the leaders of the congregation decided the only way to solve the problem was to ask each person in the church to purchase at least one hymnal. Since the individual books were not too expensive, that seemed like a reasonable solution and one they thought would be acceptable to the members of the church.

The elderly minister was asked to make the announcement at the next church service, which he agreed to do. In the later years of his ministry, the old Southern preacher had become slightly hard of hearing, which created some interesting scenarios. At the next service, the minister informed the congregation that the new hymnals were being ordered and would be purchased individually by members of the church. He said he hoped the members would support the effort with joy so their singing praises to God could continue.

When the minister had finished his announcement, the deacon of the church arose to remind the audience that the following Sunday was the regular day for blessing new infants born into their congregation during the past year.

The minister, not hearing clearly what the deacon had said and thinking he had made reference to the hymnals, hastily added, "All you who haven't any can get as many as you want for seventy-five cents each by calling me."

Dear Lord, please help me to hear your Spirit clearly when you speak to me. I want to be in tune with your will and your plan for my life. Amen.

Making Headlines

Everyone will see the Son of Man coming on the clouds with great power and glory.

MARK 13:26

The editor of a small-town newspaper had cherished for many years a set of old-fashioned wooden type in a huge sixty-point size. On more than one occasion his assistants had tried to induce him to use it for one story or another, but he always firmly vetoed the idea.

One summer the old man went away for a short fishing vacation, leaving his assistants in charge of getting the newspaper out in his absence. While he was away, a tornado struck the little town, tearing the steeple off the Baptist church, ripping roofs from several prominent houses, sucking a couple of water wells dry, and scattering pieces of a few barns. No bigger calamity had ever hit the town.

Figuring this was their chance, the editor's assistants reverently got down the treasured giant type from the top shelf and set a sensational front-page headline: "TORNADO RIPS TOWN APART!"

Two days later the editor came back from his fishing trip and stormed into the office. "Balls of fire!" he shouted. "What d'ye mean by taking down that type for a little old tornado?"

"But, sir," the assistants stuttered, "it's the biggest story ever to happen here. We just thought—"

"It's the biggest story to happen here *so far*," huffed the editor. "All these years I've been saving that type for the second coming of Christ!"

That editor was right about one thing—no bigger story will ever happen than Christ's return. However, because the Bible says it will happen "in the blink of an eye" (1 Corinthians 15:52), I doubt the editor will have time to set a headline about it.

Lord Jesus, we wait with eager anticipation for your return, knowing that when you come back, you will take us to heaven to be with you. Come soon, Lord! Amen.

July 27

How Do You Spell Grace?

God saved you by his grace when you believed.
And you can't take credit for this; it is a gift from God.

EPHESIANS 2:8

Once a mother took her little girl to a lesson with Edgar Degas, the French Impressionist painter and sculptor. While they were there, the mother reproved the little girl for making mistakes in her spelling.

"Why do mistakes in spelling matter?" the child protested.

"Why do they matter? Because they do, and it is very naughty in a little girl to make them, isn't it, Monsieur Degas?"

Peering sideways at the mother, he responded appropriately, "Very naughty."

Then, when the mother had left them, Degas said to the child, "Which would you like best—to know how to spell or to have a box of candy?"

"Candy!" cried the little girl without hesitation.

"Well, so would I," replied Degas. "But if you were to have to ask for candy in writing, and if you could not spell the word *candy*, what do you think that would mean?"

"Well, I guess it might mean that I would get something other than candy."

"I see," said Degas knowingly. "So do you now think that mistakes in spelling matter?"

"Oh, y-e-s!" said the little girl seriously.

And so it is with other things in our lives. They become more important to us when we understand *why* they matter. For instance, it is extremely important to understand God's grace, and yet many of us don't "get it." We understand it intellectually, perhaps, but not really with our hearts.

Then one day we come to understand that we are *saved* because, through his Son, God has given us his undeserved favor, and the importance of grace becomes primary in our lives.

So let me ask you, how do you spell *grace*? I spell it *J-e-s-u-s*.

Thank you, Father, for saving me from my sins through your wonderful grace and love. I would surely be eternally lost without them. Amen.

Which One?

All who are victorious will be clothed in white.
I will never erase their names from the Book of Life.

REVELATION 3:5

Having been blessed to publish several Christian books through the years, I am always humbled when someone I meet for the first time recognizes my name. Over time, though, I have also come across another author with my same name. The difference is that she writes much more scholarly books than I do, on such topics as Renaissance England and other historical subjects. (I'm not jealous, though!)

Once in a while, someone will ask me if I wrote one of the other woman's books. That always makes me smile, and I take it as a great compliment because I know I am not on her intellectual level. And I always wonder how she feels if someone asks her whether she wrote one of mine, such as *Polka Dots, Stripes, Humps 'n Hatracks.* She probably cringes at the thought and is highly insulted.

A similar thing happened to Dr. John Erskine, an acclaimed educator and author, who once went to give a lecture at the University of Pennsylvania. He traveled to the appointment by train, and the president of the university went to the station to meet him. But he had never actually met Dr. Erskine before, so he did not immediately succeed in finding him.

When the two men had at last identified each other, the university president said, "I asked one gentleman coming off the train if he was Dr. Erskine, and he said emphatically, 'I should say not!' Then I asked another gentleman if he was you, and he said, 'I wish I were.' That proves that at least one of them has read your books."

"Yes," said Erskine, "but which one?"

Religious people around the world expound on a multitude of different theological perspectives, all supposedly based on the Bible. Do you think God ever wonders *which ones* actually read his Book?

Dear Father, I know that you alone are the Author of life, and I pray that I will spend my life reading your Book and sharing it with others. Amen.

Landing the Part

There are many parts, but only one body. . . .
Some parts of the body that seem weakest and least
important are actually the most necessary.

1 CORINTHIANS 12:20, 22

Little Tyler was so excited. The director of his summer day camp had announced that the campers would present a play on the last night of the session, and all the children could audition for parts. Tyler wanted so badly to be chosen for one of the parts. He worked hard to learn the lines in the tryout passage. At last he had the lines down perfectly.

Tyler's mother knew he had his heart set on being chosen for a part in the play, but she was afraid he would not be chosen because he had a slight speech impediment and his speech was not always clear. So, when she dropped Tyler off at camp, she said gently, "Tyler, you know that not everyone can have a part. There just aren't that many to go around. So don't get your hopes up too high."

The auditions were held on Friday; the parts were to be assigned over the weekend, and the cast list would be posted on Monday. By Monday, Tyler was so excited he could hardly wait to get to camp to see whether his name was on the cast list. His mother tried not to think about how disappointed he would be if he did not get a part. After camp that day, she went to pick him up.

Tyler came running to the car looking excited. Then he said some words his mother never forgot: "Hey, Mom, guess what?"

"What, honey?"

"I was chosen for a part!"

"Really? That's wonderful, honey! What part did you get?"

"I've been chosen to clap and cheer!"

Think about it: Even if you play the lead, it's no fun if there's no one to clap and cheer when the play is over.

O Lord, thank you for giving special parts to some of us. Help us to be grateful for our gifts and to use those gifts to glorify you. Amen.

The Last Drop

Give to Caesar what belongs to Caesar, and give to God what belongs to God.

MATTHEW 22:21

The local truck-stop customers were so sure that their cook was the strongest man around that they offered a standing wager of one thousand dollars. The cook would squeeze a lemon until all the juice ran into a glass, then hand the lemon to a contender. Anyone who could squeeze just one more drop of juice out of the lemon would win the money.

Many people (burly truck drivers, weight lifters, longshoremen, and the like) had tried to win the wager, but nobody had been able to do it, which had left the cook the lemon-squeezing champion for several years.

One day a thin, balding little man, wearing thick, black-rimmed glasses and a double-knit polyester leisure suit, came into the truck stop. He ordered a glass of milk and then announced to the cook in a tiny, timid voice, "I'd like to try that wager, if you please."

After the laughter had died down, the cook said, "Okay, if you're really serious."

"I am, sir," said the challenger.

The cook grabbed a lemon and squeezed away. Then he handed over the wrinkled remains of the lemon. The little man clenched his fist around the lemon, and the crowd's laughter turned to silence as one drop fell into the glass—then another and another. Six drops in all were squeezed from the lemon.

As the crowd cheered, the cook grudgingly paid the thousand dollars. Then he asked the winner, "Say, what do you do for a living? You're obviously not a lumberjack or a weight lifter."

An almost imperceptible smile came across the little man's lips as he replied in a quiet but satisfied voice, "I work for the IRS."

O God, you have blessed me so richly, and I am thankful for every good gift you have given me. Help me to honor you with my money and to pay my taxes with honesty. Amen.

July 31

Did God Hear You?

We are confident that he hears us whenever we ask for anything that pleases him.

1 JOHN 5:14

Sunday was an extremely frustrating day for Susan. She had forgotten to set her alarm the night before, so she overslept. Everything went downhill from there. The kids were slow getting ready for church, Susan burned the waffles and had to start over, and she couldn't do anything with her hair. On the way to church all the traffic lights were red. When Susan's family slipped into their pew about ten minutes late, they drew the critical eyes of the people around them.

Susan managed to sit through the church service, but she was distracted by her morning aggravations. On the way home after the service, she complained about how long the sermon had been. She griped when the traffic moved at a snail's pace. And at the restaurant where they stopped for lunch, she fussed about the waitress and how long they had to wait to get their food.

When their lunches were delivered at last, Susan said, "Let's pray," and she led a prayer of thanks to God.

Throughout the morning Susan's little girl had been watching her. As they began to eat, she said, "Mommy, did God hear you when you fussed about the sermon?"

"Well," stammered Susan, "yes, I guess he did."

"Did he hear you when you yelled at the traffic and complained about the waitress?"

"Yes, I'm sure he heard me, dear."

"Well, Mommy, did God hear you just now when you prayed?"

"Yes, sweetheart, of course he did."

"Then, Mommy, which one did God believe?"

Now *that's* a good question, isn't it? The truth is, God hears everything we say, whether we are praying or not. (It makes me want to put a zipper on my lips!)

O God, please forgive me for speaking words that do not glorify or please you. Help me to be more careful about my speech as well as my actions. Amen.

Name That Place

The LORD came down in a cloud and stood there with [Moses]; and he called out his own name, Yahweh [the Lord].

EXODUS 34:5

Names of people and places are an interesting study. And that is more than true in Louisiana where I used to live. We lived in Monroe, which the locals call "MUN-row," but outside Louisiana, it is called "mun-ROW." We had a family in the church named Heber, which they pronounce "HE-bur." If you drive south a few hours toward New Orleans ("Newawlins"), their name is pronounced with the French influence: "AY-bare."

In Texas there's a small town named Mexia, which the locals call "ma-HEHR" but outsiders tend to pronounce the Spanish "May-HEE-ya." One man was on vacation with his family, and they went to Mexia for a visit with family. He thought, *This will be a good chance to help the kids learn the way to say* Mexia *correctly.*

Coming into town, they stopped at a Burger King to eat before going to their relatives' home. *Now's my chance*, he thought. When the cashier delivered their hamburgers, he said to her, "Wait a minute, please. Before you leave, would you please tell my kids where we are? And I want you to say it very, very slowly. Pronounce it exactly as it is supposed to be pronounced."

She looked rather puzzled and asked, "Really?"

He said, "Yes, please. Just say it very slowly."

"Okay, if that's what you want," she said, shrugging her shoulders. Then turning to the kids, she said, "It's Burrr-gurrr King."

Yes, names are important. God himself wants people to know his name, "Yahweh," and he carefully writes his children's names in the Book of Life (see Revelation 21:27). The Bible also says that someday every person will bow down at the name of Jesus (see Philippians 2:10). So we can wear his name with honor.

Lord Jesus, we bow at your name and in your honor because we know your name is above all names. We praise your holy name! Amen.

Moving Day

He led me to a place of safety;
he rescued me because he delights in me.

PSALM 18:19

Moving day arrived for my housemates and me. Besides the three of us, my mom also volunteered to help. We started out strong in the early morning, but by the middle of the afternoon, we were dragging as we moved boxes in anticipation of the movers handling the major furniture pieces.

My mom was a real trouper and was working as hard as the rest of us, only she did not know where things needed to go. And apparently neither of my housemates could answer her questions, because every time I turned around, I heard, "Stevie, where does this go?"

"Stevie, is this right?"

"Stevie, can you help me?"

"Stevie, should this go in this car?"

"Stevie, show me how this goes."

"Stevie," "Stevie," "Stevie," "Stevie." I grew to hate my name.

All of us were tired, because it had been a long day, and my name was hanging heavy and often in the air. I rolled my eyes and escaped to the truck with another load. I sat down in the driver's seat to take a break, and at the point of screaming, I gripped the steering wheel.

Dear, dear God, you know I love my mother with all my heart. And I know that someday I am going to want to hear her call my name just one more time. However, today is not that day. If ever a prayer needed to be answered quickly, Lord, this is it. Please give me the wisdom and patience to make it through this day. Amen.

And he did!

—Stevie Stevens

Father, I love the fact that you delight in me. Thank you for rescuing me from the little irritations in my life, and thank you for never tiring of hearing me call your name. I love you with all my heart, Lord. Amen.

Again This Year?

All of you can join together with one voice,
giving praise and glory to God.

ROMANS 15:6

When I was a kid, we lived in a small, two-bedroom house typical of homes in the 1950s—wood floors, wallpaper, little insulation, no air-conditioning, screen doors, and a wraparound front porch. Next to the kitchen was a hallway—about ten feet long and six feet wide. My dad envisioned taking out the wall between the kitchen and hall to make a larger eating area.

Every spring Dad would say, "When it gets a little warmer, I'm gonna take out that wall and make this room bigger. Don't you think that's a good idea, honey?"

Mom—a witty but wise woman—would reply sweetly, "Yes, dear, I think that's a great idea. When should you start?"

Dad would reply without commitment, "Oh, when it gets a little warmer." And then he never got around to the project.

This conversation was repeated every spring for six or seven years. It was predictable. Part of the family routine.

One year, spring popped out, and the wall conversation came up at dinner one night. Dad said, "When it gets a little warmer, I'm gonna take out that wall and make this room bigger. Don't you think that's a good idea, honey?"

This time, Mom peered over the top of her glasses at Dad, grinned impishly, and said, "Oh boy, we gonna do that again this year?"

Dad, surprised and a little offended, looked up at her, saw her grin, and laughed in embarrassment. Then he laughed. "Maybe when it gets warmer." He never did take out that wall.

Ever since then, when things don't get done as planned, someone laughs and says, "Oh boy, we gonna do that again this year?" It's a favorite family joke.

Don't you know God wants to say that to us, too, when we keep *planning* to do things for him but we just don't get around to them?

Father God, thank you for second chances and continuing opportunities to do things that bring glory to you. Amen.

August 4

Who Are You Going to Call?

Everyone who calls on the name of the LORD will be saved.

ACTS 2:21

For our daughter Isabelle's second birthday, my husband and I bought her a toddler bed to make the crib available for our three-month-old son. When Isabelle opened her present, she was overjoyed and climbed right in, snuggling up to her new pillow and bedspread. The joy lasted until later that night, when she realized she actually had to sleep there.

Her first nap in the new bed was no easy task either. The girl who usually went down for a nap without a peep resisted. A few minutes after leaving the room, my husband and I heard her cry, "Mommy! Mommy! Mommy!"

Then, a few minutes later, she switched to "Daddy! Daddy! Daddy!"

These we expected. What we did not expect was her next line of attack. "Nelda! Nelda! Nelda!" she called out.

My husband and I looked at each other. "Is she saying what I think she's saying?" I asked, and we both started laughing.

Nelda is Isabelle's great-aunt, who lives more than seven hundred miles away. Nelda was fresh in Isabelle's mind because she had sent a present for Isabelle's birthday. So when Mommy and Daddy did not answer quickly enough, Isabelle was willing to call on anyone she could think of who might be able to help her.

Aren't you thankful to be the child of a Father who is near enough to answer when you call? And aren't you glad he loves you so much that he wants to answer you every time you ask? Our God is so compassionate and good.

—Lisa Bartelt

Father God, thank you that you hear me when I call and are close enough to answer when I cry out to you. Forgive me when I seek anyone other than you to save me. Amen.

Bible Fairy Tales?

Look! I stand at the door and knock. If you hear my voice and open the door, I will come in, and we will share a meal together as friends.

REVELATION 3:20

It is always interesting to me how folks tend to get Bible stories and other kinds of facts and fiction intertwined. I remember hearing about one little girl who was relating the story of Jezebel. She said Jezebel fell out of a window, her insides spilled out all over the ground, and people gathered up twelve basketfuls of pieces. Hmmm. I don't think that's exactly how it happened.

Sometimes we even mix up Bible stories and commercials we hear. For instance, one little boy said he knew Jesus rode a motorcycle. When his teacher asked him how he knew that, he pointed out that the Bible says, "He rode around in great triumph." It does say that, of course, but . . .

At age three, one little girl began to learn all the traditional fairy tales, such as "Goldilocks and the Three Bears," "Little Red Riding Hood," and "The Three Little Pigs." Her mother and father taught her the familiar Bible stories as well, such as "Noah and the Ark," "Daniel in the Lions' Den," and "David and Goliath." And the young girl's mind was like a sponge, soaking up all these stories and trying to understand and assimilate them.

One day her mother read to her Revelation 3:20, which says, "Look! I stand at the door and knock." When finished reading the verse to the little girl, her mother asked, "If Jesus is knocking at your heart's door, will you open the door and let him in?"

Without a moment's hesitation, the little girl answered, "Not by the hair of my chinny-chin-chin!"

O Lord, we love the wonderful stories in your Word. Please help us to read them often enough that we can remember them accurately and apply their lessons to our lives. Amen.

August 6

A Fantastic Idea

Your word is a lamp to guide my feet
and a light for my path.

PSALM 119:105

Can you imagine life today without a telephone? Me, neither! I love my iPhone and Bluetooth. But early on, Alexander Graham Bell offered to sell his telephone invention to Western Union for what today would probably seem like a joke.

Out of respect for Mr. Bell, Western Union formed a committee to review and consider his seemingly ridiculous invention and offer. After thinking it through, here's what the committee had to say:

> *The telephone is named by its inventor, A. G. Bell. He believes that one day they will be installed in every residence and place of business. Bell's profession is that of a voice teacher. Yet, he claims to have discovered an instrument of great practical value in communication that has been overlooked by thousands of workers who have spent years in the field. Bell's proposal to place his instrument in almost every home and business is fantastic. The central exchange alone would represent a huge outlay in real estate and buildings, to say nothing of the electrical equipment. In conclusion, the committee feels that it must advise against any investment in Bell's scheme. We do not doubt that it will find users in special circumstances, but any developments of the kind and scale that Bell so fondly imagines is utterly out of the question.*

Oops! Wouldn't you love to be a fly on the wall if that same committee could meet and reconsider that decision today? Wouldn't you hear a giant, collective "Duh"? That's what I call a magnificent mistake.

Yet, God probably looks at some of the shortsighted spiritual decisions we make in our lives and shakes his head in disbelief too. Again, the giant divine "Duh" is hard to miss. When we take our eyes off the Guide, we stumble and fall.

Thank you, Lord, for your long-suffering patience and forgiveness. I know I make so many bad decisions, and I need your ongoing help and guidance. Please protect me from myself, Lord. Amen.

Bug Off

[Jesus said,] "My purpose is to give [my sheep] a rich and satisfying life."

JOHN 10:10

The Terminix man arrived at my house for a routine pest inspection. Let's just say my kids were not on their best behavior that day. The bug guy kept saying, "You sure have your hands full."

First he met Shepherd, my three-year-old with fire engine–red hair and a personality to match. Shepherd was screaming because I would not let him watch a movie. Toys were strewn everywhere as if they had exploded out of the toy box in *Toy Story*.

Then Mr. Terminix noticed my two-year-old, Owen, in his high chair happily eating graham crackers (yes, for breakfast—oh, well). In disbelief he said, "Whoa, didn't even see *him*. You've got two? Boy, you *sure* have your hands full."

Since Mr. Bug Hater needed to throw something away, he asked "Red" where the trash was. Recalling that the garbage can was an overflowing, stinky mess, I quickly intervened.

"Uh . . . just set it on the counter. I'll take care of it later."

No could do for the helpful bug man. He found the disgusting dump site. "Can I take your trash out for you?"

"Uh . . . no. I can handle it." Thanks, buddy, for making me feel incompetent. Sorry you had to smell it once, but I'm certainly not going to make you smell it twice—much less touch it. This guy was really starting to bug me. That day I decided that bugs do not bug me nearly as much as the stinky trash or the aggravating bug man.

Actually, I am thankful for the toys strewn everywhere, the screaming children, and, yes, even the ants that are attracted to all the crumbs. There is life in my household—rich and satisfying life.

—*Marla Livers*

Thank you, Lord, for the sometimes-messy blessings that are evidence of life in my home and of your great blessings. Amen.

Perspective

Everything else is worthless when compared with the infinite value of knowing Christ Jesus my Lord.

PHILIPPIANS 3:8

A university coed wrote the following letter to her parents:

Dear Mom and Dad,

I just thought I'd drop you a note to clue you in on my plans. I've fallen in love with a guy called Jim. He quit high school after grade eleven to get married. About a year ago he got a divorce.

We've been going steady for two months, and we plan to get married in the fall. Until then, I've decided to move into his apartment (I think I might be pregnant).

At any rate, I dropped out of school last week, although I would like to finish college sometime in the future.

On the next page the letter continued:

Mom and Dad,

I just want you to know that everything I've written so far in this letter is false. None of it is true.

But, Mom and Dad, it is true that I got a C– in French and flunked Math. It is true that I'm going to need a lot more money for my tuition payments.

Love, Jonie

The girl made her point! Even bad news can sound good if it is seen in comparison to worse things or seen from a different perspective. The difficulties of life are, indeed, nothing when compared to the glories of heaven.

—Erwin Lutzer

Righteous Father, I stand in awe of your majesty and glory, and I dream of being in your radiant presence for all eternity. Help me to look past the troubles of this life and keep my eyes fixed on you. Amen.

Skin-Deep Beauty

Charm is deceptive, and beauty does not last;
but a woman who fears the LORD will be greatly praised.

PROVERBS 31:30

Lying out in the sun makes me resemble sweet-and-sour pork more than a swimsuit model. Though I would love to grace the decks of a swimming pool with my version of Chinese takeout, who has the time?

Nervously, I entered a tanning salon to begin my transformation into Farrah Fawcett, poster girl. The receptionist looked me over and recommended I purchase a special set of nose plugs with tiny holes in them. This device and the short instructional video should have made me change my mind. But I was determined to fulfill my tanning fantasies without the aid of Revlon.

In a private room I removed my clothes, smoothed lotion on any dry extremities to prevent the tanning spray from clumping, and donned the standard-issue goggles. I stepped into the spray booth, striving to remember every detail of the video. Legs shoulder width apart, arms bent, fingers curled back, I managed to press the green start button.

An amber mist blasted my body, moving steadily upward. As it hit my face, I remembered that my special nose plugs were sitting on the table next to my clothes.

Snort. Gag. Gulp. *I can't breathe!*

The spray ended as I gasped for air, my nostrils now filled with their own summer glow. Turning around, I tried to recall how much time I had before the vulgar, spitting machine continued engulfing me in the suffocating spray for which I had paid so dearly.

Snort. Heave. Wheeze.

Like a woman in labor, I puffed and panted, finally exploding from the booth.

Then I knew it was true: Charm is deceptive and beauty, like a spray-on tan, does not last.

—Jennie Nagy

Lord, help me foster lasting beauty that resonates from within my heart, a sweet offering to you in whose image and likeness I was created. Amen.

Too Close

You have been believers so long now that you ought to be teaching others. Instead, you need someone to teach you again the basic things about God's word. You are like babies who need milk and cannot eat solid food.

HEBREWS 5:12

Friday had been a very long day for little Jerrod. It was his very first day of kindergarten. And even though they had taken a nap after lunch, by the time he got home from his school excursion, he was exhausted.

Jerrod's mom gave him a healthy after-school snack. Then she said she needed to run some errands. So they set off in their SUV. First they went to the dry cleaners to pick up his dad's suits. Then they ran by the public library to take back some books they had borrowed. Next they stopped at the video store to get some movies for the weekend.

Then it was time for Jerrod's Little League practice. Jerrod's mom dropped him off at the baseball field, where he practiced with his team for about an hour. After his mom picked him up from practice, they went to the grocery store so she could do the shopping for the week.

By the time they got back home, little Jerrod was really dragging. He could hardly keep his eyes open. He ate his supper, took a hot bath, put on his pajamas, and crawled into bed between his favorite Batman sheets. He instantly fell asleep.

In just a few minutes, Jerrod's dad heard a loud thump down the hall. He ran down to Jerrod's room to find him lying on the floor.

"What happened, Son?" asked his dad, picking him up and putting him back into bed.

"I don't know, Dad," said Jerrod sleepily. "I guess I just laid down too close to where I got in at."

As the writer of Hebrews noted, a lot of us in the church do that too, huh?

—Clyde Shrode

Faithful Father, please help me to grow up in my spiritual life and not lie down too close to where I came in. Amen.

The Bribe

Anyone who wants to come to [God]
must believe that God exists and that he
rewards those who sincerely seek him.

HEBREWS 11:6

In the Bible is an interesting theology that is primarily overlooked by most Christians. It is sometimes referred to as "reward theology." You can see it revealed in the Scriptures in many places where God says to us, "If you do this, I'll do that." For example, Genesis 4:7 says, "You will be accepted if you do what is right. But if you refuse to do what is right, then watch out! Sin is crouching at the door, eager to control you." So, *if* we do what is right, we will be accepted by God. Great reward.

In 1 Chronicles 28:9 we see that "if you seek [God], you will find him." And John 15:10 says, [*If*] "you obey my commandments, you remain in my love." So we are rewarded richly for doing God's will God's way.

At a certain children's hospital, a boy gained a reputation for wreaking havoc with the nurses and staff. One day a visitor who knew about his terrorizing nature made him a deal: "If you are good for a week," she said, "I'll give you a dime when I come again."

A week later she stood before his bed. "I'll tell you what," she said, "I won't ask the nurses if you behaved. You must tell me yourself. Do you deserve the dime?"

After a moment's pause, a small voice from between the sheets said softly, "Gimme a penny."

And so it is with our Christian lives. God offers us the great reward of heaven if we follow his guidelines, but we can never *earn* it—he gives it to us as a gift, free and clear. It's called *grace.* What a reward!

—Lewis and Faye Copeland

Father, thank you so much for rewarding us with a home in heaven with you. We know we can receive it only by the gift of your grace. And we are humbled by your sweet gift. Amen.

The Serpent

Eve was deceived by the cunning ways of the serpent.

2 CORINTHIANS 11:3

If you're like me, you probably did not know there is a musical instrument called "the serpent." I had never heard of it until recently. Interestingly, the serpent makes a harsh and fairly unpleasant sound compared to more-melodic instruments.

The first time the serpent was used at a London concert, over which the German composer George Frideric Handel presided, he was so surprised at the coarseness of its tones that he called out sharply, "Vat de devil is dat?"

On being informed that it was the serpent, he replied, "It never can be de serpent vat seduced Eve!" And he was, no doubt, correct. The Scriptures say that Eve was "beguiled" by the devil, which indicates a soothing, tempting voice rather than a harsh, coarse one.

My aunt Bethel was particularly easy to frighten. And my brother, who is a bit of a tease, loved to give her a scare just to liven things up.

One day we were all at my grandparents' house. Grandmother, Aunt Bethel, and Mom were cooking lunch while the rest of us played games or just sat on the porch. Looking for some excitement, my brother hid an old jointed toy snake under his shirt and wandered into the kitchen. When nobody was looking, he dropped it into the pot of beans cooking on the stove. Then he sauntered out onto the porch to wait for the reaction.

Suddenly Aunt Bethel started screaming and burst out of the kitchen onto the porch, running as if the devil himself were chasing her. She had stirred the beans and stirred up the toy serpent. She had just about been a runaway. She wouldn't go back into the kitchen for the rest of the day.

Aunt Bethel had one thing right: When the devil is after you, run for your life!

Dear God, please help us to identify the beguiling voice of the devil when he is whispering in our ears. And let us run to you for protection. Amen.

Dawg Huntin'

Today is the day of salvation.

2 CORINTHIANS 6:2

Pulitzer Prize–winning author and dramatist Booth Tarkington, while stopping at an inn in a little Indiana town, lost one of his dogs.

"Have you a newspaper in town?" he asked the landlord.

"Right across the way, there, back of the shoemaker's shop," the landlord told him. "The *Daily News*—best little paper of its size in town."

The editor, the printer, and the printer's devil were all busy doing justice to Mr. Tarkington with a paragraph about his being in town when the novelist arrived.

"I've just lost a dog," Tarkington explained after he had introduced himself, "and I'd like to have you insert this ad for me: 'Fifty dollars' reward for the return of a pointer dog answering to the name of Rex. Disappeared from the yard of the Mansion House Monday night.'"

"Why, we were just going to press, sir," the editor said, "but we'll be only too glad to hold the edition for your ad."

Mr. Tarkington returned to the hotel. After a few minutes he decided, however, that it might be well to add "No questions asked" to his advertisement, and he returned to the *Daily News* office.

The place was deserted, save for the skinny little freckle-faced devil, who sat perched on a high stool, gazing wistfully out of the window.

"Where is everybody?" Tarkington asked.

"Gawn to hunt th' dawg, o'course," replied the boy, without removing his gaze from the distant fields.

Silly question! When there's a great prize to be had, don't just sit around—get after it! And the greatest prize of all is salvation, which we must pursue with all our hearts.

Dear God, we know that salvation comes from you, and we offer you our praise and thanksgiving for your marvelous gift of love. Amen.

August 14

What Would You Be?

Job replied to the LORD:
"I know that you can do anything,
and no one can stop you."

JOB 42:1-2

Theodore Roosevelt was making a political speech during one of his campaigns, when a heckler from the large crowd interrupted him with a repeated and slightly inebriated cry, "I am a Democrat!"

Mr. Roosevelt was generally a dangerous man to heckle. Pausing in his speech and smiling with unction, he leaned forward and said, "May I ask the gentleman why he is a Democrat?"

The voice replied, "My grandfather was a Democrat, my father was a Democrat, and I am a Democrat."

Roosevelt said, "My friend, suppose your grandfather had been a horse thief, and your father had been a horse thief, what would you be?"

Instantly the reply came back, "A Republican!"

What can you say? Politics is a crazy business, and only the strong can survive.

In a similar way, during Jesus' volatile ministry his political enemies—the Pharisees, Sadducees, and others—heckled him. They posed tricky questions to him. They threatened him. They challenged him at every turn until, finally, when they could not make him look bad through their vocal attacks, they had him murdered.

In truth, they killed him out of jealousy and fear. His runaway popularity among the people and his declaration that he was, in fact, the Son of God terrified them, and the only way they could deal with it was to have him killed. Little did they know that Jesus' death was the astounding finale to the symphonic plan God had been conducting for hundreds of years to save . . . you and me. It was his plan all along, and his plans cannot be thwarted. Hallelujah!

O Lord, my Savior, I am so humbled by your sacrifice for me. I want to live my life in service to others out of gratitude to you. Thank you. Amen.

Be Alert

Now we see things imperfectly, like puzzling reflections in a mirror, but then we will see everything with perfect clarity.

1 CORINTHIANS 13:12

One morning as I sat down at my computer, an e-mail subject line captured my attention: "Bear Alert in Subdivision." My eyes widened as I opened the e-mail. Photos showed my neighbors' steel bird feeder ripped to the ground; the metal cables dangled like kite string in their tree. Five years earlier a furry, black vandal had destroyed an identical feeder.

This copycat crime was big-time news. I updated my Facebook status: "Sue Ferguson was informed there's been a bear in her subdivision!" Comments accumulated rapidly. Excited about the bear and the comment-catching status, I grabbed my camera, hoping for a furry photo shoot.

For several days I peered out the window and enjoyed my friends' clever comments on my status updates. No bear came.

One afternoon, while still in watch-out-the-window mode, I noticed a skunk sleeping on our back property line. *Is that really a skunk?*

While on bear watch, I had seen birds, bunnies, and squirrels, but never a skunk. I snatched my camera and zoomed in for a closer look. *Yep, it's a skunk.*

Thrilled, I updated my status: "Sue Ferguson never saw the neighborhood bear but has spotted a skunk sleeping at the edge of the woods!"

Not wanting to miss any developing news, I stared at my wildlife discovery. Moments later I left the window to post the following update: "Sue Ferguson is embarrassed. When that skunk woke up, it was a cat!"

—*Sue Ferguson*

Father, I often act foolishly because of what I think I see. I need your eyes. Help me to be alert to your prompting and to trust your eternal perspective. Amen.

Never Mind

The Lord will deliver me from every evil attack and will bring me safely into his heavenly Kingdom.

2 TIMOTHY 4:18

Are we there yet?" If you are a parent, you have probably heard those words repeated over and over from little voices in the backseat on vacations and trips. I confess that I am not much better. As my mother often says, "I'd like to just be able to wiggle my nose, like Samantha on *Bewitched*, and be there."

One older woman, on her way to a summer resort, kept pestering the train conductor to tell her when they reached Ellenville. Finally, harried by her frequent questioning, he pleaded with her to bother him no more and promised he would tell her as soon as they reached the town.

Becoming busy with all his duties, the conductor forgot all about the elderly woman until the train had reached and passed Ellenville. Suddenly recollecting her anxiety about the place, he reversed the train, and as it backed into the little station, he hurried to find the woman and told her, "Here you are now—in Ellenville. I'll help you with your baggage."

"Oh, thank you," she replied. "But I'm not getting off here. My daughter told me that when I got to Ellenville, it would be just about time to take another of my pills."

Life, too, is a long road trip of sorts. And we're the kids in the backseat, with God in the driver's seat. The destination is heaven, and I can hardly wait to get there, because I know it will be fabulous. As the old hymn says so well, "This world is not my home; I'm just a'passin' through."

I don't know about you, but I look out the window at the unfolding scenery of life, and sometimes I want to ask, "Hey, Dad, are we there yet?"

Abba, Father, we are in your hands and in your care, and we know you will bring us safely to your home in heaven. Thank you for loving us, Lord. Amen.

In the Driver's Seat

There is a path before each person that seems right.

PROVERBS 14:12

By the time I was nine, my older brothers were gone from home. I learned to drive the truck and the tractor in order to help my dad on the farm. He was accustomed to the boys knowing how to do things, but it took him a while to learn that his blonde little girl was not as savvy as her older brothers.

One hot August day, as we prepared for hay-baling season, my dad's tractor would not start. He asked for my help as he attached a tow chain on our old truck and then to the front of his small Massey Ferguson tractor. He wanted me to pull the tractor until the engine started. I hopped in the truck, excited that I would get to put my newly learned skills to work.

My dad assumed that I would ease forward and gradually let the slack out of the chain. He was mistaken. Thinking the tractor would be hard to pull, I revved the engine of the old Ford, shifted it into gear, and gunned the gas. I am sure my dad was bewildered as he saw the slack in the chain quickly disappear.

Knowing what was going to happen, Daddy barely had time to grip the steering wheel before the slack vanished. The abrupt jolt realigned the front of the tractor and both our necks. Daddy thought the tractor had problems *before* I helped him, but afterward it needed a total overhaul.

Don't you know, God often feels as my dad did? He has high hopes for what we, as his children, will be able to accomplish. And then, when he sees our immature actions and lack of wisdom, he just shakes his head and smiles, knowing we need him to get through life.

—Pam Whitley

Father, when others ask me for help, please don't let me assume I know what is best. May I always consult you and then follow your instructions. Amen.

August 18

Healing Power

[Jesus] welcomed them and taught them about the Kingdom of God, and he healed those who were sick.

LUKE 9:11

Many years ago an English sailor who had broken his leg was advised to send to the Royal Society an account of the remarkable manner in which he had healed the fracture. He did so.

His story was that, having fractured his leg by falling from the top of a high mast, he had dressed it with nothing but tar and oakum, which had proved so wonderfully effective that in only three days he was able to walk just as well as he had before the accident.

This remarkable story naturally caused some excitement among the members of the society. No one had previously suspected tar and oakum of possessing such miraculous healing powers.

Several letters accordingly passed between the Royal Society and the humble sailor, who continued to assert most solemnly that his broken leg had been treated with tar and oakum, and with nothing else.

The society might have remained puzzled for an indefinite period of time had not the man added an interesting postscript to his last letter, which said the following: "I forgot to inform your honors, by the way, that the leg I broke was a wooden one."

A broken leg—even a wooden one—being healed in only three days would, indeed, be remarkable. Compare that, however, with Jesus' miraculous healings of real withered arms, deaf ears, mute tongues, and even the dead. Consider his calming of storms, disappearing from amid crowds, and healing of people who only touched his robe as he passed by.

The healing power of God is incomparable!

Dear Lord, I come to you with gratitude for your healing touch on my heart and life. I know that you and you alone are the great Physician. Amen.

Should Have Looked

Teach us to realize the brevity of life,
so that we may grow in wisdom.

PSALM 90:12

In 1933 George Rafferty and his family were taking a long summer vacation. They began in San Diego, California. Then they drove north along the glorious Pacific coast in their open roadster. They enjoyed wonderful times swimming in the ocean, picnics on the beach, and many other excursions.

During the trip George was especially interested in the historical sites along the way. He loved learning interesting tidbits about the places they visited. When they reached their hotel in the Yosemite Valley, George found out that an old man in the office had been one of the company of people who had discovered Yosemite in 1851.

Eagerly George seized the opportunity to find out what it was like to be among the first explorers to behold one of nature's most marvelous works.

"It must have been wonderful," George said, "to have the valley burst suddenly upon you! Tell me, please, what you remember about that moment."

The old man spat over the edge of the veranda and looked reflective for a moment, trying to remember the time in question. "Well," he said finally, "I'll tell ye, son. If I'd'a knowed this here valley was going to be so famous, I'd'a looked at it."

Sometimes life flashes by me like the scenery out the window of my car as I drive down the highway at seventy miles per hour. I get glimpses of color and flickering shadows, splashes of rain, and sunshine and rainbows, but I rarely stop long enough to really look at my life's events individually. I don't take them in and explore them.

Like the old man, someday I may look back sadly and think, *If I'd'a knowed this here life was going to pass by so fast, I'd'a looked at it.*

Slow me down, Lord, and help me to look at and appreciate the glories you put along my pathway every day. Amen.

August 20

I'm Coming Out Now!

The angel spoke. . . . "I know you are looking for Jesus, who was crucified. He isn't here! He is risen from the dead."

MATTHEW 28:5-6

The call to worship had just been pronounced, starting the Easter service in an East Texas church. The choir started the processional, singing "Christ Arose" while marching in perfect step down the center aisle to the front of the church.

The last woman was wearing shoes with very slender heels. Without a thought for her fancy heels, she stepped onto the grate that covered the hot-air register in the middle of the aisle. Suddenly the heel of one shoe sank into the hole in the register grate. In a flash, she realized her predicament. Not wishing to hold up the whole processional, without missing a step she slipped her foot out of her shoe and continued marching down the aisle.

There was not a hitch. The processional continued to move with clocklike precision. The first man after her spotted the situation and, without losing a step, reached down and pulled up her shoe—but the entire grate came with it! Surprised but still singing, the man kept on going down the aisle, holding in his hand the grate with the shoe attached. Everything still moved smoothly.

Still in tune and still in step, the next man in line stepped into the open register and disappeared from sight. The service took on a special meaning that Sunday, for just as the choir ended with "Hallelujah! Christ arose!" a voice was heard under the church shouting, "I hope all of you are out of the way, 'cause I'm coming out now!"

The little girl closest to the aisle shouted, "Come on, Jesus! We'll stay out of the way."

O Father, thank you for giving your Son as a sacrifice for our sins and for raising him up from the grave to be our living Lord. We are so humbly grateful for your great love and grace. Amen.

Meeting the Train

God loved the world so much that he gave his one and only Son, so that everyone who believes in him will not perish but have eternal life.

JOHN 3:16

When I was in college in the early 1970s (okay, you don't have to calculate to figure out how old I am), I loved to play the guitar and sing folk songs. One of those songs was called "This Train." The lyrics included this line: "This train is bound for glory—this train!" And I always thought, *I want to be on* this *train.*

Somehow, though, riding other trains can be a bit more challenging, and their destinations can be less definite than the one for "this train." For instance, after having been absent from home for several days, Alice Hathaway, the first wife of Theodore Roosevelt, wired her husband to meet her at a certain train station.

Hurrying to be on time to meet her, Colonel Ted arrived at the train station just in time to see the train whiz past at great speed, not slowing down at all, much less stopping to allow passengers to disembark.

Somewhat bewildered, Ted stared at the speeding cars and was even more astonished to see his pretty wife standing on the very back platform frantically waving an important-looking envelope in her hand. Spying him, she threw it at him, and then she waved, disappearing with the train as it rounded the corner.

Scrambling about in the bushes into which the envelope had fallen, the colonel finally found it and quickly opened it. He was amused and somewhat relieved to read the following note: "Dear Ted, This train doesn't stop here."

Fortunately for us as Christians, the train that is bound for glory does stop here. It stops right in front of us and allows us to climb aboard and ride nonstop through the gates of heaven into eternal glory with God. And oh, what a destination that will be!

All aboard!

Thank you, Lord, for the trip of a lifetime! It has been a glorious ride so far. Amen.

August 22

On Average

They will be called "children of the living God."

ROMANS 9:26

Traveling around the world is both an exhilarating and a frightening experience, especially for first timers. Going from country to country presents many challenges, such as changing languages, changing types of money, changing foods, and especially changing customs and cultures. You can get yourself in hot water in a hurry, if you're not careful.

The issue of tipping or not tipping is always tricky to me. In some places you are expected to tip; in other places tipping is considered inappropriate. And keeping this straight is not easy. For instance, in Germany you are expected to tip the attendant in the public restrooms. Who would've thought of that? (I certainly didn't the first time.) But when you're traveling with a tour group, you don't usually tip the waiters because the tip has already been included in the price you paid for the trip. *Sigh.*

In the early 1920s, a gentleman who had very little experience in travel had made a transcontinental trip by train. As he was about to leave the train, he was in some doubt as to how much he should tip the Pullman porter who had catered to him throughout most of the journey.

"Sam," he asked, "what is the average tip you receive from passengers who travel with you cross-country as I have?"

"Five dollars," replied Sam with a grin.

The passenger promptly pulled a five-dollar bill from his wallet and handed it to Sam, saying, "Thank you so much for your good service, Sam."

Overcome and embarrassed, Sam shuffled his feet for a moment, and then he said, "Well, sir, I reckon I ought to tell you that, so far, you are the first one that's come up to the average."

Happily, when it comes to being a Kingdom traveler, there is no such thing as *average.* We all have safe passage as sons and daughters of the King!

Father, we are so blessed to be your children and on our way to live with you eternally. Thank you for adopting us into your family. Amen.

Every Word of It

By his divine power, God has given us
everything we need for living a godly life.

2 PETER 1:3

Words are my stock in trade. I love working with them, fitting them together, listening to their rhythm, their inflections, and their texture. Words fascinate me and entertain me day after day.

Mark Twain, the famous American writer and humorist, loved words too. Occasionally he attended the church services of Dr. Doane, who was later the bishop of Albany but at the time was rector of an Episcopal church in Hartford, Connecticut.

One Sunday morning Mr. Twain said to Dr. Doane at the end of the service, "Dr. Doane, I enjoyed your service this morning very much. I welcomed it like an old friend. You will find it interesting to know that I have a book at home containing every word of it."

"You have not," said Dr. Doane indignantly.

"I have so," said Twain confidently.

"Well, you send that book to me, then. I'd like to see it," said Doane.

"I'll send it," promised Twain, shaking the rector's hand and heading for home. The following day he sent Dr. Doane an unabridged dictionary.

There is another Book that contains every word that we need "for living a godly life." It gives us guidelines for happy living. And yet, so many people today do not believe that Book is sufficient for them. They try to supplement it with all kinds of other writings, teachings, and philosophies. As a result, because other teachings do not fully match God's Word, these people end up confused and frustrated.

When you want the words of life, stick to the Word of God.

I know that you, Lord, are the true Author of life and that your Book is the only one upon which I should base my life and my hope for life hereafter. Help me to share its message with everyone I can. Amen.

Oh Dear, What Can the Matter Be?

The LORD God placed the man in the Garden of Eden to tend and watch over it.

GENESIS 2:15

My dad was a great gardener. He loved watching things grow and taking care of them—he grew everything from food to flowers and enjoyed every minute of it. He was also a minister who preached the gospel for more than fifty years. There, too, he loved to watch young lives and converted hearts begin to blossom and grow. So gardening stories often worked their way into his sermons as illustrations.

One day later in life he said, "I guess I ought not to be surprised by anything at my time of life, but one member of our congregation did manage to take my breath away.

"I was preaching about God's tender wisdom in caring for us all, and I illustrated it by saying that the Father knows which of us grows best in sunlight and which of us must have shade in order to thrive.

"I said, 'You know that you plant roses in the sunshine, as well as heliotrope and geraniums. But if you want your fuchsias to grow, they must be kept in a shady nook.'

"After the sermon, which I hoped would be a comforting one, a woman came up to me, her face glowing with pleasure that was evidently deep and true. She said, 'I am so grateful for that sermon,' clasping my hand and shaking it warmly.

"My heart glowed for a moment, while I wondered what tender place in her heart and life I had touched. It was only for a moment, though.

"'Yes,' she went on fervently. 'I never knew what was the matter with my fuchsias.'"

Dear God, thank you for tending to our lives, pruning our hearts, and helping us to grow into the kind of people you know we can be. We love you, Father. Amen.

Hit Him Again!

You must each decide in your heart how much to give.
And don't give reluctantly or in response to pressure.
"For God loves a person who gives cheerfully."

2 CORINTHIANS 9:7

The small country congregation had been worshiping in their old wooden church building for more than fifty years. Together they had weathered many storms, both spiritual and earthly. The timeworn structure had hosted their church assemblies, weddings, funerals, celebrations of new babies, revivals, and so much more. For the long-term members of the church, the comfortable place truly felt like home every time they came in the doors.

After all those years, though, the wonderful old building was in need of some major repairs. It was literally falling apart. The roof was leaking in a few places, which in turn had damaged the beautiful hardwood floors in the lobby. The front doors were warped by rain and wind. And the red carpet that ran down the center aisle was worn and faded.

The church leaders met to find a way to raise the funds required to make the repairs. On Sunday, the minister, stirred by very real emotion and having been connected with the congregation for nearly twenty years, made a great, moving speech.

Much to his and the other members' surprise, the most wealthy but miserly member of the church suddenly stood up near the back and offered to kick off the fund-raising effort with a contribution of five dollars. As he spoke, a piece of plaster fell from the ceiling and hit him on the head.

A trifle dazed, the miser rose again and said, "Reckon I'd better make that fifty dollars."

From the back of the hall came a pleading voice: "Hit him again, Lord!"

Lord, when I am less than generous with you and your people, please forgive me. Help me to open my heart and my hands out of love and compassion. Amen.

The Way to Heaven

Jesus [said], "I am the way, the truth, and the life. No one can come to the Father except through me."

JOHN 14:6

My friends will tell you that I am directionally dysfunctional. I get lost going around the block, even more traveling cross-country. The big joke is that, no matter where we're really trying to go, if I'm driving we'll end up in Texarkana. I read somewhere that direction dysfunction is some kind of learning disability (I guess that's better than just being a directional num-num).

So my new best friend is Google Maps. I just love being certain that I know the way to my destination before I ever set out.

It is incredibly frustrating to be lost. Believe me, I know, because I've been there, done that, many times. And while it is funny to my friends, it is frightening to me at times not to know which way to go to get home.

I'm not the only one who gets lost, though. Jerome D. Engel, when conducting one of his celebrated revivals in Philadelphia, stopped a small newsboy one day and asked him the way to the nearest post office.

"It's down the street three blocks, then turn to the left."

"You seem to be a bright little fellow," said Engel, a man of considerable self-esteem. "Do you know who I am?"

"Naw."

"I am the famous preacher who is holding the revival over in the big tabernacle. If you will come to my meeting tonight, I will show you the way to heaven."

"Aw, go on," said the youngster, "you don't even know the way to the post office."

The boy was right—when you need directions to an important destination, it is vitally important to go to the right source to get those directions. And there is one source that beats Google Maps every time. Seek the Source!

Father, thank you for giving us perfect directions to get us home to heaven and eternity with you. We love your Word, Father. Help us to read it carefully. Amen.

Doctor, Doctor!

Christ is the visible image of the invisible God.

COLOSSIANS 1:15

Once a doctor was awakened in the middle of the night by a phone call from a man to whose family he had not rendered medical treatment for quite some time.

"Doctor," said the excited man, "please come to my house right away. My wife is in great pain, and I'm sure it's appendicitis."

The doctor had been sleepily mulling over the medical history of the family and said, "Well now, it probably isn't anything like that. I'll come around first thing in the morning. Don't worry. It's probably just indigestion."

"But, Doctor, you've got to come now. I'm positive it's appendicitis," protested the alarmed husband.

"Oh, come now, Mr. Johnson," the doctor said, somewhat irritably, "I took out your wife's appendix almost two years ago. You know as well as I do that she doesn't have another one."

"That's all true, Doctor," said the husband, "but I've got another wife!"

Sometimes things are not as they first appear. My German heritage blessed me with blonde hair, blue eyes, and pale skin. My best friend's American Indian background graced her with dark eyes, dark hair, and beautiful olive skin (I envy her). The strange thing is that people are always asking us if we are sisters. Go figure! After being best friends for twenty-five years, we have evidently grown to look alike, even though we think we look *nothing* alike.

Once, a woman in Harrods department store in London asked if we were *twins*. We just looked at each other and laughed. In fact, so many people have asked us through the years if we're sisters that we have just started saying yes. We are, after all, sisters in the Lord.

While it's fun for us to look alike, it is more vital that we grow to look like "the visible image of the invisible God" so others can find him too.

Dear God, please hear my prayer: I want to look like you, Lord. Just like you. Amen.

August 28

Many Are Called

Many are called, but few are chosen.

MATTHEW 22:14

Many are called, but few are chosen" might well be the motto emblazoned above the doors of Hollywood casting directors. They put out the casting call for actors to audition for specific roles in their movies; many actors audition, but the number of roles and actors chosen is limited.

One hopeful young actor was turned down time and again by the same company for the roles for which he auditioned. Despairing yet determined, he made a last-ditch effort. Approaching one of the film directors, he said with as much moxie as he could muster, "It's now or never, sir, if you want me in one of your pictures. I now have many companies after me."

"Oh, really?" asked the director, his interest aroused by this statement. "Exactly which companies would that be?"

"Well," said the actor seriously, "there's the telephone company, the electric company, the gas company, the milk company . . ."

The director laughed, and the creative actor got the role.

In a similar way, the casting call has gone out to everyone in the world for parts in heaven's drama. Fortunately, there are roles available for each of us who answers that divine call. The great Playwright has carefully crafted a script that allows us to use our particular gifts and talents on life's stage, and acting experience is not required.

The drama is a once-in-a-lifetime opportunity for those on stage, calling us to give the greatest live performance possible. And the finale will be out of this world! So study your lines carefully—they're available in the Playwright's special Book, which he has made available to us all.

My Lord and my God, I pray with all my heart that I will play my part in your drama with joy and excitement. And when the finale comes, may I be found in my place onstage. Amen.

A Good Minister

The time is coming—indeed it's here now—when true worshipers will worship the Father in spirit and in truth.

JOHN 4:23

It is always fascinating to me that we humans seemed to have split the true religion of God into many segments and parts. Have you noticed that too? Some of us are more comfortable with quiet, calm worship services; others among us like more spirited, exciting services. Some people like a minister who speaks calmly with reason; others prefer a minister who shouts and moves around a lot. "Different strokes for different folks" is the way the phrase goes.

Yet, I sometimes wonder if God is really concerned about our *comfort.* Rather, he may be more concerned with our *spiritual completeness.* And when we throw out the parts of his complete truth to suit ourselves, in order to be comfortable, do we not also throw out vital parts of the whole?

One well-known minister, Edgar DeWitt Jones, once addressed this issue by propounding the specifications of what he thought made a good minister:

> *He should get religion like a Methodist; experience it like a Baptist; be sure of it like a Disciple; stick to it like a Lutheran; pray for it like a Presbyterian; conciliate it like a Congregationalist; glorify it like a Jew; be proud of it like an Episcopalian; practice it like a Christian Scientist; propagate it like a Roman Catholic; work for it like a Salvation Army lassie; and enjoy it like a Charismatic.*

The question is, why do we have to give up anything? Why can we not include all the elements of truth? That way, no one would be comfortable or uncomfortable all the time, but we could all be complete all the time. What do you think?

Dear Father, forgive us for treating your worship like a meal at the cafeteria—just picking and choosing the parts we like. Instead, Father, please help us to worship you wholly, in spirit and in truth. Amen.

A Fair Trade

You can enter God's Kingdom only through the narrow gate. The highway to hell is broad, and its gate is wide for the many who choose that way. But the gateway to life is very narrow and the road is difficult, and only a few ever find it.

MATTHEW 7:13-14

My friend Rick Atchley, the preaching minister in Texas of a large congregation of four thousand members, once remarked, "We spend more time praying to keep saints out of heaven than we do to keep sinners out of hell." And for the most part, he's right.

For instance, when great old saints become ill, we call in all the prayer warriors to plead with God not to take them home. Meanwhile, how many times have we called in the prayer warriors to pray for people who are spiritually ill in order to keep them out of hell? (Ouch! I just stomped on my own toes.)

One time a new minister in town sought the medical services of the reputed best local physician, a man who was sadly irregular in his church attendance. The medical treatment became prolonged, and the young minister, worried over the accumulating medical expenses, asked the doctor about his bill.

"I'll tell you what I'll do," said the doctor. "I hear you're a pretty good preacher, and you seem to think I'm a fair doctor. So let's make a bargain. I'll do all I can to keep you out of heaven, and you do all you can to keep me out of hell, and it won't cost either one of us a red cent."

I'm not sure that is a trade the Lord would particularly like. The truth is, no one else can do anything to keep us out of hell. That's up to each of us individually through our faith in the grace of our loving God that saves us. Without that faith, without that grace, there would be no salvation for any of us.

And by the way, just in case you're wondering, God does not do horse trading.

Dear God, thank you for providing the way for us to be saved. We are, indeed, eternally indebted to you. Amen.

Who Do You Know?

All the animals of the forest are mine,
and I own the cattle on a thousand hills. . . .
All the world is mine and everything in it.

PSALM 50:10, 12

In the 1970s I worked for H. L. Hunt—the oil tycoon and, at the time, the world's richest man. I served on his personal staff as a writer.

On a trip with Mr. and Mrs. Hunt to Los Angeles, where he was to appear on *The Merv Griffin Show*, we stayed at the Beverly Hilton hotel. After registering, Mr. Hunt asked the bell captain to have a table set up in the lobby to display some political comment materials, as he did everywhere he went.

The bell captain—a young man who had never heard of Mr. Hunt—explained that there was a convention in the hotel so he could not comply with Mr. Hunt's request.

Mr. Hunt patiently explained to the young man why it would be advantageous for him to put up the table, but he continued to politely refuse. Finally Mr. Hunt said to me, "We'll go to our rooms now."

In Mr. Hunt's suite he said, "Please get Mr. Hilton on the phone."

"Yes, sir!" I answered, thinking, *This should be interesting.* I knew that Mr. Hunt had a six-foot mahogany table in the lobby of the Dallas Hilton hotel where his materials were continually displayed.

"Mr. Hunt for Mr. Hilton, please," I said to the assistant.

"Of course! One moment, please."

"Conrad Hilton."

"Mr. Hilton, I have Mr. Hunt for you."

"Well, put him on!"

"Hiltie, this is H. L. Hunt. I'm in your hotel in California, and they won't let me put my table up in the lobby."

I couldn't hear Mr. Hilton's response, but Mr. Hunt then said, "Now, Hiltie, you know I've been known to *buy* hotels." And he hung up.

In less than five minutes, I heard *knock, knock, knock*! I went to the door. There stood the red-faced bell captain, who said, "Mr. Hunt, we have your table up in the lobby!"

Dear Father, we know that you own the whole world, and we are so blessed to know you. Amen.

A Touching Story

I pray that God, the source of hope,
will fill you completely with joy.

ROMANS 15:13

An elderly man lay dying upstairs in his bed. He gathered his remaining strength and lifted himself slowly from the bed. Leaning against the wall, he made his way out of the bedroom. With even greater effort, he forced his bony fingers to grab the handrail, and he let himself down the stairs, one painful step at a time.

With labored breath, he leaned against the door frame and gazed into the kitchen. Were it not for his agony, he would have thought himself already in heaven. There on the kitchen table, spread out in neat rows on wax paper, were literally hundreds of his favorite gooey chocolate chip cookies. Was he already in heaven, or was this one final, heroic act of love from his devoted wife of sixty years, seeing to it that he experienced one tasty indulgence so he could leave this world a happy man?

Mustering his last bit of strength, he threw himself toward the table, landing on his knees. His parched lips were parted in anticipation. He could almost taste the wondrous, moist, chocolaty cookie. His withered hand, driven by one last, gritty effort, made its way shakily toward a large cookie at the edge of the table, only to withdraw when his wife smacked it with a spatula.

"Stay out of those," she ordered. "They're for the funeral!"

Father, we know that heaven will be filled with delights beyond our imagination. Help us to concentrate on the joys to come and to stay focused on our eternal rewards rather than allow ourselves to be distracted by earthly pleasures. Amen.

In Residence

The twelve gates were made of pearls—
each gate from a single pearl! And the main street was pure gold,
as clear as glass. . . . And the city has no need of sun or moon, for
the glory of God illuminates the city, and the Lamb is its light.

REVELATION 21:21, 23

An old gospel song says, "I'm satisfied with just a cottage below, a little silver and a little gold. . . . I've got a mansion just over the hilltop in that bright land where we'll never grow old." And wouldn't we all be so much better off if being content with less were true of us? If only we could be satisfied with a little rather than always be grabbing for a lot, life would be so much simpler and less stressful.

When Patrick J. Ryan of Philadelphia was a very young priest, he was assigned to a parish in St. Louis, where Archbishop Kenrick presided over the diocese. Kenrick lived in a small, unpretentious house, scarcely in keeping with his recognized position in the church.

One day Father Ryan was passing the house of the archbishop, accompanied by a priest from Chicago who was visiting St. Louis. Father Ryan pointed out the house as the residence of the leader of the local church.

His guest said with surprise, "Why, you should see the splendid residence we have in Chicago for our archbishop!"

"Yes," said Father Ryan with a smile, "but you should see the splendid archbishop we have in St. Louis for our residence."

Ah, that's the key, isn't it? Instead of building mansions here on earth in which to live temporarily, we should be building our inner lives to make them fit to live in heavenly mansions for all eternity. "And someday yonder we will never more wander but walk on streets that are purest gold."

Heavenly Father, we wait with eager anticipation the return of your Son, who will bring us home to live with you for all eternity. Lord Jesus, come soon! Amen.

September 3

Taking the Risk

Fix your thoughts on what is true, and honorable,
and right, and pure, and lovely, and admirable.
Think about things that are excellent and worthy of praise.

PHILIPPIANS 4:8

In a small, impoverished community in the South, the only place the local church had in which to hold its services was a large room below a second-story dance hall with a wild reputation. During evening worship services, it was often difficult for the preacher to make himself heard above the music, the stomping, and the clatter from the floor above.

The building was old and ramshackle, and one night, in the midst of a sermon, a particularly vigorous jive was in progress upstairs. Suddenly the loud splintering of a plank was heard. Looking upward in alarm, the parson saw, protruding through a hole that had opened up in the ceiling, the plump leg of a woman.

In consternation, the preacher called out, "Any man what raises his eyes to the ceiling, the Lawd will strike blind!"

A hushed silence fell over the congregation. Then the quavering voice of an aged man at the rear of the congregation was heard to remark, "Waal, I'll risk one eye on it anyhow."

The old man was not unusual, was he? People are often tempted by cravings for the things they see. In today's world, we see the evidence in rampant pornography, lewd movies, and the idea that "sex sells" in every kind of ad from chewing gum to automobiles.

Yet God has warned us against following our "evil desires" (Romans 7:5) because they will surely lead us down the wrong road. So when you're thinking you'd be willing to risk one eye on something anyhow, think again!

Dear Lord, you have given us a perfect example of holiness and purity to follow. Help us to emulate you in all we do and to remain pure in our thoughts, actions, motivations, and speech. Help us to keep our eyes on you and not other things. Amen.

A Perfect Scenario

You are to be perfect, even as your
Father in heaven is perfect.

MATTHEW 5:48

When it comes to writing for publication, one of the most important aspects of the process is *re*writing. A writer doesn't necessarily rewrite a piece because there is something wrong with it. Often the rewriting is part of making a piece the best it can possibly be. As one writer said, "When my writing is not good, I typically rework it at least five times. When my writing is good, I rework it only four times." In other words, rewriting is essential if the result is to be the best it can be.

A story is told that after film producer Samuel Goldwyn read the first script submitted by a new writer attached to the movie studio, he summoned the hopeful employee to his desk.

"This is a perfect scenario," said Goldwyn. "It is the first time in my life that I've seen a perfect scenario. There's absolutely nothing wrong with it. I want you to have a hundred copies made so I can distribute them to all the other writers so that everybody can see a really perfect script."

"Really, Mr. Goldwyn?" responded the surprised writer as he turned to go and do the director's bidding.

"Yes," said Goldwyn. "And hurry before I start rewriting it!"

Our heavenly Father, as the author of our lives, rewrites and redeems the scenarios in which we live, not always because there is something wrong with us, but because he wants us to become the very best we can be.

The good news is that God sees us as perfect even though he knows we're not, because he looks at us through rose-colored glasses—stained by the precious blood of his Son on the cross.

Thank you, Father, for seeing us as we are in Christ. We are humbled in your presence and by your marvelous grace to us. Amen.

Imitations

Do not imitate what is evil but what is good.
Anyone who does what is good is from God.
Anyone who does what is evil has not seen God.

3 JOHN 1:11 (NIV)

Little children love to play dress-up. They put on coats, hats, and shoes that are much too big for them, cover their faces with makeup, and pretend to be grown up, trying to imitate their heroes—us! And we think it's funny and cute. We take pictures of them and tell our friends and families about their antics.

I wonder, though, whether sometimes it makes us a little nervous. Are we really worth imitating? After all, when we take a good look at ourselves, we can see the flaws and faults no one else knows about. So it makes sense that we would worry about the possibility of children turning out just like us—imperfect, frail, and faulty.

At a dinner in Hollywood one night to celebrate his birthday, Charlie Chaplin entertained the guests by imitating people they knew—men, women, children, his chauffeur, his Japanese servants, his secretaries.

Finally, toward the end of the evening, Charlie sang—superbly—at the top of his voice an aria from an Italian opera.

"Why, Charlie, I never knew you could sing so beautifully," someone exclaimed when he had finished.

"I can't sing at all," Chaplain responded with mock surprise. "I was only imitating Caruso!"

Perhaps Charlie's example is a good one for us to consider emulating. When you have done something good and someone else notices and praises you for it, don't take the credit and respond by saying, "Well, thanks. I do my best." Instead, say, "I'm not good at all. I was only imitating God, who *is* good."

Kind Father, teach me to always give you the credit for any praise or honor bestowed on me, for I know that you alone deserve the glory. Amen.

Just out of Reach

All glory to God, who is able, through his mighty power at work within us, to accomplish infinitely more than we might ask or think.

EPHESIANS 3:20

I love all kinds of food—Italian, Thai, Chinese, and American. But Mexican food? That's my favorite. My brother says that eating is my favorite indoor sport. (Maybe that's why I've been on Weight Watchers.)

A group of friends and I love to eat Mexican food together. Our restaurant of choice is El Rancho Grande in Fort Worth, Texas, where they have the best nachos on the planet.

One day we were at El Rancho, and while we munched on chips and salsa and waited for our food, we were talking about heaven and hell. Each one of us had a different image of these two eternal places, so we took turns describing them.

I've mentioned in an earlier devotional that my idea of heaven is sitting by the ocean with my poetry book and a pencil, composing poetry or lyrics as the waves lap against the shore. There would be sailboats on the horizon and seagulls gliding overhead, as if suspended by the unseen hand of God.

Carol said heaven to her will be a rainy day when she can sit by the fire and read an engaging book just for fun. She will hear the rain on the roof as she snuggles under a soft wool blanket. Occasionally she will drift into a nap, like the proverbial cat.

As our food arrived, Ouida said, "Well, I know what hell would be like for me. There would be this enormous banquet table filled with every kind of food I could imagine—just six inches beyond my reach."

Thank you, God, for putting heaven within our reach and for rescuing us from the powers of death and hell through your Son. We are forever indebted to you for your saving grace and love. Amen.

Centered

Fix your thoughts on what is true, and honorable,
and right. . . . Then the God of peace will be with you.

PHILIPPIANS 4:8-9

I watched Jeff walk away from me, shoulders squared under his fuzzy blue jacket. The teacher we had met at open house now greeted him by name. Miss Maxwell's eyes were warm and brown. I could imagine Jeff's bright blue ones crinkling into a shy smile.

Taking your firstborn to kindergarten is tough. This is a big world, sometimes cold and mean. And on the first day of school, the illusion of being able to protect your child seems to fly away like autumn leaves in a stiff north wind.

The first couple of days, Jeff filled the ride home with talk of classroom routines, details of who sat beside him at snack time, and verbatim quotes of just about everything Miss Maxwell said. By the end of the week, I was almost as comfortable with kindergarten as he was. Almost.

Then on Friday afternoon, Jeff buckled his seat belt and announced, "We have sinners in our classroom."

"What?" I had feared this. My child's innocence was already being corrupted by the outside world. Where did he get such a notion? Who would say this to him? "Did someone tell you that, Jeff?"

"Miss Maxwell. Mom, I think we're supposed to go now. The crossing guard is waving her flag at us."

Miss Maxwell? I had to stay calm.

"I like the sinners, Mom," Jeff was saying. Of course he did. Jeff liked everyone. "Especially art," he continued.

"Art?"

"You know, drawing and coloring and stuff. That's what you do in the art *center*. I like the block center, too, and the neighborhood center. But art's my favorite."

—*Kathleen Brown*

Lord, our fears can darken everything we see around us. Keep us from concentrating on our worries, and instead, help us to focus our attention on what we know is honorable and true. Our peace, your peace, is there. Amen.

Eyes on the Master

Don't waste what is holy on people who are unholy. Don't throw your pearls to pigs! They will trample the pearls, then turn and attack you.

MATTHEW 7:6

When the apostle Paul appeared before Festus, the governor of Judea, the ruler shouted at him, "Paul, you are insane. Too much study has made you crazy!" (Acts 26:24). And honestly, I've met a few educationally mad professors and scientists in my time, too, haven't you? Even more often than that, I've read works by highly educated authors who seem to think that vocabulary is more important than communication. My question is, why use a three-dollar word when a fifty-cent one will do?

English painter C. R. W. Nevinson once said, "It was a privilege to paint Mark Hambourg, a dear friend." He said he had never met a man with such a gift for penetrating to the heart of things, and by the use of a few vivid phrases, Hambourg could lift any conversation out of the ordinary.

Nevinson said he remembered sitting beside Hambourg at an after-dinner concert one night when the great pianist Benno Moiseivitch was playing. The audience—all men and women of culture—were anything but attentive. While Moiseivitch played, they were smoking, drinking, coughing, picking their teeth, wriggling around in their chairs, and in general, being disrespectful.

Meanwhile, the waiters and waitresses stood entranced, their eyes on the master musician.

"Look," said Hambourg, glancing around at the crowd. "Just look at the effect of education. It kills all concentration. Those considered the lower classes are the only people left who can listen and respond to the highest emotions of mankind."

It is interesting, isn't it—sometimes ignorance walks hand in hand with wisdom, and education keeps company with the foolish. Go figure!

Dear Lord, thank you for making your Word both plain and simple enough for people to understand and obey. I know heaven will be filled with educated and uneducated people who simply chose to follow your will and your way. Amen.

September 9

Baptism in Reverse

Go and make disciples of all the nations,
baptizing them in the name of the Father
and the Son and the Holy Spirit.

MATTHEW 28:19

It was a hot afternoon in early September when little Jeremy and his friends, Joey and Shelly, decided to play church. Jeremy's dad was the minister of a church that practiced baptism by immersion. The kids had learned how to sneak into the church and get to the baptistery, where, unbeknownst to their parents, they sometimes went for a swim.

On this particular day, they decided that the Great Commission was meant for them, and they needed to help the "lost" of the world be saved by baptizing them. So they gathered up their "lost" pets—Samson the Chihuahua; Twitter the canary; Hairy the roly-poly gerbil; and Sir Humphrey, the fifteen-pound tabby with a pronounced "cattitude." Smuggling them into the baptistery, they began immersing the wayward pets to "wash away their sins."

Samson enjoyed the process, getting loose and dog-paddling around the baptistery for several minutes before they could catch him.

Twitter didn't mind getting a bath, either—she flapped her wings and chirped while she was "baptized."

Even Hairy was patient while they dunked him and then dried him with a towel.

Sir Humphrey, however, was not the least bit interested in being saved if it meant getting into the water. Just as Jeremy and Joey started to baptize him, Sir Humphrey took a mighty leap over their heads, letting out a back-fence yowl that echoed through the church. That threw the boys off balance, and they both landed with a great splash in the baptistery.

Sir Humphrey was sitting on the edge of the baptistery, indignantly licking his damp paw just as the minister rushed in to see what the commotion was. *Busted!*

Father, thank you for the saving blood of your Son, who died in our place. We are humbled and grateful for your love and forgiveness. Amen.

TR and the Celestial Choir

Be filled with the Holy Spirit, singing . . . and making music to the Lord in your hearts.

EPHESIANS 5:18-19

One of the great joys in my life is singing. I came by my ability naturally because my dad was a singer with a big bass voice that he used to glorify God. So I love to hear great basses sing. They get to sing a lot of what I call the "good parts"—runs, leads, and sometimes solos.

The bass notes anchor the song and often are the notes upon which the chords of a song—the foundation—are built. Without the bass line, songs just don't feel tethered, at least not to me.

The fable is told that former president Theodore Roosevelt died and ascended to heaven. There he bustled about and made himself quite a nuisance by insisting that he be entrusted with some major responsibility. After all, he had run a huge country, so surely he should be in charge of something significant in heaven.

At last, weary of his insistence, the heavenly powers instructed Peter to authorize TR to organize and train a celestial choir to replace the old one, which they felt had gone to seed. So Peter gave TR the good news.

TR continued to be a nuisance, though, by the fierce persistence with which he pressed his requisitions for the new choir.

"I must have ten thousand sopranos," he told the bewildered and weary Peter. "And I need ten thousand contraltos, and ten thousand tenors. And hurry. Hurry! Everything is waiting on *you*."

"Yes, yes, all right," said Peter, "and how about basses?"

Roosevelt fixed Peter with a scornful glare and bellowed, "I'll sing bass!"

Perhaps TR could hold down the bass section alone, but if my dad is around, I predict TR will be sitting second chair.

Thank you for music, Father! It is a source of such beauty and contentment for me. I will sing your praises as long as I have voice. Amen.

Hailed in Horror

I will forgive their wickedness, and I will never again remember their sins.

HEBREWS 8:12

Life is full of embarrassing moments. Once one of the girls in my dorm was halfway across campus when a boy pointed out that she had forgotten to put on a skirt over her slip. She set a new world speed record sprinting back to the dorm!

Then there was the time in high school when I went on a date. We were going to the movies, but first my date took me to the local hamburger drive-in. He asked what I wanted to eat, so I asked for a hamburger and a Coke. He ordered *one* hamburger and *one* Coke. Then he sat there and watched me eat it. I was mortified!

A young lady on her way to a business meeting one morning was standing in a crowded New York bus traveling down Fifth Avenue. She was worrying over the age-old problem of whether or not her slip was showing. Unable to see for herself, she asked a small boy standing next to her.

"No, ma'am," he informed her politely.

When she reached her stop, she alighted and began to move briskly along Fifth Avenue. Then, to her horror, she heard the voice of that little boy, shouting to her as the bus went by, "Hey, lady! Your slip is showing now; it's showing now!"

We all make mistakes, and embarrassing moments are bound to come. We need to learn to take them in stride, grin and bear them, and cut one another a lot of slack until Jesus calls us home to a better world.

Father in heaven, thank you for your sweet love and forgiveness. How wonderful to be reminded that you will never call to mind the sins you have already forgiven. Help us to live in such a way that we do not embarrass you. Amen.

Mother Mary Speaking

You may be sure that your sin will find you out.

NUMBERS 32:23

I went to college at Abilene Christian University—a small, conservative, evangelical school. My parents sacrificed a lot to help me go to ACU, and I helped by working two or three jobs at a time. One of my jobs was working the switchboard in the dorm where I lived. I was also what we called a checker or resident assistant on the first floor of the dorm. That meant I had to *check* to be sure all the girls were in their rooms before curfew and to enforce the rule of keeping the noise level down in the halls during "quiet hours" so the girls could study.

Fortunately, the switchboard was right outside the main door to my floor, so I could do both jobs at once. And since the switchboard was usually inactive during quiet hours, I could also study while sitting there.

In those days we did not have phones in each room. We had only two phones on each floor, one on each end of the dorm. With three floors, that meant we had six phones in all for 218 girls. That seems incomprehensible in our smartphone, Bluetooth, text-crazy age, but that's how it was then.

On the switchboard it was easy to tell whether a call was coming from inside or outside the dorm, and we were careful about how we answered calls coming from outside: "Nelson Hall. How may I direct your call?" But when calls came from inside the dorm, we answered in lighthearted ways, just for fun.

One day I was working the switchboard, and a call came to the board from *inside* the dorm. I answered, "Nelson Nunnery, Mother Mary speaking."

There was a pause; then I heard, "Well, that's very interesting, Mary. This is *Dean Wilkinson. . . .*"

O Lord, you know my sins before I even commit them. And it's so easy to sin with my lips. Please forgive me when I do. Without your forgiveness, I am lost indeed. Amen.

September 13

The Man We Want

Humble yourselves before the Lord,
and he will lift you up in honor.

JAMES 4:10

Shug Jordan, former coach of the Miami Dolphins, asked one of his linebackers, Mike Kollin, to do some recruiting for the team.

Mike said, "Sure, Coach. What are you looking for, exactly?"

"Well, Mike, you know there's that fellow you knock down and he just stays down?"

Mike said, "Yeah, Coach. We don't want him, do we?"

"No, that's right. Then there's the fellow you knock down, and he gets up. You knock him down again, and he stays down."

Mike said, "We don't want him, either, do we, Coach?"

Coach said, "No, Mike. But there's a fellow you knock down, and he gets up. Knock him down again, and he gets up again. Knock him down, he gets up. Knock him down, he gets up."

Mike said, "That's the guy we want, isn't it, Coach?"

The coach answered, "No, we don't want him, either. I want you to find that guy who's knocking everybody down. *That*'s the guy we want!"

While I was writing this book, I was spending time in the hospital with my ninety-two-year-old mom, who had fallen and broken her hip. Then she had a mild heart attack. You might think that was it for her, but that would mean you don't know my mom.

Before she fell, Mom was living in her own home, driving her car, working in her yard, baking for every church event, and simply doing her life. She and her *older* sister, who is ninety-five, take care of each other. (Don't you love it?) Mom also had been married to my vagabond-preacher dad for seventy years. I told you, she's no quitter! And to her, this hip fracture was just a speed bump on the road of life. In no time at all she was back on her feet and walking!

When life knocks you down, do you stay down or get back up?

Dear God, you are the one who lifts me up when I fall and keeps me going when I want to quit. I'm so grateful for your strength in my weakness. Thank you, Father. Amen.

An Unmentionable Mishap

Everything is naked and exposed before [God's] eyes.

HEBREWS 4:13

Because I'm a pastor's wife, Sundays are hectic and stressful. And that's *before* I get to church! My husband leaves early to manage the details of Sunday service, which leaves me at home with our young kids, doing my best to get everyone—including me—up, dressed, fed, and out the door on time.

One Sunday morning I was home with our two-year-old, Brittany, and our newborn, Julia. Bleary eyed from late-night feedings, I poked around in the clean laundry pile to find something for Julia to wear, wondering how someone so tiny could generate so much laundry.

Despite my best efforts to get everyone ready, we were behind schedule. I threw my hair in a ponytail and dabbed on some lipstick before getting everyone into the car.

Thankful for a front-row parking spot, I hastily began to grab my things—infant carrier, diaper bag, purse, Bible, and notebook. Meanwhile, Brittany skipped to the front door, where John, a man from our community group, said hello and opened the door for her. Spying me only a few steps away, John knelt down to chat with Brittany, keeping her close until I could catch up.

When I approached, he burst out laughing.

As I walked through the front door, I saw the reason for John's guffaw. Apparently Brittany had played in our laundry that morning and thought it would be fun to try on Mommy's panties. And, apparently, she did *not* know about gravity—my underwear had dropped around her ankles, right there in the church lobby, for God and everyone else to see!

Cheeks burning, I untangled my panties from Brittany's legs and tucked them into my purse. John chuckled good-naturedly and said, "Don't worry, Jen. You're in church! You can't hide anything from God."

Indeed. God knows everything about us—even our "unmentionables"—and loves us anyway.

—*Jennifer Stair*

Father, please help me to remember that I can't hide anything from you. My life is an open book to you. Help me to make it worth reading. Amen.

September 15

Coming or Going?

Jesus [said], "A prophet is honored everywhere except in his own hometown and among his relatives and his own family."

MARK 6:4

Sometimes it's hard to tell whether you're coming or going, isn't it? Actually, through the centuries, that phrase has been turned around. Originally, the phrase was "going or coming," because women of old watched their husbands, fathers, and sons *going* off to war and then waited impatiently to see them *coming* home again. But because the armies could be seen for great distances, it was often hard to tell whether they were "going or coming."

Me? Some days I do well just to remember whether I was going up the stairs or coming down. Do you ever have that problem?

One young man named George, who had come to the Dallas/Fort Worth Metroplex from a small rural community, had worked hard for several years until at last he had gained some prominence in the banking world. His name often appeared in the financial section of the large city's newspaper, and he was invited to all the major social events.

Finally, George returned to his hometown for a visit. Considering his new notoriety, he half expected that the greater part of the community would come out to meet him at the station and that some considerable fuss would be made over the local boy who had made good.

To his great disappointment, though, there was not a single soul around when he got off the train onto the station platform. He waited doubtfully as several people came and went, none of them giving him so much as a glance. At last an old baggage handler recognized him and shuffled forward to look at him with some interest for several seconds.

"Hello, George," he said at last. "You goin' away?"

Dear Lord, help us to be content with who we are in you, knowing that even you were not honored by your relatives and friends. Let us realize that our identity as your children is all we will ever need. Amen.

The World's Greatest Violinist

[Jesus said,] "Take my yoke upon you. Let me teach you, because I am humble and gentle at heart, and you will find rest for your souls."

MATTHEW 11:29

There is a legend about the time Jascha Heifetz—one of the world's most famous violinists—made his triumphant New York debut. Among those in the audience were violinist Mischa Elman and distinguished pianist Joseph Hofmann.

It was a glorious New York evening in the spring, and the concert hall was packed. Many prominent New Yorkers filled the prestigious private boxes.

The concert progressed well, and as usual the audience was spellbound by the genius of Heifetz. As the music continued, Mischa Elman became increasingly fidgety, running his finger around the inside of his collar and mopping at the perspiration on his forehead with a handkerchief. In the pause between two musical selections, he leaned over and whispered to Joseph Hofmann, "Awfully hot in here, isn't it?"

Hofmann smiled and whispered back, "Not for pianists."

Jesus, too, made it *hot* for the proud and haughty people around him. His humble spirit and gentleness drew people to him like metal to a magnet. His popularity grew exponentially as he traveled from place to place proclaiming the Good News. But Jesus' popularity was viewed as a major threat by the religious establishment, who did not understand that his Kingdom was not a worldly one.

You can imagine the Pharisees and Sadducees listening to Jesus' words—words that portrayed a life diametrically opposite of theirs—becoming uncomfortable, like Mischa Elman, running their fingers around the necks of their robes and mopping the sweat from their brows. It was *hot* for them, all right.

But it wasn't for Jesus' true disciples—the humble, gentle followers of the gospel of love and peace.

Lord, thank you for the example you are of how to live. Please help me every day to become more like you in every way. Amen.

September 17

Lingerie and Long-Bed Trucks

Plans go wrong for lack of advice.

PROVERBS 15:22

My husband's brother, Loren, was a missionary in Thailand for about thirty years. Loren and his wife, Penny, along with their four children, were happy there and did wonderful work for the Lord. Once in a while they got to come to the States on furlough.

One summer they were going to San Francisco before heading home to Kansas. To help them save the airfare from California to Kansas—a lot of money for six people—I agreed to drive our big fifteen-passenger van from Louisiana to California, pick them up, and take them to Kansas to my in-laws' farm. When they arrived in San Francisco, we loaded the van to the gills, finally tying bigger pieces of luggage to the rack on top. We looked like the Beverly Hillbillies!

Somewhere in Colorado we stopped for the night. The next morning Loren loaded the luggage, and we were on our way again. We were clipping down the side of a mountain when Loren and Penny's daughter Kim yelled, "Hey, there goes our luggage!"

I looked in the rearview mirror just in time to see two big pieces of luggage bounce onto the road, burst open, and send clothes flying everywhere. I stopped as quickly as possible and then carefully backed up to where the luggage lay in ruins.

"How did the luggage come loose, anyway?" I asked.

Loren, a little red faced, admitted, "I thought the big pieces were heavy enough that they wouldn't need to be tied down, so I didn't secure them."

We told the kids to stay in the van while the adults got out and gathered up my pajamas and other unmentionables and stuffed them back into the suitcases, all the while keeping an eye out for some long-bed truck barreling down the hill. The scene looked like an *I Love Lucy* episode! Fortunately, we survived the mishap with laughter and were left with a great memory.

Dear Father, thank you for protecting us when our lack of planning causes difficulties and even sometimes puts us in harm's way. Keep us safe in your care, and help us to take the time to plan wisely. Amen.

A Returned Favor

How can you think of saying, "Friend, let me help you get rid of that speck in your eye," when you can't see past the log in your own eye? Hypocrite! First get rid of the log in your own eye; then you will see well enough to deal with the speck in your friend's eye.

LUKE 6:42

Ouch! Does that Scripture verse stomp on your toes the way it does mine? Somehow I can always see in others—magnified and much worse, of course—the same problems that plague me personally. For instance, I tend to notice people who look as if they need to be on a diet. (I've been on the Weight Watchers program.) I fuss at drivers who do not seem to know where they are headed. (I am directionally dysfunctional and get lost a lot.)

I think about those things, and then I remember the words of the apostle Paul, who humbly identified himself as the worst of sinners (see 1 Timothy 1:15-16). I think I could run him a pretty good race.

I'm reminded of Ignacy Paderewski, the great Polish pianist and composer, who was visiting Boston some years ago. As he walked down the street during his free time before the concert, he was approached by a shoe-shine boy, who called, "Shine, mister?"

The great pianist looked down at the young man whose face was streaked with grime and boot polish and said, "No, my lad, but if you will wash your face, I will give you a quarter."

"All right!" exclaimed the boy, looking sharply at him. He ran to a nearby fountain, where he washed his dirty face until it shone. When he returned, Paderewski held out the quarter.

The boy took the quarter and then returned it, saying gravely, "Here, mister. You keep it and get your hair cut."

Dear God, forgive me for being critical of others when what I really need to do is look deep inside and work on my own faults and sins. Help me daily to work on getting the log out of my own eye. Amen.

A Finicky Eater

[God] richly gives us all we need for our enjoyment.

1 TIMOTHY 6:17

I was a finicky eater as a kid. I loved ketchup but not tomatoes. I liked potatoes but not most green vegetables. I would say, "I don't like that," even when I had never tasted a particular food. Fortunately, I eventually gave up those childish ways and learned to eat many wonderful foods.

There's a story about a very finicky eater: One day, a customer entered the most famous and expensive bakery shop in New York City. He ordered a cake baked in the shape of the letter *s*. He insisted on various details of its decoration and specified that it must be ready by a certain date.

The day before the deadline, the customer dropped by and found that his cake was finished and being decorated.

"This is all wrong!" he said, flying into a rage. "You've baked it in the shape of a capital *S*. I wanted it to be a *small* one. The whole thing will have to be done over, and you'll have to have it ready by tomorrow anyway!"

He created such a fuss that the apologetic manager assured the customer they would make every effort to satisfy him. They would redo the cake, even though they felt the mistake had been a natural one.

The following day the customer returned and found his lowercase *s* cake decorated exactly as he had requested.

"That's fine," he said, much mollified. "That's just right."

He took out his wallet and paid for the cake.

"Now, sir," said the proprietor, "where shall it be sent, or shall I box it so you can take it with you?"

"Oh, that's all right," said the customer with a wave of his hand, "I'll just eat it here." And he did!

For your wonderful gifts and blessings, Father, I thank you with all my heart. May I accept them with joy and share them happily with others. Amen.

Godly Potato Chips

God loved the world so much that he gave his one and only Son, so that everyone who believes in him will not perish but have eternal life.

JOHN 3:16

When I was in first grade, I was often chosen to carry messages to the office or to other teachers. One day I was asked to carry a note to Mrs. Williams, who was known for spanking naughty students.

As I approached Mrs. Williams's room, I heard the familiar wailing of a student being spanked. After the spanking, Mrs. Williams wrapped her big brown arms around the sobbing child. She whispered something to him as her other hand reached inside her desk drawer and brought out a big bag of potato chips. I let out a gasp as she gave the bag to the little fellow.

"What do you want?" Mrs. Williams asked loudly as I inched toward her desk and presented her with the note. She wrote something on it, and I was soon running back to my classroom. I was still shaking as I hurried home after school.

I ran into the house, yelling, "Mamma, Mamma, guess what they do at that school?"

Mamma's eyes widened, waiting for me to continue.

"If you ask for a bag of potato chips there, they beat you."

Mamma shook her head in disbelief and then began to laugh as I described the incident.

This experience often reminds me of our loving God, who sent Jesus to take our "spankings" so we would one day have eternal life. He takes our place in the principal's office and accepts the punishment that should be ours. And because he does, we can be confident of having all the "potato chips" heaven can offer.

—*Gwen Williams*

Thank you, God, for loving a sinner like me and for your gift of eternal life. Amen.

Exaggeration

The LORD detests lying lips,
but he delights in those who tell the truth.

PROVERBS 12:22

So the story goes, Mark Twain once asked a baggage handler in the railroad station in Washington, "Is that satchel strong enough to go in the baggage car?"

The baggage man lifted it high above his head and smashed it to the ground with all his might. "That," said he, "is what it will get in Philadelphia."

He picked it up and bashed it against the side of the car four or five times. "That is what it will get in Chicago."

He next threw it high in the air, and when it landed, he jumped on it vigorously. It split open and scattered its contents across the platform. "And that is what it will get in Sioux City. If you are going any farther than Sioux City, you'd better take it in the Pullman with you."

Twain was sometimes given to exaggeration. Writers like to call it "poetic license." Others call it "stretching the truth." But when you get right down to it, exaggeration is nothing more than a form of lying. Entertaining? Yes. But lying just the same.

I admit it is tempting to make the most of a story by embellishing it with exaggerated "facts" and delightful super-deeds that fascinate readers. And yet the Bible is clear when it says that "the devil . . . is a liar and the father of lies" (John 8:44). The last thing we want to do is imitate the devil.

An interesting consideration to me is that exaggeration about God is virtually impossible. He is already *omnipotent* (all powerful), *omniscient* (all knowing), and *omnipresent* (in all places all the time). So if we concentrate on telling God's story rather than lesser stories, we can use every superlative in the dictionary and still not begin to come close to the truth about him.

Dear Lord, when you know that I am about to speak dishonestly, please just shut my mouth. Replace those exaggerations with words of love and truth. Amen.

An Unlikely Bridge

Remember, it is sin to know what you ought to do and then not do it.

JAMES 4:17

Do you remember when gentlemen routinely opened doors for women? And women thanked them politely for doing so? Whatever happened to that kind of courtesy? It just does not seem to exist much anymore, and I miss it.

I tend to feel that many men stopped acting like gentlemen when women stopped being ladies. Many women campaigned for "equal rights," and we got what we *thought* we wanted, but in many cases it did not turn out to be what we expected it to be. Men are no longer sure how to act, and some err by doing nothing at all. As Dr. Phil says, "How's that working for you now?"

Sir Walter Raleigh—the gallant example of courtesy and gentlemanliness—would have had to devise different techniques if he lived today. In Philadelphia one day, an obviously authentic descendant of Sir Walter encountered three girls who were marooned on the curb of a downtown street. A violent cloudburst had left a deep puddle in the poorly drained street, stretching nearly all the way between them and the trolley they wished to board.

Two of the girls had attempted to jump the puddle only to land in water over their ankles. The third was still standing on the curb in despair when a sedan rolled up and stopped directly in front of her. With a flourish its driver opened the rear door on her side, then opened the other rear door. Catching the idea, the young lady proceeded to step through the car and onto the trolley, perfectly dry. Tipping his hat, the driver closed his doors and proceeded to drive away. The girl called out, "Thank you!"

What happened to chivalry? It's still alive and well in Philadelphia!

Gracious Father, help me to show courtesy and politeness to those around me, because I know that those attributes are reflections of you. And please help me to take every opportunity to do good. Amen.

Gratitude Remembered

Don't be misled—you cannot mock the justice of God. You will always harvest what you plant.

GALATIANS 6:7

My mom is a woman of gratitude. No matter what small gift you give or act of kindness you do for her, she immediately sits down and writes a thank-you note or calls you on the phone to say thank you. Maybe she goes a little overboard, because she even writes thank-you notes for greeting cards she receives, but better too much gratitude than not enough, right?

Another example of gratitude is a story about a hunter who came across a huge elephant that was limping. The hunter followed the elephant for quite some time until, unable to walk any farther, it finally stopped and lay down.

Throwing caution to the wind, the hunter gingerly examined the elephant's feet. In one he found a large thorn, obviously the cause of the limp he had observed. He carefully removed the thorn, and the elephant got up and walked away, looking back at the hunter as he left.

Years passed, and one day the hunter was sitting in a cheap seat at the circus. Eventually the elephant troupe entered the arena. During one of the turns, a huge elephant reached out with its trunk, encircled the hunter's waist, lifted him from his cheap seat, and carefully set him down in a seat in a private box. After the hunter recovered from his surprise, he realized it was the same elephant he had helped in the jungle.

"An elephant never forgets" is an attribute we could all stand to emulate, especially when it comes to remembering others' kindness and showing gratitude for someone else's care.

I am so grateful, Lord, for your constant care and kindness to me, and I thank you for always being there for me when I need help. I love you, Lord. Amen.

The Bakery

Keep on asking, and you will receive what you ask for.

MATTHEW 7:7

Alex thought God had really blessed him when he bought the run-down bakery on Fourth Street. Mr. Bonner—the delightful old baker who had made the shop famous—had died and the business had closed. Evidently no one else in the family could carry on the old man's work.

After weeks of renovating, Alex excitedly announced the reopening of Bonner's Bakery in the Sunday paper—an announcement he knew the town would cheer. The only remaining problem was how to provide baked goods that even came close to Mr. Bonner's mouthwatering, secret-recipe cinnamon rolls and delectable red velvet cakes. Alex had searched extensively, but none of the bakers he had interviewed seemed right for the beloved old shop. *God, I really need your help, please.*

Suddenly, a young woman knocked on the door. She wore a nostalgic smile, as if enjoying a fond memory.

"May I help you?" Alex asked.

"I was hoping I might help *you*," she said, smiling. "I'm Tina Bonner. Mr. Bonner was my grandfather."

"Really! Come in."

"You've made some wonderful improvements," Tina said. "Have you found a baker yet?"

"No. Your grandfather's a hard act to follow. Why do you ask?"

"My husband recently died of cancer, and I need a job to support my two little girls. I worked here for several years as Pop's apprentice; he taught me how to make all his recipes."

"Even the secret-recipe cinnamon rolls?"

"Yes!" she laughed. "Even Pop said I was almost as good as he was."

"Hallelujah!" shouted Alex, dancing around the bakery. "If you can be here in the morning at six o'clock, you're hired!"

"Oh, I'll be here. You can count on it."

Local residents flocked to the bakery the next day, perhaps because a Bonner was still the baker. Alex got the help he had asked God for at just the right time.

Dear God, thank you for always answering when we call out to you for help. Amen.

September 25

All Roads Lead to Texarkana

Jesus [said], "I am the way, the truth, and the life."

JOHN 14:6

A few years ago, my friend Charlotte and I took a trip to Hot Springs, Arkansas. Since Charlotte is not a morning person, I drove first. And about the time we crossed the Red River going north, she fell asleep.

Charlotte hadn't traveled with me very much at that point, so she didn't know that when God handed out *compasses*, I thought he was giving out "rumpuses" and asked for a very small one. If I make two turns, I'm lost. I can even get confused going to my office (ordinarily, that wouldn't be funny, but I work at home).

I'd been driving about two hours when Charlotte roused. She seems to have a built-in radar device in her brain. She can be asleep, but if you start going the wrong direction, she senses it and wakes up.

"Where are we?" Charlotte asked.

"Still going north on Highway 19."

"Then why does that sign say twenty-one miles to Texarkana?"

"I don't know," I said defensively. "I haven't made a single turn."

"You must have turned somewhere, because we're going south, not north."

I stopped, and Charlotte studied the map for a minute. Then she began laughing.

"What's so funny?" I asked.

"Well, friend, we've made a grand circle, and we're almost back where we started."

"No way! Well, I'm not very good at directions."

"No kidding!" Charlotte laughed. "Next time I'd better drive."

"Drive! You couldn't even stay awake."

Since that trip, my friends like to joke that whenever Mary drives, all roads lead to Texarkana.

Savior and Lord, help me to remember that I am never lost as long as I'm with you. Be my compass and help me to stay on the right path. Amen.

We Surrender!

Jesus Christ is the same yesterday, today, and forever.

HEBREWS 13:8

As I grow older, I am trying really hard not to become an old fogy. I want to age gracefully and stay current on things. I do not want to become a grouchy old woman who spends her time criticizing others and complaining about how life is changing.

For the most part, I think I handle newness fairly well. I have an iPhone, a Macintosh laptop, a satellite Internet connection, and WiFi at my house. And I drive a red convertible just to defy creeping age. (It's my belief that everyone should have a convertible at least once!)

Still, there are some new things that escape me, and I catch myself responding like Scarlett O'Hara in *Gone with the Wind*: "I'll think about it tomorrow." I know I'm not alone in this, because my friends tell me they struggle with some contemporary developments as well.

Twentieth-century American composer Deems Taylor told a similar story about the first Carnegie Hall performance of the modernistic *Ballet Mécanique,* by George Antheil. The composition might be classified as an extreme of extremes. Among the numbers of unorthodox instruments augmenting the orchestra were ten grand pianos, six xylophones, a player piano, a fire-alarm siren, an airplane propeller, and several automobile Klaxons.

The audience, who had been well mannered up to that point, began to fidget after the start of the music. The general excitement and consternation mounted until finally, after eight minutes of the offending composition, a man in the front row raised a white handkerchief tied to his cane and the entire audience burst into laughter.

When faced with the myriad changes that come along seemingly every day, I, like that man in the front row, sometimes want to raise a white flag and shout, "I surrender!"

I'm so happy that Jesus remains constant in my life. He never changes, and I can count on him always to stay the same. What a relief!

Heavenly Father, thank you for being my Rock, my Fortress, and my Protector. When I'm afraid of the changes life brings, help me to remember that I can always run to you. Amen.

Need Any More?

A gentle answer deflects anger,
but harsh words make tempers flare.

PROVERBS 15:1

For about twelve years I served as the managing editor of a newsletter called *TEACH*—a twenty-page, hard-hitting publication for Christian teachers and leaders, chock full of informative and practical tidbits and helpful ideas. Included in each issue were about ten full-length articles for teachers and leaders who worked with different age groups in the church and related ministries.

In one of the early issues, before I really had all the processes and procedures down, I published an article written by a man in a neighboring city. I inadvertently neglected to get written permission from the author to use the article, however. So when the issue came out, he found his article and was upset that we had "stolen" his work.

We shortly received a rather irate letter from the man, and I realized immediately that the fault was mine. I wrote to him, apologizing profusely for my oversight in not seeking permission to use the article, and I included a check for one hundred dollars, our standard payment for the longer articles, hoping that would appease him.

During the ensuing days, I waited nervously for his response, praying that he would not want to press the matter further. About two weeks went by, and I finally received a rather large envelope from the offended author. Fearing that it might be filled with legal papers and that we were in for some kind of battle, I opened the envelope and pulled out about twenty-five additional articles he had written, with a note that said, essentially, "Thanks for the check. Do you need any more articles?"

I'm happy to say that all was forgiven, and he and I developed an excellent long-term working relationship.

As Snoopy used to say, "A kiss on the nose turneth away wrath."

Loving Savior, thank you for the privilege and joy of being forgiven. Help me to return the favor when others offend me. Amen.

A Gift for Everyone

Christ suffered for our sins once for all time.
He never sinned, but he died for sinners
to bring you safely home to God.

1 PETER 3:18

One day Abraham Lincoln was feeling ill. However, a young man who was seeking an appointment to the post office was visiting with him and stayed until President Lincoln grew fidgety.

While the young man was extolling his own virtues, Lincoln's physician entered the room and observed the president's discomfort.

"Doctor, what are these blotches?" asked Lincoln, holding out his hands for the doctor's inspection.

Understanding that Lincoln needed to be rescued from his visitor, the doctor said seriously, "That's varioloid—a mild smallpox."

"They're all over me," said Lincoln. "Is it contagious?"

"Oh yes, very contagious," replied the doctor, nodding solemnly.

Lincoln's caller suddenly leaped to his feet. "Well, I can't stay, sir. I just wanted to see how you were doing. I'll be going now."

"Oh, don't be in such a hurry," said Lincoln, grinning good-naturedly.

"Thank you, sir," said the visitor. "I'll be sure to call again when you're feeling better." And in a flash he was out the door.

The doctor looked at Lincoln and they both laughed.

"There is one good thing about this," Lincoln observed after the man was gone. "I now have something I can give everybody."

Jesus, too, had something that he could give to everybody—the astonishing gift of life ever after, because of his beautiful grace and mercy!

Like the young man who visited Lincoln, we can accept the remarkable gift, or we can leave without it. It's up to us. And the consequences of our decision are life altering. Have you accepted the gift Jesus offers?

Precious Lord, I bow in humble gratitude for your amazing gift of salvation. I will spend the rest of my days expressing my thanks in praise and service to you. Amen.

A Small Catastrophe

Do to others as you would like them to do to you.

LUKE 6:31

My mother was the second of six beautiful sisters raised on a farm in East Texas. As my dad often said, "There wasn't a clunker in the bunch."

Now in their nineties, the two oldest sisters love to reminisce about their growing-up years, including stories of pranks they played on each other and on unsuspecting visitors.

It seems that the senior sister, my aunt Zelma, had a friend spending the night with her. An uncle was also temporarily living there and working for my granddad. He was using as his bedroom "the little room"—a long, narrow room with a door at one end and one window at the other.

The uncle hated cats, and my grandparents kept a healthy crop of them to help eliminate rats and other vermin that crept in from the surrounding woods. So he was constantly complaining about the meowing and squalling that comes naturally to the annoying, leg-rubbing fur balls.

Knowing his passionate dislike for cats, Aunt Zelma and her friend crept around the house and positioned themselves just below the uncle's window. Because the weather was hot, the screenless window was open to allow some cooler air in. Aunt Zelma's friend, who had a knack for making the sound of a squalling Siamese cat, proceeded to yowl.

"Meoooow, meoooow."

"Scat!" said the uncle.

"Meoooow!"

"Scat, I said!"

"Meoooow, meooooow!"

Now totally frustrated, the uncle, yelling "Get outta here!" grabbed one of his work boots and threw it out the window.

Of course, the boot hit Aunt Zelma's friend in the face and gave her a huge black eye. Aunt Zelma says that explaining that black eye the next morning was pretty hard. And they didn't soon repeat their prank because, she says, "It was a big *cat*astrophe!"

Father, please help us to be more considerate of others and to learn to treat them with the same kindness we would like to receive. Amen.

Where Are You?

I press on to . . . receive the heavenly prize for which God, through Christ Jesus, is calling us.

PHILIPPIANS 3:14

When I worked for H. L. Hunt—then the world's wealthiest man—he once said to me, "Sometimes I wish I could just give all my money away and see if I could make it again. It's no fun *having* the money; it's only fun *making* it."

Twentieth-century missionary and theologian E. Stanley Jones wrote about a fictional person who lived out a fantasy life. All he had to do was think of something, and—*poof!*—it happened. So he stuck his hands in his pockets, leaned back, imagined a mansion, and—*poof!*—he had a fifteen-bedroom mansion with soft-footed servants to wait upon his every need.

A place like that needs fine cars, so he closed his eyes and imagined the driveway full of the finest cars money could buy. He sat in the back of one of them as a chauffeur drove him wherever he wished to go.

There was no other place to travel, so he returned home and wished for a sumptuous meal—and there it was in front of him. But always there was something more he "needed."

Finally he grew bored and unchallenged, and he whispered to one of his attendants, "I want to get out of this. I want to create something. I want to earn something. I even want to suffer some things again. I'd rather be in hell than here."

The servant replied, "Sir, that is where you are."

It's the goal that makes life interesting. And that is why heaven is the perfect goal—it's just out of our reach, calling us ever upward. As poet Robert Browning said, "Ah, but a man's reach should exceed his grasp. Or what's a heaven for?"

For a life worth living here, focus on life hereafter.

Heavenly Father, I want my eternal home to be with you in heaven. Help me to stay focused on that goal and to finish the race well. Amen.

October 1

Rescued Lamps and Lives

He has rescued us from the kingdom of darkness and transferred us into the Kingdom of his dear Son.

COLOSSIANS 1:13

One of my favorite relaxations is resale shopping with my best friend, Marcia. As we were browsing at a place charmingly named Bearly Used one Saturday, I poked about looking for old wooden frames for my decidedly amateur acrylic paintings. Instead of frames, I spotted a row of lamps.

One lamp had a bird design on it. Then I saw there were two lamps with the same design, which looked strangely familiar. *Where have I seen that design before?* I realized it was on the large soup tureen and platter in my home, a gift from my husband, Byron, to his beloved first wife, Louise.

Carefully, holding my breath and expecting to find "Made in China" on the base, I looked underneath and almost gasped aloud. "Herend. Handpainted. Hungary."

Without lamp shades or finials, but otherwise perfect, they were priced $7.99. I carried them to the high school kid at the counter and said, "Are these $7.99 apiece, or for the pair, because they match. See?" He said for the pair, so I scurried off with my gorgeous $4 lamps, which I kept telling myself were probably knockoffs.

The next day, I bought lovely silk shades and shiny brass butterfly finials, and then I looked on the Herend website and found that this lamp, the Rothschild pattern, was still available at $1,450 each. Mercy me!

Then I realized my own life was like one of my prized, rescued lamps. In 1986 I fell in love with golfer Byron Nelson. He baptized me into Christ on October 15, we were married on November 15, and we had nearly twenty beautiful years together. Now my life has the chance to shine and glow and shed light wherever I am because I'm connected to that eternal source of power, Jesus Christ.

—*Peggy Nelson*

My Lord, how can I ever thank you for rescuing me from my sins? I will praise and worship you all my life. Amen.

A Special Honor

Everyone will honor the Son, just as they honor the Father.

JOHN 5:23

The late actress Helen Hayes is one of my all-time favorites. She showed such class, humor, and dramatic ability during her acting career. She had, of course, been honored many times for her acting and stage performances.

When Helen was portraying Mary of Scotland, though, she received the most touching tribute an actress could ever hope to get. After the matinee one winter's afternoon, as darkness was falling and the bitter cold was setting in, she left the theater by the stage door. Outside, standing in the cold, was a small boy who gazed at Helen adoringly. She thought it odd, but when he quickly ran away, she dismissed the incident and went home.

For several days, after each afternoon matinee, the young boy faithfully appeared again outside the stage door. She would smile at him, and he would run away, not daring to speak to her.

Finally one day, as she came out to get into her car, the little boy impulsively ran up to her and thrust something into her hand, then fled down the street at a dead run. Miss Hayes watched him go and wondered about him, then she glanced down at her hand to find herself holding a small box. Opening it carefully, she found a little gilded medal bearing the inscription, "Scholarship Medal, Public School 42, 1933." Her heart melted. She knew she had been exceedingly honored by her young admirer because he had obviously given her his most prized possession.

Our heavenly Father also honored us beyond imagination when he gave us his most prized possession—his Son, Jesus. And while we can't hold him in our hands, we can hold him in our hearts for all eternity. In that way we can honor both the Father and the Son in return for the marvelous gift they have given us.

Gracious Father, I come to you in humble thanks and awe that you would give your precious Son for me. I promise to hold him in my heart forever. Amen.

October 3

The Vote

Dear brothers and sisters, when troubles come your way, consider it an opportunity for great joy.

JAMES 1:2

Fellow citizens," said the candidate running for political office, "I have fought against the Indians. I have often had no bed but the battlefield, and no canopy but the sky. I have marched over the frozen ground until every step has been marked with blood."

His story told well, until a dried-up-looking voter came to the front to speak to him.

"Did you say you fought for the Union?"

"Yes!" replied the candidate with pride.

"And agin the Indians?"

"Yes, many a time, my good man."

"And that you slept on the ground with only the sky for a kiver?"

"Certainly, sir, over and over again."

"And that your feet bled in marching over the frozen ground?"

"Yes, that they did," cried the exultant candidate.

"Then I'll be switched if you hain't done enough for your country. Go home and rest. I'll vote for the other fellow."

The apostle Paul was not running for office, but he was required to defend himself in the public arena on more than one occasion. He, too, found it necessary to rehearse the struggles and difficulties of his life—beaten with rods, stoned, left for dead, shipwrecked, lost at sea, robbed, and other painful experiences—all for the name of Jesus.

When I read that list, I wince to think that I have never suffered any of those things for my Lord. And yet, I sometimes hear myself whining about insignificant offenses that come my way—an insult, a criticism, an oversight. I want so much to face my trials with the joy that comes from suffering for Christ. And I pray that I will smile in the face of troubles so others can see him in me.

Suffering Savior, please forgive me for my weakness and self-serving attitude. I bow in humility and sincere repentance before you. Help me to reflect your joy in all circumstances. Amen.

Making a Difference

Go and make disciples of all the nations,
baptizing them in the name of the Father
and the Son and the Holy Spirit.

MATTHEW 28:19

Needing a break, a businessman and his wife escaped for a few days of relaxation at an oceanfront hotel. One night a violent storm lashed the beach and sent massive breakers thundering against the shore. The man lay in his bed, listening and thinking about his own stormy life of never-ending demands and pressures.

The wind finally died down, and shortly before daybreak the man slipped out of bed and took a walk along the beach to see what damage had been done. As he strolled, he saw that the beach was covered with starfish that had been thrown ashore and helplessly stranded by the great waves. Once the morning sun burned through the clouds, the starfish would dry out and die.

Suddenly the man saw an interesting sight. A young boy who had also noticed the plight of the starfish was picking them up, one at a time, and flinging them back into the ocean.

"Why are you doing that?" the man asked the lad as he got close enough to be heard. "Can't you see that one person will never make a difference—you'll never be able to get all those starfish back into the water. There are just too many."

"Yes, that's true." The boy sighed as he bent over and picked up another and tossed it back into the water. Then as he watched it sink, he looked at the man, smiled, and said, "But it sure made a difference to that one."

No one can save all the lost of the world, but each one of us can touch one other life with the sweet message of salvation. And think what a difference it will make to that one!

—Denis Waitley

I want to be more like you, Lord. I want to reach out and touch the heart of someone near me with your love and grace. And I know you will help me. Amen.

A Strange Flower

God blesses those who patiently endure testing and temptation. Afterward they will receive the crown of life that God has promised to those who love him.

JAMES 1:12

Miss Clara Morris, a well-known star of the stage, once found herself in a difficult onstage position. It was years ago, when she was playing Camille. In the first scene, the unfortunate Armand was supposed to take a camellia from Camille as a token of her love. They had almost reached that point in the scene, when Miss Morris glanced down and saw that the flower was missing from its accustomed place on her blouse.

What could she do? On the flower hung the strength of the entire scene. However, "the show must go on," so she continued delivering her lines in an abstracted way while she began hunting the stage for the missing camellia or for some substitute. Her gaze wandered until she spotted some celery on the dinner table. Moving slowly toward it, she grasped the celery and twisted the tops into a camellia form. Then she began the fateful lines:

"Take this flower. The life of a camellia is short. If held and caressed, it will fade in a morning or an evening."

Hardly able to control his laughter, Armand spoke his lines, which were, "It is a cold, scentless flower. It is a strange flower." And Miss Morris agreed with him.

As Shakespeare pointed out, life is also a stage, and we are the players. Just as it happened for Miss Morris, things sometimes go wrong on life's stage as well, and we have to improvise because "the show must go on."

Life seems to be a series of problems we need to solve. How we approach those dilemmas—whether with despair or joy—often determines how complicated they become. Even when problems last, if faced with joy they are more bearable and may "fade in a morning or an evening."

For our problems, Father, we thank you, because we know they help us to grow stronger. Help us to face them with joy. Amen.

Garlic in the Church

Our lives are a Christ-like fragrance rising up to God. But this fragrance is perceived differently by those who are being saved and by those who are perishing.

2 CORINTHIANS 2:15

We had the pleasure of sharing the life of our church with many university students. After the morning service each Sunday, we would have a fellowship lunch, and various groups were on the roster to cook. One Sunday a group of students from Singapore, Hong Kong, and China prepared one of their cultural dishes for the lunch. The meal was delicious and laced with garlic. Those present loved it, and there were no leftovers!

That night a number of church members who had been at the lunch returned for the evening service, which was held in the chapel a short distance from the dinner hall. Welcoming visitors and others who had not been to the lunch, we noticed their noses twitching, and their eyes seemed to be asking questions their lips would not utter.

Someone asked, "What is that strange and strong smell that met us as we entered the building?"

It was not the flowers, and we do not use incense. Because we who had eaten the meal were saturated by and contributing to the garlic-flavored atmosphere, at first we did not grasp what they were going on about. We were totally unaware of the odor that surrounded us, but others certainly noticed it. That night visitors and regular members entered into a different but aromatic service!

The garlic aroma soon faded. However, the spiritual object lesson has remained to remind us to consider what kind of fragrance our lives are to God and those around us.

—Raymond N. Hawkins

Lord, I often wonder how strong a spiritual fragrance flows in and through me and touches the spiritual noses of others. May I feed my inner life on the manna of heaven so that it permeates my life and makes others hungry for you. Amen.

And Now, Mr. Mayor

If you claim to be religious but don't control your tongue, you are fooling yourself, and your religion is worthless.

JAMES 1:26

My athletic prowess knows no bounds. Unfortunately, my best talent seems to be tripping over my tongue. I go along quite well for some time, and then one day I open my big mouth and insert my foot right up to my ankle. And while I'm busy choking on my foot, I also manage to offend someone important to me. I'm really good at it, too, because I've had a lot of practice through the years. *Sigh.*

The Bible cautions us to control our tongues, probably because God knew that it would be one of our most difficult tasks as fallible human beings, as this story demonstrates:

When her boys were very small, Mrs. Johnson gave a party at which one of the guests was to be the mayor. The boys were to be brought in, introduced, and ushered out.

Mrs. Johnson's great fear was the possibility that Tory, the more outspoken of her two boys, might comment rudely about the mayor's celebrated and conspicuous ears. So beforehand she explained to Tory that personal observations were impolite and cautioned against his making any comment about the mayor's ears, no matter what he might think of them.

When the moment came and the boys were brought in, Mrs. Johnson held her breath as she saw Tory's gaze fix upon the mayor's prominent feature and remain there. Nonetheless, the introduction was made without incident. The little boys came in, were introduced, bowed politely, and were sent on their way.

With a sigh of relief, Mrs. Johnson turned back to her duties as hostess and inquired of her guest, "And now, Mr. Mayor, will you have cream or lemon in your ears?"

Father, please help me to be careful about the things I say in every situation. I want my words always to glorify you. Amen.

Joy Remembered

I pray that God, the source of hope,
will fill you completely with joy and peace
because you trust in him.

ROMANS 15:13

Sunlight cascaded over the slats of wide metal blinds, landing on the faded cushions of the familiar green-flowered couch. The upright piano stood brown and solemn by the staircase. Its hinged cover, the finish worn from decades of opening and closing, concealed keys that were already uneven and yellowed when my preschool hands had played them.

Each time I visit Aunt Grace and Uncle Robert, I rejoice again that their house is unchanged from the days of my childhood. Though Aunt Grace's hair is now white and Uncle Robert has Alzheimer's, their home is still a place in which to relax and be family. And, even in difficult circumstances, it's a place to laugh.

"I have a joke for you, Kak, about a farmer and his purple pig." Uncle Robert spoke slowly, but his eyes were already smiling.

"I'm ready! A purple pig?"

Behind him, my aunt lightly smacked her hand to her forehead and rolled her eyes. We had heard that joke at least three times that afternoon. Uncle Robert delighted in describing the purple pig; we had laughed for him every time. But finally Aunt Grace tried to intervene.

"Now, Robert, you just told Kak that joke a few minutes ago," she said.

"I did?" My uncle sounded astonished.

"You did."

He looked at his hands, at the autumn sunlight in the window, and finally back to us. Then he said in his most convincing tone, "Well, maybe she forgot."

Aunt Grace and I dissolved in laughter louder than even the purple pig could evoke. Victorious, Uncle Robert joined in.

—*Kathleen Brown*

Lord, you offer your joy to us as a strength, a shield against despair, a sign of your presence and love. Remind us to expect joy, to be watchful for it everywhere and all the time. Thank you, Father. Amen.

Let Them Know!

[Jesus said,] "I tell you the truth, everyone who acknowledges me publicly here on earth, the Son of Man will also acknowledge in the presence of God's angels. But anyone who denies me here on earth will be denied before God's angels."

LUKE 12:8-9

During the American Revolution, a British unit was marching through the countryside when they came upon a ramshackle old house in the woods. Thinking it would yield little in the way of supplies or horses, they planned to just march on by to the more palatial house in the distance.

Suddenly, out of the house hobbled a little old man. As fast as his limp would allow, he shuffled toward the British army, shaking his cane above his head.

Then from the house came a young woman, running to catch up with the old man and shouting, "Grandpa! Grandpa! What are you doing? Get back here! You can't take on the whole British army alone!"

As the old man kept advancing toward the Brits, he hollered back to his granddaughter, "Well, I know that, but I can at least let them know whose side I'm on!"

Similarly, when the Pharisees and Romans came to arrest Jesus, one of the men with Jesus stepped up, pulled out his sword, and sliced off the ear of the high priest's slave in defense of Jesus.

In response, Jesus— a man of compassion and healing—said, "No more of this." And Jesus touched the injured man's ear and healed him. (Can you imagine the slave's astonishment?)

In today's world of toleration and let's-just-get-along-no-matter-what attitude, we often hesitate to stand up next to Jesus and let people know whose side we're on. Instead, when the time comes to be counted among the faithful, we tend to do a Peter act as if to say, "Who, me? I don't really know him."

Does the world know whose side you're on?

Give me courage, Lord, to stand up and be counted for you, knowing the eternal consequences are far greater than the earthly ones. Amen.

Who's Helping Whom?

Let your compassion quickly meet our needs,
for we are on the brink of despair.
Help us, O God of our salvation!

PSALM 79:8-9

When I was a kid, my family loved to watch *The Andy Griffith Show*. One of the first episodes in that series was touchingly funny.

Following the death of his wife, Sheriff Andy Taylor decided to invite his spinster aunt Bee to come and live with him and Opie, thinking that she would add the missing feminine touch. Surprisingly, Opie was not too pleased to have Aunt Bee come in and "replace" his mother.

Andy tried to help the situation by inviting Aunt Bee to go fishing and frog catching with them so that Opie could become better acquainted with her and, perhaps, become more attached to her. Instead, she failed miserably at fishing and frogging and later at football.

Finally, late one night after Opie was in bed, Aunt Bee talked Andy into taking her to the bus station because things were not working out as they had hoped.

Opie heard her crying beneath his bedroom window and guessed that she was leaving. So he ran down the stairs and out to the truck, exclaiming to Andy, "We can't let her go, Pa. She needs us. She can't even catch frogs, take fish off the hook, or throw a football. We've got to take care of her, or she'll never make it."

I wonder if Jesus said something similar to God when he looked down at us in our sin and misery. "Father, we can't just leave them to their own devices. I've got to go down there and rescue them, or they'll never make it."

It's true—we need to be rescued. And thank God he came.

Father, please let me remember that I am constantly in need of your help and I need your salvation. Without you I am nothing—pitiful, weak, and lonely. Help me, Lord. Amen.

The Sum of All Trials

We can rejoice, too, when we run into problems and trials, for we know that they help us develop endurance. And endurance develops strength of character, and character strengthens our confident hope of salvation. And this hope will not lead to disappointment. For we know how dearly God loves us.

ROMANS 5:3-5

She dragged her preteen body into the study, eyes downcast, shoulders sagging. I glanced up from my computer in time to see her collapse to her knees, throw her arms before her, and bury her face in the carpet.

Her voice escaped from under the mop of hair: "Mom, why do we have to do algebra?"

Stifling a laugh, I answered, "Because we all need something to torture us, so when it is behind us, we are thankful."

Her voice saturated with disgust, she replied, "Well, it's working."

For her it is algebra. For me it is weight loss. For a friend it is her mother's declining health. For each of us it is something bigger than ourselves, so big it drops us to our knees wondering why this and why us, asking how we will get through, but knowing whom to go to with our questions.

Right now she hates algebra, and she just wants out of the pain it causes. I understand. However, I also know she will survive.

I will survive too. I know it.

I looked at the frustrated heap in front of me and said, "Honey, your hair looks like dead Cousin Itt from *The Addams Family* TV show. It's sort of creeping me out."

Laughter bubbled forth. A smiling face popped up. A quick hug. "Thanks, Mom. I know I can always count on you to make me feel better."

And I know I can always count on my Father to make me feel better.

—Jerri Kelley

Dear Lord, thank you for trials that lead me right to you, the one I can always count on. Amen.

The Toy Store

Jesus said, "Let the children come to me. Don't stop them! For the Kingdom of Heaven belongs to those who are like these children."

MATTHEW 19:14

After several cold, rainy days, the weather was beautiful in Colorado, so Marcy decided to take her rambunctious three-year-old, Ethan, to the large shopping mall for an outing. They would shop and then have lunch in the food court, both of them enjoying getting out of the house for a change. She loaded Ethan into their SUV and drove the few blocks to the mall.

After traipsing through several stores, Ethan began to get restless, so they went to the food court for lunch. To renew his interest in shopping, Marcy said, "Hey, honey, how would you like to go to the toy store?"

"Yes! Let's go! Hurry, Mom!" And away he ran as fast as his little short legs would take him, headed in the direction of the big toy store.

To keep up with Ethan, Marcy broke into a trot, which drew the attention of other shoppers in the mall. As they approached the toy store, Marcy almost caught up with Ethan and said, teasingly, "I'm going to beat you!"

Misunderstanding, Ethan stopped dead in his tracks, faced Marcy, and screamed, "Please don't beat me, Mama! Please don't beat me! I'll be good! I promise!"

Marcy said the looks she got from the other shoppers, who had turned to stare at them, were full of shock and fear for this poor, mistreated child. They also looked surprised when she broke into laughter.

Kids! They are the delight and the scary plight of parents and grandparents alike. As my elementary-teacher friend says, "I wouldn't give a plug nickel for that kid . . . but I wouldn't trade him for a million dollars."

For the blessing of children, Father, we thank you. Help us to care for them the same way you care for us—with love and joy and tenderness. Amen.

A Warm Welcome

Cheerfully share your home with those who need a meal or a place to stay.

1 PETER 4:9

Russian history reports that when Czar Nicholas ruled Russia, he decided to test his people's hospitality to strangers. Against the advice of his family and administrators, he dressed himself in beggars' clothing and went out to the countryside. For an entire day he went from door to door, asking for food and shelter. He was refused by most and cursed at by many as they slammed their doors in his face.

Finally, as it began to get cold and dark, he knocked on the door of the humble cottage of an old peasant and his wife. The peasant was extremely poor, and his wife was ill. Still, he invited the beggar inside.

"We have little," said the peasant, "but what we have, we'll share with you."

The peasant gave the czar a small amount of warm, wholesome food. Then he prepared a sleeping mat for him on the floor near the fire, with apologies that the mat was the best he could do. They all settled down at last for the night.

When the peasant arose the next morning to prepare the remainder of the food for his family and the beggar, he found that the beggar had disappeared.

Late the next afternoon, the peasant and his wife sat on the porch of their small cottage and saw a group of soldiers coming toward them. Behind the soldiers was a beautiful carriage.

"Oh, Wife!" exclaimed the peasant. "What have I done? They must be coming to arrest me!"

The royal carriage stopped. Czar Nicholas stepped down, smiling graciously, and greeted them warmly.

Suddenly the peasants' fears turned to joy as the czar told them it had been he whom they had welcomed as a beggar. Then he showered them with rich rewards—so many, in fact, that they never had to work or worry again.

King of heaven, I welcome you into my home and into my heart. May you always feel welcome here. Amen.

Right Back at You!

Never pay back evil with more evil. Do things in such a way that everyone can see you are honorable.

ROMANS 12:17

My dear friend Paula is one of the few people I know who can really wear a hat with class and style. She can sport a wide-brimmed picture hat with the flamboyant confidence and sweet grace of the original Southern belle. She looks great and knows it. And she really doesn't care whether anybody else likes her hat or not.

Me? I feel like an idiot in a big hat. I just don't have what it takes to wear one well. I talked to Paula about it one day, and she said it's not so much about the hat itself—it's the *hattitude* with which you wear it that makes it work. And she's right!

In London, England, the famous artist Whistler was standing bareheaded in a prestigious hat shop. He was waiting patiently while the clerk of the shop was searching for the right hat in Whistler's size.

Suddenly the shop door flew open, and a short, red-faced man with a large waistline burst into the shop. Mistaking Whistler for the shop clerk, he exploded, "See here, you. This hat does *not* fit!"

Whistler, not at all flustered by the rude man, casually eyed him from head to foot. Then he drawled out, "Well, frankly, sir, neither does your coat. What's more, if you'll pardon my saying so, I'll be hanged if I care much for the color of your trousers."

The temptation to respond in kind to rude people is strong, isn't it? At times we really like the old "eye for an eye" rule. And yet, Jesus taught us to turn the other cheek and not repay evil for evil. He called us to respond in unnatural ways—to show the world what honor looks like.

Thank you, Lord, for your example of how to treat other people, even the rude ones whom we encounter. May we always respond with honor and love. Amen.

October 15

Mission: Possible

Work willingly at whatever you do, as
though you were working for the Lord. . . .
The Master you are serving is Christ.

COLOSSIANS 3:23-24

I stared in amusement at the photo of my twenty-year-old son carrying groceries up the stairs in a ghetto-like apartment complex. His face was beaming as if he were on a ride at Six Flags rather than carrying out a chore for a missionary.

I thought of the times I had asked him to run to the store to pick up something for me. I do not recall seeing that roller-coaster grin on his face then. I usually got some lackluster response, such as, "Why can't Laura do it?"

My husband, Mark, reminded me that John was on a mission for God in the Dominican Republic, so every task, no matter how mundane, became significant and meaningful. I figured that getting work out of my family meant I needed to frame it in the context of their being on a mission for God, and since I was painting my daughter's bedroom, I suggested to Mark that God might be calling him to help me paint. He laughed loudly, but then he picked up a roller and dipped it into the paint.

How often has God asked me to serve him, and I have asked why someone else couldn't do it or ended up doing the job reluctantly with a less-than-cheerful attitude? Do I do my chores heartily as if I were working at God's house?

Regardless of whether we are on a mission trip in a faraway land or we're here at home, the work we do to help others is work we do for Christ. Ultimately he is the one we serve.

—Paula Hemingway

Dear God, help me to serve you with all my heart, regardless of the task or where I am. Amen.

Taking the Elevator

Peter [said], "I see very clearly that God shows no favoritism."

ACTS 10:34

Through the years, I have been privileged to know some prominent people. Most of them are kind, humble people who just happened to be blessed with great wealth or fame. Rarely do they play the look-who-I-am card to gain special attention or garner favors.

For instance, I recently attended the Byron Nelson Championship golf tournament in Dallas with Mrs. Byron Nelson. She could have played her celebrity card, sat in her honorary private box, been waited on hand and foot, and watched the tournament from the eighteenth green. Instead, she wore a volunteer uniform, packed lunches, and served the golfers in the heat. She's the real deal, as was her husband.

The great violinist Jascha Heifetz once arrived in great haste at Radio City in New York, perilously close to being late for a radio concert with the NBC Symphony Orchestra. He hastened into the elevator carrying his violin in its case.

The elevator operator looked at Heifetz's violin case and said, "You'll have to go in the freight elevator with that."

"I have no time," said Heifetz. "I'm in a hurry."

"I don't care," said the operator. "All musicians with instruments have to ride the freight elevator. That's the rule."

Exasperated, Heifetz played what he thought was his trump card: "But I'm Jascha Heifetz."

And the operator looked him up and down and replied without blinking, "I don't care if you're Rubinoff; you have to ride in the freight elevator."

Like the elevator operator, God does not show favoritism. He says Jesus is the way to come to him. You can't travel there by some other route. No matter who you are, if you want to spend eternity with him, you have to follow the one and only way.

Help me, Lord, to follow the Way to heaven. I want to be humble enough to do what you have asked me to do. Amen.

Radiant Beauty

Let all that I am praise the Lord;
may I never forget the good things he does for me. . . .
He redeems me from death
and crowns me with love and tender mercies.
He fills my life with good things.
My youth is renewed like the eagle's!

PSALM 103:2, 4-5

I was a young high school English teacher desperate to gain all the wisdom I could in order to survive the school year. Because of this, I gravitated toward older women who worked at my school, knowing I badly needed the insight, counsel, and wisdom they could offer from their years of experience.

I approached Sandy shortly after I met her. She was new to town, and I overheard her saying she used to meet with a teacher from her former school to walk and pray each morning. *That's it!* I thought. I asked her if we could walk and pray together, which she readily agreed to do.

Sandy was in her midfifties, but she was one of the most radiant women I had ever seen. Not only was she beautiful, but she reached out to students and faculty in a fearless, unself-conscious way. After walking our laps in the gym and praying one morning, I asked her, "How did you get to be so radiant? You look like a woman in her thirties instead of her fifties!"

Sandy's face looked thoughtful as she answered, "Well, I had a difficult childhood and a wild young adulthood. When I became a Christian as a grown woman, I asked God to restore the years of my youth. He did!" She tilted back her head and laughed her short, bubbly laugh.

Then she paused and looked at me, saying with a mischievous grin, "And always drink eight glasses of water a day!"

—Erin Hobbie

Lord, thank you for having the power and compassion to restore our youth. Help us to learn to be radiant people who reflect your glory. Amen.

Who Is the King?

At just the right time Christ will be revealed from heaven by the blessed and only almighty God, the King of all kings and Lord of all lords.

1 TIMOTHY 6:15

The lion was exceedingly proud of his mastery of the animal kingdom. One day he decided to make sure all the other animals knew he was the king of the jungle. He was so confident that he bypassed the smaller animals and went straight to the powerful bear.

"Who is the king of the jungle?" the lion asked.

The bear replied, "Why, you are, of course."

Next the lion asked the dangerous Bengal tiger, "Who is the king of the jungle?"

The tiger quickly responded, "Everyone knows that you are, mighty lion."

Next on the list was the massive elephant. The lion faced the elephant and addressed him with this question: "Who is the king of the jungle?"

The elephant immediately grabbed the lion with his trunk, whirled him around in the air five or six times, and slammed him into a tree. Then he pounded him on the ground several times, dunked him under water in a nearby lake, and finally dropped him out on the shore.

The lion—beaten, bruised, and battered—struggled wearily to his feet. He looked at the elephant through sad and bloodshot eyes and said, "Look, just because you don't know the answer is no reason for you to get mean about it!"

Sadly in today's world, when asked who the King is, many people do not know the right answer. Some would say it is Elvis, some would say the president, and some would not even have a guess. They just don't have a clue.

The day will come, though, when the King will return, and everyone on the earth, above the earth, and below the earth will acknowledge that Jesus Christ is King. Hallelujah!

Come soon, Lord Jesus! And take us with you to your home in heaven, where we will be allowed to worship you for all eternity. What a glorious day that will be! Amen.

Trained to Hear God's Voice

The Holy Spirit says,
"Today when you hear his voice,
don't harden your hearts."

HEBREWS 3:7-8

Someone with a hard heart is often full of pride and unable to listen to anyone else. This statement, however, does not describe my dog. Nappy (short for "Napoleon") is a pretty smart fellow, and he is a good listener, too. He has been trained to understand the meaning of many different words in the English language. When he hears *snack*, *walk*, *bone*, *ride in the car*, or *bun-bun* (bunny), he stops whatever he is doing, looks around, and listens intently.

While I was eating my lunch in the cafeteria at work one day, I was suddenly overcome with a bout of hiccups. Nothing seemed to get rid of them until my friend Mary leaned across the table and asked me, "When was the last time you saw a white horse?"

I stopped and thought for a moment, then gave her my answer. Sure enough, my hiccups were gone!

Not too long after that, Nappy sat next to me on the couch. His soft ears were bent back, his head leaned forward, and two sad eyes pleaded for help as his little body convulsed with hiccups.

"Nappy," I said in an authoritative voice, "when was the last time you saw a bun-bun?"

He turned to face me, staring hard and not moving a muscle as he listened. His hiccups were cured!

In the same way, life is full of hiccups. Bumps in the road. Detours. If we listen carefully to the voice of our Father when we are having some kind of problem or facing a difficulty, he can guide us to find a cure for our troubles.

—Gloria J. Wallace

Father God, thank you for the many times you speak to us. I pray that you would train our hearts to soften and our ears to hear as you lovingly direct our steps. Amen.

I Owed a Debt

God showed his great love for us by sending Christ to die for us while we were still sinners.

ROMANS 5:8

Film producer Gabriel Pascal once acquired the film rights to George Bernard Shaw's plays—a gold mine of entertainment material that practically every producer in Hollywood had tried to buy at one time or another. But the way it happened is utterly implausible.

In 1935, after spending six months in Hollywood doing practically nothing, Pascal, who had made one successful picture in England and a succession of film shorts, left in disgust. Once he arrived in London, out of a clear blue sky he called on Mr. Shaw, whom he had never met, saying he wanted to produce his plays on film.

When Mr. Shaw asked Pascal how much capital he had to do it with, Pascal replied, "Fifteen shillings and sixpence . . . but I owe a pound."

Delighted as much with Pascal's brashness as with his obvious admiration for Shaw's work, Mr. Shaw gave him a pound to pay his debts, and then he agreed to the film experiment. The result was the very successful *Pygmalion*, which has become a well-loved classic.

In comparison, the mountain of spiritual debt I owed was incomprehensible! It was a debt I could never pay, no matter how I tried. It had me completely overwhelmed and buried alive. And then I discovered that Jesus had paid the debt for me—dying in my place on the cross—and nothing has ever been the same for me again.

So it is for all people who give their debts of sin to him to bear on their behalf. Have you given him your debt to pay? If not, do yourself a favor by releasing your burden to him to carry. It will change your life forever!

For your sweet forgiveness of my enormous debt, Father, I bow in humble gratitude. Thank you for taking away my sins and giving me grace in place of my debt. Amen.

October 21

Broke but Blessed

Weeping may last through the night,
but joy comes with the morning.

PSALM 30:5

Early in my freelance career, work was scarce, and I was scraping by financially. I subsisted on popcorn, potatoes, and eggs—the least expensive and most filling foods I could find. And yet, I still believed that I was doing what God had called me to do.

One morning I went to the mailbox and found a small refund check for an overpayment I'd made to an insurance company. The check was for $13.60. Even that small amount was a welcome sight in those lean days. Since I was supposed to meet a potential client for lunch, I cashed the check and hoped the money would be enough. When the bill came for my lunch, including the tip it came to $13.40. *Whew! Thank you, God.* I could imagine his smiling and saying, "When will you learn to trust me?"

The day before, I had received an e-mail from my Weight Watchers coach asking me to please bring a few of my children's books to the next day's meeting. She wanted to buy some as a shower gift. So I did, and she paid me $45.00 for the books—in cash. I tucked it into my pocket with gratitude.

When I got into my car to head home, I remembered that I needed gasoline—my car was running on fumes. So I drove to the nearest economy gas station and filled up. It cost $42.50. I looked up at heaven and said, "Thank you, Father!" (*Did I hear him laugh?*)

Before going home, I stopped to buy some eggs and potatoes. The total came to $2.60. I had a whole dime left over!

This time, *I* laughed! Through the years, I've learned that only God has twenty-twenty *foresight*, and I've often thought that his humorous solutions to my life struggles were laughable in my limited *hindsight*.

Gracious Father, please forgive me for not trusting you. Thank you for your constant care and provision. I love you, Lord. Amen.

The Lord's Prayer

Our Father in heaven,
may your name be kept holy.
May your Kingdom come soon.
May your will be done on earth,
as it is in heaven.

MATTHEW 6:9-10

One day Bobby and Tony—missionary kids in New Zealand—were walking down Tinakori Road in Wellington. Always doing the one-upmanship routine, Bobby and Tony challenged each other at every point in their friendship, usually teasing.

Tony tagged Bobby on the shoulder with a friendly punch and said, "Hey, Bobby, I'll bet I know more Bible verses than you do."

"No way!" replied Bobby, shoving Tony back easily.

"Man, I'll bet you can't even recite the Lord's Prayer," teased Tony.

"What's that got to do with anything?"

"I just bet you don't know the Lord's Prayer."

"Of course I do: 'Now I lay me down to sleep, I pray the Lord my soul to keep. If I should die before I wake, I pray the Lord my soul to take.'"

"Oh! Well, I apologize. I didn't think you knew it."

My preacher dad used to say that the prayer in Matthew 6 was not really the Lord's *personal* prayer. Instead, this was the Lord's *example* prayer. It was the pattern he gave us to follow as we learn to pray on our own.

The Lord's real *personal* prayer is in John 17—his plea to God for his followers to "be one, just as you and I are one" (verse 21). The Lord prayed for unity among his believers so that the world would know who he really was. By unity his disciples present a solid front against Satan and his angels. Without that unity, so much is lost.

It seems to me that we've done a great job of memorizing the Lord's example prayer and repeating it. There's nothing wrong with that. My question is whether we have learned the prayer of his heart—his desire for unity. What do you think?

Father, I pray that we will all be one, just as you and Jesus are one, so that the world will believe and be saved. Amen.

Waging War

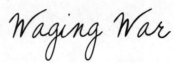

If God is for us, who can ever be against us?

ROMANS 8:31

I recently waged war against one of my toughest opponents—a megaweed! My opponent stood three feet tall, with thorns like fangs. As I dug around the base to loosen the roots, the weed stood with its leaves crossed, unwilling to budge. I became convinced this weed was attached to the gates of hell.

Once I realized the digging was getting me nowhere, I dropped the shovel, blew the hair out of my eyes, and used a new strategy—pull like crazy! I put all my best moves on that weed as I imagined it saying, "Is that all you've got?" Our game of tug-of-war seemed to last forever.

After twisting and pulling, prying and straining, I found myself losing traction and landing flat on my bottom with a thump. I could practically hear the mega weed and all its little weed friends laughing at me.

I sat for a moment, not sure what felt worse—my sore body or my broken spirit. I cried out to God, "Lord, can you please help me here? I can't do this on my own." A few minutes later, I felt a renewed energy and restored confidence. I was taking this weed down! I repeatedly thrust my shovel as hard as I could deep into the soil until all the roots were uncovered. I pretended the weed gave a defeated cry as I grabbed its tangled roots and pulled it out of the ground. There I stood, holding the weed over my head in triumph as I let out a victory yell.

No battle is too large or too small for God to help us.

—Jennifer Mersberger

Heavenly Father, thank you for hearing me when I cry out to you. Please help me to remember that you're on my side and can equip me for any battle I face. Thank you for the victory you have already claimed for me. Amen.

Room for One More

[Jesus said,] "Hypocrites! . . . Outwardly you look like righteous people, but inwardly your hearts are filled with hypocrisy and lawlessness."

MATTHEW 23:27-28

Jesus encountered hypocrites at every turn during his life and ministry. The religious leaders tried to trick him, spoke lies about him, and plotted against him. He knew what they were doing, and he did not hesitate to call them out, shouting, "You snakes! You hypocrites!" That was, obviously, not a very popular thing to say, and it eventually contributed to his being murdered by his enemies.

Hypocrites also populate the church, because the church was established for sinners, not perfect people. And every kind of sinner is invited to bring his or her knapsack of offenses to the fellowship of sinners. In truth, at one point or another in our lives, each of us is a hypocrite about something. As Pogo the cartoon character says, "We have met the enemy, and it is us!"

A great lord was once patronizing the bishop of Hereford and speaking to him with astonishing insolence.

"I never go to church," boasted the lord. "Perhaps you have noticed that, Bishop?"

"Yes, I have noticed it," answered the bishop gravely. "And would you tell me why that is true?"

"Well, the reason I do not go to church is that there are so many hypocrites there."

Smiling blandly, the bishop said, "Oh, don't let that keep you away. There is always room for one more."

Ah, now there's the rub—the lord's accusation fits each of us, which effectively eliminates the excuse entirely. As my dad used to say, "If you stay away from church because there are hypocrites there, the hypocrites are closer to God than you are."

Merciful God, please forgive me for my hypocritical attitudes and ways. I want to be pure hearted and holy, but I know that's possible only with your help. So I come to you now in repentance and praise, asking for your help. Amen.

Batting a Thousand

[Jesus announced,] "The Kingdom of God is near! Repent of your sins and believe the Good News!"

MARK 1:15

George Foster went to the local practice field. As a Little League coach, he knew it was important to keep his own skills sharp so he could do a good job of teaching the young boys the right way to do things.

Walking into one of the batting cages, George noticed a little boy in the cage next to his. As George donned his batting gloves, he heard the boy talking to himself.

"I'm the greatest hitter in the world." He tossed the ball into the air, swung, and missed. "Strike one!"

Undaunted, the boy picked up the ball, threw it into the air, and said, "I'm the greatest baseball hitter ever" as he swung at the ball again. And again he missed. "Strike two!"

The young batter paused a moment to examine his bat and ball carefully. Then a third time he threw the ball into the air. "I'm the greatest hitter who ever lived," he said. He swung the bat hard again and missed a third time. Then he cried out, "Wow! Strike three—what a pitcher! I'm the greatest pitcher in the world!"

George turned to the boy and said, "Hey, kid, how would you like to be on my team?"

Belief! That is the key to so many good things in life.

The Bible says, "God loved the world so much that he gave his one and only Son, so that everyone who *believes* in him will not perish but have eternal life" (John 3:16, emphasis mine). It is not because we can *prove* that Jesus is God's Son. It is not because we can *demonstrate* that he is God's Son. It is because we *believe* it. Have faith in it. Trust it.

When you believe in the one who can save you, you're batting a thousand, spiritually speaking.

Father, I believe that Jesus Christ is your Son, and I put my faith in him to lead me to you. Help my unbelief. Amen.

The Red Sea

What are you waiting for? Get up and be baptized. Have your sins washed away.

ACTS 22:16

William Hogarth was a famous English painter and engraver. In fact, he was one of the leading British artists of the first half of the eighteenth century.

Once a miserly, old English nobleman wanted Hogarth to paint on his staircase a picture of the destruction of Pharaoh's hosts in the Red Sea when in pursuit of Moses and the Israelites. He did so much haggling over the price that Hogarth finally agreed to do the work for about half of what it was really worth.

After two days' work, to the great surprise of the nobleman, Hogarth announced that the painting was ready. When the curtain was removed, there was nothing to be seen but the stairway painted red all over.

"What have you here?" cried the miser. "I ordered a scene of the Red Sea!"

"The Red Sea you have," replied the artist, indicating the red expanse before them.

"But where are the Israelites?" questioned the nobleman.

"They have all gone over to the other side."

"And where are the Egyptians?"

"They have all drowned."

The financial adage says, "You get what you pay for"—a truism in all arenas of life except one. When it comes to salvation, we do not pay for it at all. Instead, we get what *Jesus* paid for—our spiritual freedom. It comes to us as a free gift from the Father of love.

We often have a difficult time accepting this marvelous gift because our Puritan work ethic says we have to work for everything we receive. But we cannot work to earn God's grace. It's not for sale. It's not for barter. It's free.

Just as the Red Sea washed away Pharaoh's army, God's grace washes away the dirt of our sins, making us new creatures, clean and safe for all eternity.

For washing away our sins, dear Lord, we praise and thank you with all our hearts. We love you, Father. Amen.

Good Night, Violet

God is light, and there is no darkness in him at all.

1 JOHN 1:5

One summer I spent several weeks as a cook at Green Valley Bible Camp, just outside Rogers, Arkansas. The sweet lady in charge of the kitchen was named Violet, and one of the young women who helped in the kitchen was named Charlene.

At night Charlene and I shared a cabin up on the side of the hill. When it's dark in the valleys of Arkansas, it's nearly pitch black—unless there's a bit of light from the moon. Our beds were flat on the floor, but fortunately, someone had attached a long piece of twine to the chain attached to the light so we could reach it after we had gotten into bed.

One night Charlene began talking and walking in her sleep. I awoke to see her headed for the door, saying, "Push him in the hole, George! Push him in the hole!"

It took me a few moments to realize what was going on, but then I lay quietly, listening to find out if she was going to settle back down. She didn't.

"I see him coming, George," she whispered desperately, looking out the door. "When he gets here, push him in the hole! He's going to kill me, George. Quick, push him in the hole!"

I thought, *This has gone on long enough.* So I pulled the light string, illuminating the cabin. Then I called, "Charlene! Wake up!"

She did not wake up, so I said again, "Charlene! Wake up!"

She shuddered slightly and turned to look at me as if she were a deer caught in the headlights. "What is it? What's wrong?"

"You were talking and walking in your sleep. I got a little nervous. Are you awake now?"

"Yes, I'm fine. Thanks."

"Okay, then let's go back to sleep."

She nodded, sat down on her bed, reached over and took the light string, turned off the light, and said, "Good night, Violet!"

Hmm.

Father, thank you for always being there for me. Even when it's dark and I'm frightened, I know I can count on you to light my way. Amen.

Have You Heard?

We were not making up clever stories when we told you about the powerful coming of our Lord Jesus Christ. We saw his majestic splendor with our own eyes when he received honor and glory from God the Father.

2 PETER 1:16-17

Once upon a time there was a great storyteller named Mark Twain. One day he was talking about storytellers who persistently interrupt themselves to ask their listeners if they have already heard the story they are telling. Twain, being critical of those people, told of an encounter he had with the actor Henry Irving.

The actor asked Twain if he had heard a certain story.

"No," replied Twain politely.

Irving proceeded with the story, but after a bit once again made the same inquiry: "Have you heard this story before?"

"No, I haven't," said Twain a little more emphatically.

Proceeding almost to the climax of his story, Irving again stopped to ask if Twain had heard the story previously.

Irked by this poor habit of Irving's, Twain finally said, "I can lie once, I can lie twice for courtesy's sake, but I draw the line there. I can't lie the third time at any price. I not only *heard* the story, I *invented* it!"

Some people claim that the stories told about Jesus are fictional, made-up stories. Yet the people who told them proclaim that they were not "making up clever stories" when they related the tales about him because they "saw his majestic splendor" with their own eyes. They were, in fact, eyewitnesses—the most powerful kind of testimony used in a court of law today.

So you can be confident in telling the story of Jesus, knowing that the facts are true, the Man was real, and the God of heaven backs you up.

Father God, we love to tell the story of you and your Son. Please give us the courage to tell it to everyone we know so they, too, can find your grace and salvation. Amen.

American Hamburgers

I try to find common ground with everyone, doing everything I can to save some.

1 CORINTHIANS 9:22

In 1981 my husband and I were missionaries in New Zealand. There are many things I loved about New Zealand, but after three or four months of eating lamb chops and fish, I was positively desperate for an honest-to-goodness, Texas-style hamburger.

They had a McDonald's in Wellington, but the beef tasted a little different, and combined with their favorite kiwi juice, their burgers just didn't satisfy my craving.

One day my friend Lydell, another American, and I spied a sign in a small restaurant window that said, "Real American Hamburgers." I almost flipped the car over wheeling into the parking lot, and we both jumped out of the car and practically ran into the restaurant.

We ordered two American hamburgers, fries, and Cokes and sat salivating while we waited impatiently for them to be brought to us. Finally they came.

I sat up straighter, put my "serviette" (napkin in New Zealand) in my lap, and smiled at the waitress as she put the plates in front of us. Then she set down our Cokes, saying "There you go, love," and walked away.

We looked down with anticipation at the hamburgers and were completely dismayed. Their "hamburgers" were two slices of white sandwich bread with thin ketchup, limp lettuce, a soggy tomato, and shaved ham. And the Cokes, in typical New Zealand fashion, had one ice cube for the whole glass.

Lydell and I looked at each other, looked back at the *unburgers*, looked back at each other, and burst into laughter. We took one sip of the warm Coke, paid the bill, and walked out without taking even one bite. The waitress was a little surprised when I said, "Love, you've got a lot to learn about American hamburgers."

Those wimpy sandwiches were downright un-American! Dell and I drove straight to McDonald's.

Thank you, Father, for missionaries who are willing to give up their homes and preferences in order to touch the hearts of those who are lost. Amen.

Which Came First?

In the beginning God created the heavens and the earth. . . . God said, . . . "Let the skies be filled with birds of every kind."

GENESIS 1:1, 20

Which came first—the chicken or the egg? How many times have you heard that discussed through the years? Seemingly, though, no one can come to any conclusion.

Recently a story appeared in London's *Daily Express* with the title "The Chicken Came Before the Egg, Researchers Discover." The story noted that researchers at the University of Sheffield and the University of Warwick had actually found that a protein called ovocleidin-17 (OC17), produced in a pregnant hen's ovaries, is crucial to the formation of eggshells. From this discovery they concluded that the chicken had to have come first. The statement that made me giggle, though, was, "However, the research does not come up with how the protein-producing chicken existed in the first place." I can just hear God saying, "Gotcha!"

I am convinced that God allows "great scientists" to discover what they consider new facts and findings, which consistently verify what the Bible has said all along. And it seems the further we get from Creation and Bible times, the more dramatic the findings are.

For instance, a few years ago archaeologists unearthed a great ancient library. And while we sometimes think people in those times were not as well educated as we are, that library contained more than ten thousand volumes in seven different languages.

One day I believe those persistent explorers of the Mountains of Ararat in Turkey will actually find Noah's Ark. When they do, I wonder how the scientists will explain it away?

The Bible says, "God created the heavens and the earth." Since that's true, it seems to me that he would be able to write an accurate book about it. Perhaps the scientists should just learn to read. You think?

Almighty Creator, we bow before you, knowing that you are our Maker and Lord. We worship you and praise your great majesty. There is no other god like you. Amen.

God's Left Hand

I have placed my rainbow in the clouds.
It is the sign of my covenant with you.

GENESIS 9:13

When my niece Dawn was five years old, I was staying with her while my sister was away for a few hours. We were playing games, eating snacks, and having fun.

Suddenly a huge thunderstorm rumbled into town. Dawn and I snuggled together on the sofa, listening to the crashing thunder and watching brilliant lightning flashes.

After almost an hour the storm finally stopped, and we headed to the kitchen for an ice cream sundae as a reward for surviving the storm. As I walked into the breakfast nook, I saw a magnificent rainbow through the big bay window. The entire rainbow, from end to end, was visible in all its glory.

"Hey, Dawn," I called, "come and look at this!"

"Wow! It's so pretty," she said with feeling.

"Dawn, do you know the story of the rainbow in the Bible?"

"Well, of course!" she said indignantly.

"Would you tell it to me? I think I've forgotten some of it."

"Well, one time God got really mad at everybody on earth. So he decided to make a flood. The only people he wasn't mad at were Noah and his family. So God told Noah to build a big boat and put all the animals on it. (I don't know how they did that part.) Anyway, it rained and rained, and the big boat floated around. Then it finally stopped raining, and God was sorry he had gotten so mad. Then with his left hand he drew a big rainbow in the sky and promised he'd never do it again."

"Yes, now I remember. But why do you think God used his *left* hand to draw the rainbow?"

"Well, don't you remember that the Bible says Jesus was *sitting* on God's *right* hand?"

—Foy O. Jackson

Father, thank you for reminding us that you love us. Thank you for saving us and for keeping us safe. Amen.

Follow My Example

[Paul said,] "You should imitate me,
just as I imitate Christ."

1 CORINTHIANS 11:1

My three-year-old son adores his older sisters, and he loves to mimic everything they do—often to the chagrin of his father, who doesn't enjoy seeing his only son rocking out to Hannah Montana or sporting watermelon lip gloss.

Sometimes the youngster's antics are hilarious, and other times they get him in lots of trouble.

Take, for instance, the time our oldest daughter rolled her eyes in disgust at the dinner table. We strongly reprimanded her and informed her that eye rolling was unacceptable in our home.

I didn't realize how closely our son had observed that interaction until the next day, when I gave him an afternoon snack. As I handed him one of his favorite treats—vanilla yogurt with M&M'S—he squealed in delight.

"Thank you, Mom!" he said gleefully, followed by a dramatic sigh and a big eye roll.

Trying to keep a straight face, I explained to him that, first of all, eye rolling is not permitted in our home—and second, if he was going to roll his eyes, at least he should learn *when* to do it.

At his young age, our son had no idea what eye rolling was all about. He just saw his sister do it, so he wanted to try it too.

Though his mistake gave me a hearty laugh, it was a good reminder of how closely our children are watching us and following our examples. As we go about our day-to-day lives, are we setting a Christlike example for our children, our families, and those around us?

—Jennifer Stair

Father, help me to remember that others are watching me and imitating what I do. Teach me to follow your example and reflect your love to everyone around me. Amen.

Hand over Hand

[Jesus said,] "You are so careful to clean the outside of the cup and the dish, but inside you are filthy."

MATTHEW 23:25

The story is told that when the great orator Daniel Webster was a boy, he was not noted for tidiness. His teachers were constantly after him to straighten up his desk, tuck in his shirt, wash his face and hands, and attend to other personal hygiene tasks. Daniel, however, was not the least bit concerned about these mundane things, so the teachers' admonishments often went unheeded.

One day the teacher told him that if he appeared again with such dirty hands she would thrash him. Although Daniel had a momentary look of repentance, he did, indeed, appear in the same condition again the next day.

"Daniel," said the teacher, "hold out your hand."

Daniel spit on his hand, rubbed it on his pants, and held it out. As usual, it was filthy.

"Daniel," the teacher said, "if you can find me another hand in this school that is dirtier than that one, I will let you off."

Grinning, Daniel promptly held out his other hand.

When Jesus faced the Pharisees, he did not see dirty hands and faces. He saw dirty hearts. And he did not hold back from telling them so: "You are like whitewashed tombs—beautiful on the outside but filled on the inside with dead people's bones and all sorts of impurity" (Matthew 23:27).

Little boys are hardly concerned about dirty hands and faces, but often their hearts are clean as they bring Mom a bouquet of fresh-picked flowers from the garden.

Religious "children," however, are concerned about *looking clean* while hiding the impurity in their hearts. Dirty hearts win the unacceptable award over dirty hands every time.

Purify my heart, Lord, and make me clean in your sight. Amen.

My Weekend Barbecue

Topheth—the place of burning—
has long been ready for the Assyrian king;
the pyre is piled high with wood.
The breath of the Lord, like fire from a volcano,
will set it ablaze.

ISAIAH 30:33

My mouth watered at the thought of the prime rib. In an hour it would be cooked perfectly—done enough to keep it from mooing but still retaining the natural juices of the fat. I held the sixteen-ouncer up to eye level and examined it. The marbling glistened in the sunshine. *Mmm. Poetry in meat. The smell of cooked steak ought to be recognized as the official state flower*, I thought.

I took mental inventory. *Do I have enough charcoal? Yes. Lighter fluid? Yes. Just one more squirt to help the charcoal light evenly.*

Ignoring the vapors that were blurring my view of the neighbor kids' swing set, I struck the match. There was a huge flash, like ten thousand suns shining in my hand, and then my vision blurred even more. I felt a slight push against my face and chest.

I could smell something cooking, but it was definitely *not* the prime rib.

You can call the explosion a vision, maybe a warning, but the words of Isaiah 30:33 came instantly to mind. It took a couple of seconds for me to realize that the buzzing noise I heard was the sound of smoke detectors coming from inside the house.

After the emergency medical technicians left, the investigating fire marshal told me, "Next time, use less lighter fluid, and wait thirty seconds to let the fumes exhaust before striking the match."

"Thanks," I said, "but I'm buying a smoker. Electric."

—*Al Speegle Jr.*

Father God, sometimes we fail to see what's right in front of us. Help us not to be so blind and to pay closer attention to the people and events around us. Give us wisdom for our daily living. Amen.

November 4

Booming Voice

When [John] saw many Pharisees and Sadducees coming to watch him baptize, he denounced them. "You brood of snakes!" he exclaimed. "Who warned you to flee God's coming wrath?"

MATTHEW 3:7

Many pastors get really fired up when delivering a powerful sermon. They use dramatic gestures and pace back and forth as they preach. The pitch and volume of their voices rise to match the urgency of their message.

Speaking loudly is a good way to wake up a sleepy congregation—it makes nodding off a lot more difficult. If the women in the congregation are thinking about the noon meal, the pastor's booming voice calls their focus back to the spoken Word.

Our small congregation is made up mostly of elderly folks, but occasionally young children also attend, even though a nursery is available for those who wish to make use of it. Parents or grandparents typically care for the little visitors when small children come to "big church"—they snuggle up in a lap, look at books, or draw pictures. It is a good church-learning experience. All ages are welcome in our worship services. And if children become rambunctious, the pastor just speaks a little louder.

On one particular Sunday morning, Brother Joe got very excited about his message, and he nearly raised the roof. When three-year-old Malakai heard the pastor's booming voice, he raised his own and boomed out, "Is he mad?"

I don't really remember the morning message that day, but I will never forget the logical response of Malakai.

Those listening to John the Baptist might have reacted the same way. His unorthodox clothes, eating habits, and bold words made people sit up and listen—no snoozing when John spoke. His message about Jesus was too important.

—*Pam Ford Davis*

Heavenly Father, help me to remember the urgency of your message. I want to listen with attentive ears and a receptive heart. Amen.

These Shoes Weren't Made for Walking

*A cheerful heart is good medicine,
but a broken spirit saps a person's strength.*

PROVERBS 17:22

I was at the mall, helping my son buy a winter jacket. I had just finished drinking a twenty-ounce coffee, so I was energized and ready to hunt for bargains. We had been shopping for more than an hour when my legs and lower back started bothering me. I tried to ignore the discomfort as I walked, because shopping often helps a woman overcome her sensitivity to pain. Right?

After purchasing the jacket, we headed back to the car. I just happened to look down at my feet. To my complete embarrassment, I saw that I was wearing two different shoes. I quickly glanced around to make sure nobody was watching me. Then I started to laugh. No wonder my lower back was bothering me—one shoe had a much higher heel than the other. I sounded like a Clydesdale. I guess that is what happens when you get dressed in too great a rush. I had worn two different-colored socks before, but never two different shoes!

Can you believe the humorous things we do in our everyday lives? When today's verse talks about a cheerful heart being "good medicine," that's not just an interesting metaphor. Research has proved that our bodies release calming endorphins when we laugh, so laughter is actually good for our health. Our funny situations are too. The next time you find yourself in an embarrassing situation, stay cheerful and try to laugh. I suspect that God will be smiling with you.

—Lisa M. Garvey

God, help us to be able to laugh at ourselves more and be less uptight over things that likely don't matter much in the grand scheme of things. We want to show your joy to the world around us. Amen.

Crackerjack

[Adam] gave names to all the livestock, all the birds of the sky, and all the wild animals.

GENESIS 2:20

One of the most interesting pets I ever had was a conure parrot named Crackerjack. He was beautiful, with bright green feathers, a brilliant orange comb, and sunny yellow on his chest and underwings. He had snapping black eyes and loved to talk in his gravelly voice. If you asked, "What's your name?" he replied, "Crackerjack! I'm a crackerjack!"

One evening we had dinner guests. Crackerjack was jabbering in his normal happy manner. Our guests had not been to our house before, so they were unfamiliar with Crackerjack's wide vocabulary and repertoire of tricks. We were enjoying our dessert when I heard a siren in the distance. I thought, *Hmm. This should be interesting.*

As the siren came closer and closer, Crackerjack started his favorite routine. In his cage were a number of toys, which parrots—known as "clown birds"—love, including perches, a mirror, a ladder, and a bell.

He began to run back and forth in his cage, squawking, "Help! Help!" Then he swung wildly from perch to perch screaming, "Here it comes! Here it comes!" Then he bobbed his head up and down while moaning, "Oh no, oh no, oh noooo."

By that time our guests were looking around to see what the crazy bird was doing. Knowing what was coming next, we were struggling to keep straight faces.

Finally, as the siren went screaming past our house, Crackerjack ran up and down his ladder yelling, "Fire! Fire!" and ringing his bell. "Fire! Fire!" *Ding. Ding. Ding.*

Now our guests were cracking up, we were dying with laughter, and Crackerjack was exhausted.

"How did you ever teach him to do all that?" asked one of the guests.

"We didn't," I replied solemnly. "He really thinks he's a fireman."

Thank you, God, for the joy that your creatures give us every day. They are so special to us, as you knew they would be. Help us to be good caretakers. Amen.

Joy Thread

I have told you these things so that you will be filled with my joy. Yes, your joy will overflow!

JOHN 15:11

The year my Grammy Nokie turned one hundred years old, I wrote a book of her memories. Amazingly, I found several similarities between us. Core values, faith, and a thread of joyous humor woven throughout tied us together like quilting stitches. It was clear that my life stories echoed hers.

Grammy came from a large family but was particularly connected to her younger sister, Giva. Often they were a duet of mischief. Once, their mother sent them into the woods to collect berries. Not long into the picking, they heard a bloodcurdling scream that sent them charging back to the house. As they ran, they held onto each other by their button skirts and sailor collars. When they came to the fence, they stopped, breathing hard. Their skirts were down to their ankles, and their blouses were completely disheveled.

It was a perfect opportunity for my Grammy. With wide eyes she gasped, "Oh, Giva, your hair has turned white as snow!"

Eyes full of fear, Giva grabbed one of her braids to look—and Nokie laughingly scooted under the fence ahead of her.

Later when they told their mother of their fright, she shrugged. "It couldn't have been that bad, 'cause it didn't scare the mischief out of Nokie."

Fifty years later, my mother turned to my sister and said nearly the same words about me. It seems that even a joyous confidence that comes from being in Christ was passed down from one generation to the next.

Joy is definitely contagious. Do your friends and family a huge favor—infect them with it!

—*Sandy Lackey Wright*

Father, I thank you so much for the thread of playfulness that runs through my family. I know that the joy and fun are gifts from you. Please help me to let that joy become a way for me to share you with others. Amen.

November 8

Unnecessary Fuss

Don't think you are better than you really are.
Be honest in your evaluation of yourselves.

ROMANS 12:3

Several months after President Calvin Coolidge died, Mrs. Coolidge decided to take a trip abroad to get away and see some different sights. However, she feared that there might be an unnecessary fuss made over the wife of a former American president as she traveled from place to place.

The friend with whom she would be traveling said, "Don't worry. In the little places where we'll be stopping, they don't know one president of the United States from another. People won't bother you. I've done a lot of traveling, so trust me."

"All right, if you're absolutely sure," said Mrs. Coolidge hesitantly. "I just hope the press leaves us alone."

And so they began their journey, looking forward to the quaint villages and shops they would be visiting. To Mrs. Coolidge's delight, and just as the friend had said, no one bothered them until they reached a small Italian town and received word that reservations had been made for them in the next town. This sounded ominous, but they decided to proceed with their itinerary anyway. It was, after all, a small town, so how bad could it be?

When they reached the hotel in the next town, the hotel manager received them with great pomp, bowing deeply as they entered. "We are so proud to welcome the wife of the great president of the United States! We have prepared our very best suite of rooms for you," he said.

Mrs. Coolidge extended her hand and said quietly, "Thank you, sir. We appreciate your kindness."

Then the manager gestured toward the registration desk and asked, "Will you please register, Mrs. Lincoln?"

Gentle Father, I know that you alone deserve our praise. I humbly ask that you help me to see myself accurately, as your simple servant, nothing more. Amen.

Car-Seat Caper

My eyes are always on the Lord,
for he rescues me from the traps of my enemies.

PSALM 25:15

Struggling to get free, I chided myself. *I bet I'm the only adult to ever get stuck in a child's car seat!* Visions of headlines reading "Firemen Rescue Grandma from Car Seat" danced before my eyes.

It had happened innocently enough. As I loaded my car that afternoon, I realized I had left my grandchild's car seat in the garage. Grabbing it, I cleared a spot on the backseat, passenger side, and set it in place. Clutching the car's seat belt with my left hand, I threaded it through the back of the child seat and securely snapped the buckle in place. But when I tried to remove my arm, my watch was stuck in the back of the car seat. For fifteen minutes I twisted and squirmed and tugged to get free, but to no avail.

The first ten minutes ticked by with my body hanging out of the car as I continued to scold myself for getting into such a ridiculous predicament. Finally, I saw a young man and his big dog walking by.

"Can you help me?" I called.

He looked my way but hesitated.

Again, I said, "Can you please help me?"

"What do you need?"

"I'm stuck in my grandchild's car seat."

He sauntered up but allowed his intimidating dog to trot ahead of him. Soon the dog and I were nose to nose. *Maybe I should call 911 now!*

Climbing in the other side of the car, it took the young man five minutes to untangle the watch and set me free.

He confessed, "At first I thought you might have a trap set for me."

Laughing, I told him, "There was a trap all right, but I was the one caught in it."

—Pam Whitley

Thank you, Lord, for rescuing me from the most unlikely traps, including the ones that the enemy sets. Please help me to remember that I can always call out to you for help, no matter what my predicament. I know you'll be there to answer me. Amen.

Predictions

Job replied to the LORD*:*
"I know that you can do all things;
no purpose of yours can be thwarted."

JOB 42:1-2 (NIV)

A self-proclaimed astrologer once foretold the death of a woman whom King Louis XI passionately loved. And the women did, in fact, die as the astrologer had predicted. But instead of believing that the astrologer had predicted only what was going to happen anyway, the king imagined that the astrologer's prediction was, in fact, the *cause* of his love's death.

Louis sent for the astrologer, intending to have him thrown through the window and killed as punishment. "Tell me," he said to the astrologer, "you pretend to be so clever and such a learned man, what will your fate be?"

The astrologer, who suspected what the king was planning and knew his great foibles, replied, "Sir, I foresee that I shall die three days before Your Majesty."

Believing the astrologer and rethinking his plan, the king took great care to protect the man's life.

Another King's death was predicted as well—not by an astrologer who claimed to read the stars, but by the one who created the stars. Oddly enough, that King's death was part of God's divine plan to save you and me.

Out of his extravagant love for us, God put a magnificent plan in place to rescue us from ourselves, from our sins. And as Job pointed out, no plan of God can be thwarted.

God's shocking plan to allow his own Son to be murdered as a sacrifice for us was so outlandish that people failed to believe it. Even Satan stubbed his toe on the idea that God would allow his Son to die for us. Yet that is exactly what happened, just as God had planned long before.

Jesus, the embodiment of grace, died in our place.

Thank you, Father, for your unspeakable love! Words can never convey my gratitude for what you gave up for me. Take my life, Father, and use it up in thankful praise and honor to you. Amen.

Innocence

I was in prison, and you visited me.

MATTHEW 25:36

While visiting the prison at Potsdam, King Frederick William I listened to a large number of pleas for pardon from prisoners who had grievances against the law's injustice. All of them said they had suffered imprisonment because of prejudiced judges, witnesses who had perjured themselves, or unscrupulous lawyers.

From cell to cell the tales of wronged innocence continued, until the king finally stopped at the barred door of one cell inhabited by a surly inmate who said nothing.

Surprised at his silence, Frederick said to him jokingly, "Well, I suppose you are innocent too."

"No, Your Majesty," came the startling response. "I am guilty and richly deserve all that I get."

"Here, guard!" thundered Frederick. "Come and get rid of this rascal quickly, before he corrupts this fine lot of innocent people you are responsible for."

Although it's possible for human justice to go awry and the innocent to be imprisoned for something they did not do, it is impossible for God's justice to go wrong. But truthfully, we should not want justice from God anyway. Instead, what we should want are his mercy and grace, because God's justice will mete out to us exactly what we deserve as a result of our sins, just as the man in prison stated. The Bible says, "The wages of sin is death" (Romans 6:23), but I don't want death. I want life!

In the Bible, the concepts of mercy and grace often appear together. And it is interesting to contrast them. Mercy means that God does *not* give us what we so richly deserve—the death penalty for our sins. And grace means he *does* give us what we do *not* deserve—eternal life through Jesus Christ.

So what do you truly want from God: justice, or mercy and grace? Me? I'll take mercy and grace every time!

Merciful Father, I love you with all my heart, and I thank you for your boundless mercy and grace to me. I am so richly blessed to belong to you through Christ. Amen.

November 12

Equipped for Disaster

Trust not in human wisdom but in the power of God.

1 CORINTHIANS 2:5

Two salesmen greeted us at our front door. Our typical no-thank-you response was reversed when they promised to clean our carpet if we would watch their Kirby demonstration.

"Sure, come in," we responded, smiling.

With three toddlers running around, our carpet was perfectly staged to showcase their amazing product. We would not be tempted to bust our budget because we had a reconditioned model in the closet. Maybe we could even learn how to use our attachments.

As the salesmen demonstrated their vacuum cleaner and presented their sales pitch, my husband, Randy, and I could barely contain our delight—the carpet would be clean for the upcoming holidays. The gentlemen graciously identified our odd-looking set of attachments, too, and explained how to use each one. We did not spend a penny, but those salesmen seemed to enjoy equipping us to use our own Kirby more effectively.

A couple of months passed. Our holiday guests were settled in for the night, and the children were asleep. In the kitchen, Randy and I scurried about preparing food for the next day's feast. Tired but nearly finished, my husband turned on the garbage disposal and discovered our vegetable peelings had clogged the drain.

"No problem," he said as he reminded me of our nifty Kirby attachment.

We set the machine to blow out instead of suck in, and Randy held the dome-shaped circular attachment firmly over the drain.

I watched closely; then our powerful machine spewed veggie-stained liquid over both of us and splattered the ceiling and cabinets. We were laughing so hard that we could not even stand up.

The next morning Randy was up early. Because stores were closed for the holiday, Randy, like our friendly Kirby salesmen, went door to door on our street. Finally, he came home with what we really needed—a plunger!

—Sue Ferguson

Father, help me to trust you more than I trust friendly advisers and clever gadgets. Your power is perfect. Amen.

Playing Church

I have this complaint against you. You don't love me or each other as you did at first!

REVELATION 2:4

When I was little we used to play church. We would get chairs into rows, fight over who would be preacher, vigorously lead the hymn singing, and generally have a great time.

The aggressive kids naturally wanted to be up front, directing or preaching. The quieter ones were content to sit and be entertained by the upfronters.

Occasionally we would become mesmerized by a true sensationalistic crowd swayer, such as the girl who said, "Boo! I'm the Holy Ghost!" But in general, if the upfronters were pretty good, they could hold their audience quite a while. If they weren't so good, eventually the kids would drift off to play something else, such as jump rope or jacks.

Now that generation has grown up, but most of them have not changed too much. Every Sunday they still play church. They line up in rows for the entertainment. If it's pretty good, their church may grow. If it's not too hot, eventually they will drift off to play something else, such as yachting or wife swapping.

—Anne Ortlund

Anne is right. Many people today just play church, and it's truly sad because they really don't know what they are missing.

A minister I know used to say, "Wherever you are when it's time for church, you will be worshiping your god." If you are at home asleep, then sleep is your god. If you are on the golf course, then golf is your god. If you are working, then work is your god. Or if you are in the assembly of the saints and your heart is truly engaged in worship, then God really is your God.

Aren't you happy that God was not *playing* when he offered us his grace?

Forgive me, Lord, for the times I fail to put you first in my life. I repent of my neglect and pray that you will draw me ever closer to you. Amen.

November 14

Playwright! Playwright!

The Lord *is like a father to his children,*
tender and compassionate. . . .
He remembers we are only dust.

PSALM 103:13-14

For several years, it was my delightful task to write the annual Christmas musical for our four-thousand-member church. Actually, I wrote the play, and my friend Charlotte, a world-class musician, wrote the music. By mid-November we were building the massive stage and putting up backdrops, fake buildings, and props for the early December production.

As codirector, I learned several valuable lessons: Never underestimate the unpredictability of child actors. Never expect a donkey to walk up a hollow-sounding ramp. And never, *ever* try to fly an archangel over the baptistery. (I almost forgot that one, but it's huge—really huge!)

All in all, though, the kids and the donkey didn't bother me too much. Sure, we had the usual pouting, crying, and blaming tantrums. But I felt that as the director I was entitled to them.

The real problems began when the archangel showed up for final dress rehearsal in a flowing white robe made by Omar the Tentmaker. The entire host of angels could have fit into it!

Then Joseph arrived with a broken arm in a stark-white cast that extended a foot beyond his costume sleeve, and he couldn't remember his lines because he was zoned out on pain meds.

The donkey would not go up the hollow-sounding ramp . . . again.

However, I'm happy to say that the musical came off beautifully, and the congregation loved it—except for the part when Mary tripped over one of the sheep and dropped the baby Jesus doll into the front row of the audience.

When the cry "Playwright! Playwright!" went up, I ducked out the stage door and drove so fast to get away that I got a speeding ticket. *Sigh.*

Father, please accept our paltry attempts to praise and glorify you. We really do try to do our best, in spite of the way it sometimes looks. We love you, Father. Amen.

To Tell the Truth

You will know the truth, and the truth will set you free.

JOHN 8:32

Do you remember the scene from the old *I Love Lucy* show when Lucy and Ethel decided to get part-time jobs and went to work in a candy factory? At first it was a breeze because the conveyor belt was moving past them very slowly. One at a time they picked up pieces of candy, rolled them in wrappers, twisted the ends, and then placed the wrapped pieces in a box. No problem!

Soon, though, the conveyor belt began moving more quickly. In Lucy's looniest fashion, she sped up too. "Come on, Ethel, work faster. We can do this!"

So they worked harder and faster and were barely getting the candy wrapped and into the box when . . . the conveyor sped up again.

Now the candy pieces were coming lickety-split! Lucy was grabbing them by the handfuls, throwing them into the box unwrapped, putting them into her pockets, shoving them into her shirt, and stuffing them into her mouth—anything to keep from failing or getting caught by the supervisor.

But, of course, she was fooling herself. Soon the supervisor walked in and found Lucy and Ethel with their mouths and clothes full of candy. Caught—and fired! That's what a lot of us do when we go on diets, isn't it? We try to fool ourselves and other people. When we're with our friends, we eat salads and fruits. When we're by ourselves, we eat burgers and fries.

I have finally figured out that even though we can fool our friends and family and sometimes even ourselves, we can't fool our bodies. They will respond to what we *really* eat, not to what we *fool ourselves into believing* we eat.

Faking yourself out when you're dieting is a *waist*—usually a bigger one!

Dear God, I want my body to glorify you. Please help me to be truthful about myself to myself and to you. Amen.

Playing by Ear

Anyone with ears to hear should listen and understand!

MATTHEW 11:15

One of the avocations I enjoy is music. I love to sing, and I can play by ear almost any instrument from which I can get a sound. I don't know how I do it; I just can. It's a gift from God—one I treasure. I'm no great musician, you understand; but I enjoy making music all the same.

When I was about six years old, we had dinner at the home of some family friends. In their den was an antique pump organ, and I was fascinated by it. My dad—also a musician—sat down at the old organ, started pumping away, and played a few familiar songs. I was hooked!

After Dad stopped playing, it was my turn, but I was too little to sit on the piano stool and reach the pumps and the keyboard at the same time. So I pushed the stool back, stood on the pumps, held on with my left hand under the keyboard, and played with my right hand. The grand piece I played by ear was "Twinkle, Twinkle, Little Star." My dad and his friend thought it was hilarious and laughed their heads off.

Dave Roever, a very funny performer, gives a new twist to the idea of playing by ear. When he says he plays *by ear*, he really means it. He has a prosthetic ear, which he can put on or take off at will. He tells his audience that he will play the next piece by ear; then he takes off his ear and proceeds to play with it in his hand—he's playing *by ear.* It's a crowd favorite.

As Christians, we need to *live by ear*—to listen intently to the Word of God and apply its timeless lessons to our lives. When we do, we create a grand symphony of praise in which God will take delight.

Thank you, Father, for the gift of music. It touches our lives with such beauty and sweetness. I want to sing your praises all my life. Amen.

Absentminded

Blessed are those who hunger and
thirst for righteousness,
for they will be filled.

MATTHEW 5:6 (NIV)

Former publisher of the *New York Post* J. David Stern was sometimes accused of being absentminded. He denied it, of course.

Once, as Stern walked down Fifth Avenue on his way to a meeting, he was approached by one of his old friends, who said, "David, come have lunch with me."

Stern looked at his watch, shook his head, and said, "I'd love to, but I can't. I'm already running a bit late for a meeting."

"Oh, come on, you can spare a few minutes for an old friend, can't you?"

"Well, all right, as long as we go somewhere nearby. I really do have to move along as quickly as possible."

The two men entered a restaurant, and as Stern ordered, he wondered aloud what could be the matter with him. "I am not a bit hungry today for some reason."

"Well, that's unusual for you, David," said his friend.

"I beg your pardon, sir," said the waiter, "but you just finished eating lunch here about ten minutes ago."

Sometimes I think we tend to be spiritually absentminded too. We come to the feast of the Word of God on Sunday morning, but by midafternoon we have already forgotten what we ingested, and we go on our way as if we had not partaken of the richness of his grace.

Instead of being hungry for righteousness, we hunger after wealth or power, and that hunger can never be satisfied. The more we partake of those earthly "foods," the more of them we want. Just like empty calories—they never really satisfy. But when God's Word and his righteousness fill us completely, we will never be hungry again.

Dear Lord, please grant me greater hunger and thirst for you. And then fill me, Lord, with your love and grace. Amen.

November 18

Delivering the U.S. Mail

There is no longer Jew or Gentile, slave or free, male and female. For you are all one in Christ Jesus.

GALATIANS 3:28

As a college student I worked in the campus post office. And during the summer, I landed a special student job at the post office in my hometown. My job was to drive a truck carrying special-delivery letters, CODs, and the like. When I finished those jobs, I delivered ordinary parcels to downtown businesses. So I was running all over town every day.

I was something of a novelty there. That was in the late 1960s, and in those days very few women worked in the postal system. If they did, they typically worked the customer service windows inside the post office, selling stamps and money orders. They were rarely seen walking a route or driving a postal truck. So people often did a double take when they saw me whizzing down the street in my red-white-and-blue van.

I took a lot of teasing from the mail carriers, but I didn't mind because it was a much better paying job than anything else I could have gotten. So I just teased right back, and we all had a good laugh.

Every day I met my friend Emily for lunch. She was still in high school, but we had a lot of fun together. One day while we were eating, someone tampered with my truck. Of course, damaging a postal vehicle was a federal crime, punishable by a large fine or even imprisonment. So when I discovered the result of someone's mischief, I did not know whether to laugh or panic.

On the side of the truck where it had said "U.S. Mail," someone crossed out "Mail" and written "Femail."

Fortunately, in God's system there is no distinction about who can be saved—mail or femail!

Thank you, Father, for loving everyone the same and for allowing us to be part of your family—brothers and sisters of grace and hope. Amen.

Rush Hour

Though they stumble, they will never fall,
for the LORD holds them by the hand.

PSALM 37:24

Rush hour at the gym is frenzied—it's a packed house, every machine is in motion, and TVs are blaring over the heads of sweaty bodies in overdrive.

As a new member I tried to look nonchalant while scanning the hordes for an empty treadmill. Only one. Great. Front row center. Everyone behind me could watch my, uh, technique.

Hurriedly I stepped onto the black rubber tread. Even faster I shot off the back end, narrowly missing the handlebars of the machine behind me. Fortunately I did a stomach plant. (I always wear protective padding in that area.) But the mishap occurred so fast that once I put my kneecaps back in place, I felt almost no pain.

The previous user had left the treadmill running on high speed.

Pleeeease, no one come help me! I'm fine. Embarrassed, but fine.

With what dignity I could manage, I reached to turn the switch to the off position. *No need to go all the way around . . . just step up here.* I think I became airborne that time. The impact jarred my teeth, forced my ribs into a rude collision with my backbone, and untied one shoe.

The people around me were saints. Once they saw I was okay, they just continued working out. And although surely by that time they were questioning my mental capacity even more than my physical ability, no one giggled or even smirked—well, not that I saw, anyway. I was busy retying my shoe and thinking about what to do next.

Limp away? *Not on your life!* I stepped up. Again. Right after I turned the thing off.

—Kathleen Brown

Father, why do we rush and worry through our lives? Trying to get it all done, to make sure we look good doing it, to impress others who are trying just as hard to impress us? Remind me, please, that when I hold your hand, all dignity and strength are mine. Amen.

November 20

As Close as You Can Get

God places the lonely in families.

PSALM 68:6

The last time we counted, my parents had moved forty-seven times. One of our family jokes through the years was to try to guess where we would be living the next year at the same time.

I have always admired my mom for showing enormous patience, endurance, and good humor through all those moves. She used to laughingly say that if our television accidentally got unplugged, it would run onto the front porch and wait to be loaded. Or if someone even mentioned the word *move* in our house, the furniture immediately piled itself up in the corner.

During one of those moves, the van transporting our household goods and lifelong treasures flipped over and burned. For years after that Mom would miss a kitchen utensil or some other item and say, "I guess we lost that in the fire." But even that she bore with grace and smiles.

On November 20, 1996, we celebrated my parents' sixtieth wedding anniversary. We had a nice luncheon at a restaurant with immediate family and a few close friends. It was a joyous occasion.

At one point I asked my mom and dad to tell us to what they attributed their long, happy marriage. Dad said, "Well, I know there's no such thing as a perfect wife, but your mother is as close as any woman could ever hope to get. She's followed me around all over the country and never complained. She's done everything a wife and mother is supposed to do and a lot more. *She* is the reason we have had a long, happy marriage."

The admiration my dad had for Mom was sincere and deep, and their marriage lasted yet another ten years before Dad went home to heaven. Mother obviously felt the same way about him. They had a mutual-admiration society of two, based on their individual and joint relationships with God.

Father, thank you for the joy of family laughter and love. I praise you for putting us in families for support and comfort. Amen.

Expecting the Worst

Let us come to him with thanksgiving.
Let us sing psalms of praise to him.

PSALM 95:2

The day before Thanksgiving, Jena prepared her first full Thanksgiving meal, turkey and all, for her family. Since they would be spending the next day with extended family, she wanted to have a special day just for them. Jena had never demonstrated a great talent for cooking, so the idea of her preparing a turkey on her own raised her husband's and son's eyebrows. Although they expected the worst, they still encouraged her to give it a try.

Early that morning she stuffed and basted the turkey and put it in the oven. She had read everything she could about the proper way to do it, and she was sure she had the timing just right. Surprisingly, everything went well, and she had the entire meal ready at the stroke of noon.

Knowing her own history as a cook, though, before she served the meal, she announced to her husband and son, "I know this is the first turkey I've ever cooked. If it isn't any good, I don't want anybody to say a word. We'll just get up from the table without comment and go out to a restaurant to eat." Then she returned to the kitchen.

When she entered the dining room, proudly bearing the beautifully browned turkey, she found her husband and son gone. She finally discovered them sitting in the car in the driveway with the engine running. Obviously they had very little faith in her ability!

At times we are like that about God. We have problems in life, and we pray to him for help. Then we sit back with resignation and expect the worst. We just do not seem to have much faith in him. But based on my own experience, I can say that when we exercise a little faith, we learn that no one else is as unfailingly faithful as the Lord!

Dear God, you have always been there for me, no matter what kind of trouble I get myself into. Thank you for saving me from my own foolishness. Amen.

November 22

Where There's Smoke, There's Turkey

Enter his gates with thanksgiving;
go into his courts with praise.
Give thanks to him and praise his name.
For the LORD is good.
His unfailing love continues forever.

PSALM 100:4-5

A few years ago Mark Lowry sent a smoked turkey to me for Thanksgiving. It was, according to his enthusiastic endorsement, some of the best turkey in the world.

Unfortunately, I didn't get to test that claim because I didn't take time to read the directions. Not knowing the word *smoked* meant "fully cooked," I assumed I should roast the bird the same way I do all my turkeys: in a 350-degree oven until tender, or until the firemen arrive, whichever comes first.

For the entire time that turkey was roasting, everything seemed to be going fine. There were not any dark clouds billowing out of the oven. There was no odor of burning meat. My smoke alarm did not even go off.

When I finally took that poor bird out of the oven—some fourteen hours later—and pulled back the aluminum foil, I couldn't believe my eyes. The poor thing looked as if it had been struck by lightning! Twice! It was as black as a pair of army boots and about as tender. Its poor legs were pointing in opposite directions, and the meat on each drumstick had shrunk, leaving four inches of bare bone protruding in the air. Had the SPCA seen it, I would still be paying off the fine!

Hang in there, Martha.

On this special day of thanks to God for the ways he graces us with unfathomable love, recall the many joys, hopes, and dreams he made possible through the sacrifice of his precious Son. And whether your turkey is blessed or burned, be grateful.

"Give thanks to him and praise his name. . . . His unfailing love continues forever!"

—*Martha Bolton*

We praise you, God, for your Son and for the life his death provides for us. We bow in gratitude for all you do for us. Amen.

A Flying Boat

Peter went over the side of the boat and walked on the water toward Jesus.

MATTHEW 14:29

General Ioannis Metaxas, dictator of Greece from 1936 until his death in 1941, once traveled to a Mediterranean air base to do a formal inspection. While there, he was invited to try out a flying boat. Excited to experience the new technology, he decided to pilot it himself.

Everything went well until the commander, the dictator's host, noticed that they were about to make a landing on the regular runway.

"Excuse me, General, but it would be better to come down on the sea—this is a flying *boat*."

"Of course, Commander. What was I thinking?" said Metaxas, suddenly collecting himself. He proceeded then to make a safe landing on the water.

Rising from the wheel, the general said, "Commander, I greatly appreciate the tact with which you drew my attention to the incredible blunder I nearly made." Saying that, he opened the door—and stepped into the sea.

Like the general, another impetuous man once stepped out of a boat and onto the sea. His name was Peter. We often criticize Peter for eventually sinking because his faith weakened. But I sometimes think we judge Peter too harshly, because the Bible records that he walked *on top of the water* almost all the way to Jesus.

That's amazing! I think I would have sunk on the first step. I can't imagine actually walking on water for even a few steps. But Peter did. Then he took his eyes off the Savior, saw the storm raging around him, and sank like the "rock" he was. Who wouldn't?

We all "sink" at times, but if we know the Savior, he will always be there to reach down and save us. All we have to do is call out to him, and he will rescue us.

Heavenly Father, we need you to save us, because without you we will surely drown in the sea of our sins. Keep us close to you, Lord. Amen.

Possum Stew, Lox, and Bagels

I don't really understand myself, for I want to do what is right, but I don't do it. Instead, I do what I hate.

ROMANS 7:15

It had been a lovely Thanksgiving—crisp and cool, with autumn leaves drifting down outside and Macy's Thanksgiving Day parade on television. My mom had come for a visit, and we'd had several friends over for a more-or-less traditional lunch (in Texas that often includes chips and hot sauce).

On Saturday following the Thursday celebration, I drove to East Texas to take Mom home so she could rest from being in our busy house for a few days. I got her settled at home and then started the return trip the same day.

I took a detour through a town where I once lived, just enjoying the ride, listening to satellite radio, looking at the shops, and admiring the classic courthouse on the square. As I headed back toward the freeway, I noticed a seriously mud-covered, Army-green Jeep parked on the street. I didn't pay much attention at first, because mud-covered Jeeps in East Texas are normal, but then a sign on the back window caught my eye: Red-Neck Jews.

I almost had whiplash from doing a double take. After all, some things just don't seem to go together. Do these redneck Jews wear camouflage, work shoes, and dreadlocks? Do they eat possum stew with lox and bagels? I just couldn't wrap my brain around that apparent paradox.

Then I thought, God probably shakes his head and laughs at some of the things we put together in our lives too. Joy and worry. Praise and pouting. Love and criticism. Some things just don't go together.

Father, please forgive me for the contradictory and confusing example I must set for those who are searching for you. Help me to be more consistent in my Christian walk. Amen.

A Persian Folktale

[Jesus said,] "Don't store up treasures here on earth. . . . Store your treasures in heaven, where moths and rust cannot destroy, and thieves do not break in and steal."

MATTHEW 6:19-20

It had been too long since Horace Walpole had smiled. Too long. Life for him had become as drab as the dreary weather in England. Then, on a grim winter day in 1754, while he was reading a Persian folktale, his smile returned. He wrote his longtime friend Sir Horace Mann, an envoy of King George II, telling him of the "thrilling approach to life" he had discovered from the folktale—how it had freed him from his dark prison of gloom.

The ancient tale told of three princes from the island of Ceylon who set out in pursuit of great treasures. They never found what they were seeking, but en route they were repeatedly surprised by delights they had never anticipated. While looking for one thing, they found another.

The original name of Ceylon was Serendip, which explains the title of the story: "The Three Princes of Serendip." From that, Walpole coined the wonderful word *serendipity.* And from then on, his most significant and valued experiences were those that happened to him when he was least expecting them.

That "thrilling approach to life" is still a good one. People go searching for things they *think* are important—wealth, happiness, power. But sometimes as they search, they stumble into other things much more vital to them—God, faith, family, friends, love, peace, contentment, and joy.

At the end of life, they realize they didn't get what they *wanted*, but they had, indeed, ended up with what they *needed.*

What are you pursuing in your life? When the time comes to look back over your life, will it be what you thought you *wanted*, or will it be what you really *needed*?

Father God, thank you for guiding us to the heavenly things we truly need rather than to the earthly things we think we want. You are merciful to us, Lord. Amen.

Changes

The gray hair of experience is the splendor of the old.

PROVERBS 20:29

Legendary baseball great Satchel Paige once asked, "How old would you be if you didn't know how old you were?" What a great question! And the answer has more to do with your attitude than your age.

My friend Sher has a unique way of answering a question about age. When you say, "Sher, how old are you?" she tells you how old she *feels* that day. One day she's sixteen, the next day she's eighty-five. I like that.

One mental youngster said it this way:

> *I have become a little older since I saw you last, and a few changes have come into my life since then. Frankly, I have become quite a frivolous old girl. I am seeing five gentlemen every day.*
>
> *As soon as I wake up, Will Power helps me get out of bed. Then I go to see John. Then Charlie Horse comes along, and when he is here, he takes a lot of my time and attention. When he leaves, Arthur Ritis shows up and stays the rest of the day. He doesn't like to stay in one place very long, so he takes me from joint to joint. After such a busy day I'm really tired and glad to go to bed with Ben Gay. What a life!*
>
> *P.S. The preacher came to call the other day. He said at my age I should be thinking about the hereafter. I told him, "Oh, I do that all the time, Preacher. No matter where I am—in the parlor, upstairs, in the kitchen, or down in the basement—I ask myself,* What am I here after?*"*

We joke about getting old because we don't really think we want to get there, but the Bible says that a long life is a blessing from God. So we should celebrate it!

Bless me, O Lord, with wisdom as I grow older. Help me to be the example I need to be to those who are younger. Let them see you living in me. Amen.

The Ugliest Man

May the words of my mouth
and the meditation of my heart
be pleasing to you,
O LORD, my rock and my redeemer.

PSALM 19:14

My brother, Frank, and his wife, Kay, were hosting a party for some friends. To help Kay in the preparations, Frank said he would go to the store to get a list of things she needed. So he took their three-year-old daughter, Marcy, with him to the local grocery store.

After putting Marcy in the shopping cart and buckling her in, Frank began searching for the items on Kay's list. He was about halfway through the list when he turned the corner and started down another aisle. Although Frank did not look up, out of the corner of his eye he noticed that a rather large man had entered the aisle from the opposite direction and was pushing his cart toward them.

Just as the man came even with them, Marcy pointed at the big man and said loudly, "Daddy, that man's ugly!"

Frank froze and then said, "Marcy! That's not nice."

"But Daddy, that man's ugly!"

Frank turned beet red; sheepishly looked at the man, who was huge and truly less than handsome; and apologized, "I'm sorry, mister." Then he held his breath, not knowing what to expect in return.

The big man grinned and said, "It's all right. I know I'm not the best lookin' feller in town." Then he patted Marcy on the head and walked away whistling a happy little tune.

In a similar story Abraham Lincoln said he once met a woman who was riding horseback in the woods. As he stopped to let her pass, she also stopped, and looking at Abe intently, she said, "I do believe you are the ugliest man I have ever seen."

Abe said, "Madam, you are probably right, but I can't help it."

"No," said she, "you can't help it. But you might stay at home."

Goodness!

Forgive me, Father, when my words hurt someone else, whether by accident or on purpose. Let my speech always honor and glorify you. Amen.

Top Speed!

Once you were like sheep
who wandered away.
But now you have turned to your Shepherd,
the Guardian of your souls.

1 PETER 2:25

Do you ever wonder where we are headed as a society? I think about that a lot, because it seems to me that we are galloping at breakneck speed but have no idea where we're going. In the touching song "People Need the Lord" recorded by Steve Green, the singer weeps for the people he passes on the street every day—"Empty people filled with care, headed who knows where?" And I often feel that way. Do you?

It reminds me of the story of nineteenth-century biologist Thomas Henry Huxley, who once arrived late in a town where he was to deliver an important lecture. Hailing a cab, he jumped in and shouted to the driver, "Top speed, my man! Top speed!"

Responding quickly to Huxley's command, the cabbie whipped his horse into action, and the vehicle went bumping along the streets at a wild clip. The lack of dignity and organization in the proceedings then dawned upon Huxley, and above the clatter of the wheels he shouted again to the driver, "Here, here, good man, do you know where I want to go?"

"No, Your Honor," called the cabbie, cracking his whip all the while, "but I'm driving as fast as I can!"

We are rushing headlong toward tomorrow, not knowing what will be there when we arrive. Often not even really caring. We just want to be somewhere else—anywhere but where we are—because life is hard. We don't want to face the here and now, thinking, *Tomorrow will be better, wait and see*. So we are running . . . and running . . . to who knows where?

The good news is that we can stop running. Our Shepherd says, "Come to me, all of you who are weary and carry heavy burdens, and I will give you rest" (Matthew 11:28). Come.

Gentle Shepherd, open your arms to me so I can find rest for my tired soul. I need you, Lord. I need you. Amen.

Is That You?

Pure and genuine religion in the sight of God the Father means . . . refusing to let the world corrupt you.

JAMES 1:27

Shirley had been suffering from a serious physical problem for several months. Finally, with no other options available, the doctor recommended that she have surgery. However, he could not promise that she would live through it, because it was a tricky kind of surgery.

Fearing the worst, Shirley took a few days to get her personal affairs in order and then checked into the hospital. Under the anesthetic Shirley had a dream in which she heard God speak to her. He said, "Shirley, don't worry. You will not die from the surgery. You will have another thirty to forty years of life."

Sure enough, Shirley came through the surgery fine and quickly recuperated. Since she knew she would live so many more years, she decided to live them in style. So she had a total body makeover—a tummy tuck, a face lift, a new hair color, a pair of colored contact lenses, and a new wardrobe. Even her nearest and dearest friends were amazed at the transformation.

Then one day Shirley was crossing a downtown street when she was hit by a car and died. In the "blink of an eye" she was surprised to find herself standing before the throne of God.

Looking around, she said, "God, I thought you said I had another thirty to forty years to live."

God said, "Shirley, is that *you*?"

I sometimes wonder whether—after we have worked so hard to fit into our society and conform to the look and lifestyles of the world around us—God will recognize us as his children when we stand before him. Will he look at me and say, "Welcome, my child," or, "I never knew you"?

Hold me close, Father, and don't let me drift away from you. Draw me ever nearer to you, and keep me safe and secure in your love. Amen.

Hollering for Help

Search for the LORD and for his strength;
continually seek him.

PSALM 105:4

When we find ourselves in a desperate predicament, it is human nature to turn to any available source of help, however unreliable or implausible.

Several prominent men in the state of Illinois went one day to visit the state penitentiary. The warden personally took them on a tour of the vast institution, and they saw all the facilities.

Near the end of the tour, one fellow somehow managed to get separated from the group, and he could not find his way out.

He roamed up and down one cold corridor after another, becoming more desperate with each passing minute. Finally he came across a convict who was peering out from between the bars of his cell door. Here was salvation at last!

Breathing a sigh of relief, the man hurried up to the prisoner and hastily asked, "Say, pal, how do you get out of this place, anyway?"

That's a little bit like sending a marshmallow to put out a bonfire or asking a stockbroker if you should invest in the market. Even if you get an answer that sounds logical, you might not want to rely on it too much. Before following another person's advice, it's wise to consider the source!

We often look in the wrong places for answers to our problems. We ask for advice from friends, family, attorneys, and counselors. Sometimes we gain helpful insights; sometimes we don't. If, however, we seek the wisdom of God when it comes to the difficult issues of our lives, we get good advice every time.

When life knocks you to your knees, pray. Look up to God, not just out to worldly sages and services. God's counsel is trustworthy because his Word is reliable and true: "Your word is a lamp to guide my feet and a light for my path" (Psalm 119:105).

O God, I love your Word, and I seek you with all my heart. I cannot face life without your wisdom and guidance. Help me, Lord! Amen.

A Logical Question

The wisdom of this world is foolishness to God.

1 CORINTHIANS 3:19

My niece Kim was three years old. Her sisters, Rhonda and Julie, were five and seven. They lived with their parents, Loren and Penny, and Loren's parents, who everyone called Mom and Dad, on a Kansas wheat farm where they also raised cattle.

One morning Dad noticed that one of the cows was about ready to birth her calf, and from past experience he thought she might need help. He closed her in a stall in the barn. Sure enough, she was soon in hard labor, so Dad and Loren changed clothes and started out the door to the barn.

"Can we go, Daddy?" asked Rhonda.

Looking at Penny, he said, "What do you think?"

"They have to learn sometime," she said. "It might as well be now, I guess."

"Okay, let's go, then," said Loren, "but you have to stay out of the way so the old cow doesn't kick you."

The birthing process was a long, arduous ordeal. After forty-five minutes of huffing, puffing, and using pulling chains, they finally smiled as the little white-faced, spindly legged calf was born. Dad and Loren, not to mention the cow, were exhausted.

The two men leaned against the barn wall to catch their breath, wipe the sweat off their faces, and admire the wobbly calf. It was at that precise moment that little Kim, peering between the rails of the stall, posed a three-year-old's logical question.

"Well, Daddy," she said seriously, "just how'd that thing get in there anyway?"

Now, if you think Loren was out of breath before, that innocent question really caused him to suck air. But it was, after all, a logical question from a three-year-old's viewpoint, don't you think?

I am so grateful that God doesn't turn a deaf ear to our childlike questions. How wonderful that we always have his ear!

Father, I pray that you will give me wisdom for living. Help me to follow your guidelines for happiness and to glorify you by the way I live. Amen.

December 2

From the Heart of a Child

[Jesus said,] "Let the children come to me. Don't stop them! For the Kingdom of God belongs to those who are like these children."

MARK 10:14

I praise God for the forty-plus years I was privileged to work with inner-city children. There are no words to express the joy they have been to my life. God taught me so much from the many days of fussing, crying, and singing with these precious souls. Most of my godly wisdom came from the hearts of these little ones, "my kids."

I remember asking my kids in early December to help decorate the church for their upcoming Christmas program. Among the decorations was a ceramic nativity scene, which I warned them not to touch. I was summoned to the office to take a phone call, so they were alone in the sanctuary. I heard a noise from the office and quickly ran to see what had happened.

My eyes widened and my hands flew up in the air as I tried to process the image in front of me. There was baby Jesus lying on the floor in a million pieces. My kids began a familiar chant of "Oohs" and "Aahhs" and "Ms. Chocolate's going to get you!"

All the fingers pointed to Davie, who was staring at me with his big brown eyes, hiding his hands behind his back.

I was about to give him a tongue lashing he would never forget when he came close to me, declaring, "Ms. Chocolate, Jesus not in the manger. He's in my heart." How could I be angry? Davie brought a new meaning to Christmas that year.

God used a child to tell us once again that he came to live in our hearts.

—Gwen Williams (Ms. Chocolate)

Father, may I always listen as you speak to me through the hearts of children. Their words are so sweet and true, just as your Word is. Amen.

War in Heaven

Live in harmony and peace. Then the God of love and peace will be with you.

2 CORINTHIANS 13:11

The children had rehearsed their parts in the Christmas production for months. All went well, until the grand finale.

Mary and Joseph came onstage with the baby Jesus. Angels followed, then the shepherds. Next came the wise men. The cutest came last.

A murmur of delight greeted the twelve two- and three-year-old cherubs who walked onstage holding hands, dressed in long white robes and silver halos. They obediently formed a semicircle in front of the baby; then they sat down cross legged—with one exception.

Brad's freckled face broke into an excited grin as he spotted Granny. He pulled his hand free and waved. People chuckled. Embarrassed, the little boy pulled on his robe, revealing a pair of chubby legs and blue boxer shorts.

Three-year-old Laura decided to get things back on track. She grabbed Brad's shorts and tugged. The congregation roared. Brad grabbed his shorts; then he saw Laura. He might be only two years old, but no girl would get the better of him. He took a swing.

Laura obviously had older brothers. She scrambled to her feet and shoved him. Brad came back, both fists flailing. I jumped forward and swept Brad offstage. Another teacher grabbed Laura. The congregation was hysterical.

We completed the play, but the planned spectacular ending did not happen. Some of the children had the giggles. Ripples of laughter kept sweeping across the hall. The two littlest angels sat and glared at each other.

After the curtain closed, the pastor thanked the Sunday school for their "most unusual presentation" of the Christmas story. When the laughter subsided, he added, "In the book of Revelation we read, 'Then there was war in heaven' and some of the angels were cast down to earth" (see Revelation 12:7-9).

—*Shirley M. Corder*

Lord, I am so grateful that you don't expect perfection from us, only obedience. Amen.

December 4

Looking for the Bonus

Seek the Kingdom of God above all else, and live righteously, and he will give you everything you need.

MATTHEW 6:33

Can we play the game, Mom?" asked our daughter, Victoria. It was the Christmas season, which meant we often played a fun game while driving around town. Any home that was decorated with a wreath would gain our team one point. Persons on the right side of the car played against those on the left.

That Sunday afternoon following the church service, we had invited our pastor and his wife out for lunch. The young couple, Pastor Bob and his wife, Judy, got into our car, and the game began.

My husband drove, and he teased us, saying he would choose a different route where there were more homes on his side of the street.

"That's not fair!" protested Victoria, and I agreed.

"Oh, all right." He gave in and went on to remind us, "By the way, there's a five-point bonus if you pass a Santa Claus."

The competition gained new momentum. Pastor's team had eleven points, and ours was ahead at thirteen.

"The first team to reach twenty wins," said my husband.

"Now I have fifteen," said Pastor.

"There's a wreath on that door. We have nineteen!" said Victoria.

Then Pastor blurted out, "All we need is Santa and we're saved!"

Everyone's attention turned toward him with shocked responses:

"Ooh, Pastor."

"Santa—save us?"

A red-faced Pastor Bob graciously accepted our taunting and accepted that his team had lost the game.

In truth, most of us desire to get ahead in life and are looking for that bonus that will push us over the top.

—Gloria J. Wallace

Father, I place my ambitions in your hands. Thank you for your promise to take care of my every need as I seek after you alone. For I know if I seek your Kingdom first, you will add all these other things to my life. Amen.

Pick Three

God loves a person who gives cheerfully.

2 CORINTHIANS 9:7

The roof of the country church had been seriously damaged in a recent hailstorm, but the church coffers were almost empty. There was not enough extra money available to pay for the needed repairs, which amounted to several thousand dollars. So the congregation decided to have a Sunday box lunch and afternoon fund-raising event.

Women of the congregation decorated special boxes in which they placed lunches they had prepared. The boxes were auctioned off one at a time to the men of the church. The results of the box lunch auction added about $1,500 to the roof fund.

Later in the afternoon the members of the congregation had invited their friends and neighbors from the community to join them for a gospel singing, which would double as a time to raise some additional funds.

First the minister offered for sale some of the books from the church library. He also sold some Christian CDs and DVDs. The sale yielded about $650.

Next the youth group sold coupons for their services. Each coupon sold for $25, and the coupons could be used to purchase lawn work, car washes, or household chores from the youth. They raised another $825 in all.

Finally, the minister announced that the person who donated the most money when the collection plate was passed would get to choose three hymns during the next part of the service. Some of the deacons passed the plates up and down each pew, and people placed their checks in the plates.

When the deacons examined the checks, they found that Widow Jones had put the largest check in the plate—$1,000!

The minister said, "Come on down, Sister Jones! Now tell us which three hymns you want."

Making her way to the front, Sister Jones looked around the congregation, then smiled brightly, pointed to three different widowers, and said, "I'll take him, him, and him!"

Dear God, we have been so wonderfully blessed by you. Help us to use our blessings to bless others with a cheerful heart. Amen.

December 6

The All-Seeing Eye

Your eye is a lamp that provides light for your body. When your eye is good, your whole body is filled with light.

MATTHEW 6:22

My friend Lee Nelson is a funeral director. Since my dad also worked in the funeral business for many years, Lee and I often swap stories.

One day Lee was working with a family where the mother had died. He described them as "not very sophisticated." They were making final arrangements for her service. During the interview Lee asked the daughter, "Do you have a piece of jewelry or something you would like to put on your mother during the funeral service? We would, of course, remove it before the interment."

The daughter nodded and began digging around in her purse, saying, "Yes, yes, I have something Mom would want to wear." She finally held her closed hand toward Lee, who held out his open hand to receive the item. When she took her hand away, Lee was holding the dead woman's glass eye.

Lee quietly placed the eye on his desk and said, "Would you please excuse me for a moment?" And he left the office. Then he walked to the receptionist's desk, laughing his head off, and told her and his boss what had happened. He said it took him about ten minutes to finally get control of himself so he could return to the office and finish the interview.

Just as Lee reached his office door, his boss called out to him, "Lee, wait!" Coming to Lee, he asked, "Did they tell you what their mom's last words were?"

"No, they didn't," said Lee.

"I'll be keeping an eye out for you!"

Lee said it was another ten minutes before he could get his act together to go back into his office and face the family.

Father, thank you for always watching over me with your watchful eye and for keeping me in your great love and care. Amen.

The Ugliest Christmas Tree

We, too, wait with eager hope for the day when God will give us our full rights as his adopted children.

ROMANS 8:23

During one of my trips as a traveling salesman, I accepted an invitation to have dinner at a customer's home on a December evening in 1972. After dinner their sons were putting the finishing touches on the family Christmas tree, a most peculiar specimen of greenery.

The tree looked as if it suffered from malnutrition—its trunk was as crooked as an S curve on a country road, and its top was broken. If it were not for its greenish color, the tree would have borne no resemblance at all to a pine tree. My friend informed me that his family had decided to find the ugliest tree they could and give it a home for Christmas.

What a wonderful idea! I thought. It was the stories of the Ugly Duckling, Cinderella, and Rudolph the Red-Nosed Reindeer all rolled into one. This family had adopted a defective little tree and gave it love, dignity, and best of all, the honor of being their Christmas tree.

My family began our own "ugliest tree" tradition, which has now spanned more than two decades. Proudly we display our tree as a symbol of our love for all creation and a reminder that there was only one who was perfect and his birth is the reason we celebrate this most blessed time of the year.

—*John Ray Greif*

John's point is well made. It also occurred to me that the broken trees represent each of us as broken human beings whom God adopted, decorated with his wonderful grace and mercy, and set in the world as lights on the path of the weary, the lonely, and the lost to show them the Way home to him.

Abba, Father, we rest in the knowledge that you have adopted us into your own family. We know we did not deserve such compassion and love, but we celebrate our honored place among your children. Amen.

Will I Ever Learn?

No discipline is enjoyable while it is happening—
it's painful! But afterward there will be a peaceful harvest.

HEBREWS 12:11

I had been working hard for forty minutes at that ski lesson. Although I was sweating and off balance, Mr. Instructor Drill Sergeant ordered me to position my feet and hips so that I looked like an orangutan goof on skis. He pushed me hard, out of my comfort zone. I was fifty-two years old and had only started skiing in my late forties . . . on the beginner hill.

He firmly stated, "I'm going to take the end of your pole and pull, while you edge your skis. Really edge them. Let's go!"

"Aah. Uh. This is hard," I whined. "How can I ski like this?" *This is edging, that magic technique that gives control and speed?* My instructor was pulling me downhill while I leaned back hard on my skis to stop him from causing me to fall.

"Now turn, and do it again! Edge! Look at your tracks now. See that nice, clean line? Do it again. Do it again!" he ordered, forcing me to edge my skis. I did not at all like the way I felt off balance. I was afraid, too, but his commanding, steady tone kept me focused and trusting him enough to do as he said. At the top of the ski lift, he unbelievably told me we were going to do it all again. I momentarily imagined he was a criminal torturer from a movie.

The lesson over, I discovered that for the first time I was in control as I skied. That edge I had worked so hard to learn was giving me glide, balance, and control. Wow! I wanted to hug that nasty old drill sergeant.

—*Diane E. Kay*

Father, thank you for caring enough to teach me, even when I am not sure I want to learn. I know I will enjoy the fruits of your discipline. In Jesus' name, amen.

Gingerly Snack

She saw that the tree was beautiful and its fruit looked delicious. . . . So she took some of the fruit and ate it.

GENESIS 3:6

I had just finished lugging the last of the Christmas decorations down the stairs when the doorbell rang. I opened the door in time to wave good-bye to the UPS man and drag a big box into the house. During the holiday season my husband received numerous gifts from service companies, and the return address confirmed that this was one of those.

Often the gifts were food, and because I was famished from my busy morning, I tore into the box. It was filled with delicacies, but the label that caught my attention had "Wasabi Gingered Pecans" written on it. I loved pecans, although I was not familiar with the word *wasabi*.

I opened the can and plopped a whole pecan in my mouth. Immediately I ran for the sink as I spit the hot-as-fire morsel out. With tears streaming down my cheeks, I doused my mouth with a couple of glasses of water and then grabbed some bread to take the edge off. When my mouth finally cooled down and I regained my composure, I typed *wasabi* into the computer and found out what I had suspected—Japanese horseradish!

Later, my son stopped by and thought he would sample the pecans too.

"You'd better be careful. Those are like eating fire."

He laughed and said something about my not being able to hold my spice, but instead of popping it in his mouth, he licked it. One lick sent him dashing to the sink, where he washed out his mouth and grabbed ice water.

Hmmm, I wasn't the only one who couldn't hold my spice!

—Pam Whitley

Father, help me to realize that, even though something looks or feels good to my flesh, I had better know what it is before I partake of it, or I can get seriously burned. Amen.

December 10

They Call *Me* Crazy!

We prove ourselves by our purity, our understanding, our patience, our kindness, by the Holy Spirit within us, and by our sincere love.

2 CORINTHIANS 6:6

One unusually warm and sunny winter day in central Texas, an institution for the mentally and emotionally challenged decided to give some of the patients a day outside. The patients were enjoying the freedom of blue skies, a gentle breeze, blooming pansies, and soft grass under their feet, while staff members watched from the patio.

Two of the male patients wandered out to the edge of the fenced grounds and sat down on the grass on a little incline where they could look through the fence and watch people passing by. They talked about the pretty weather and what it would be like to take a long trip outside the fence to the Gulf Coast and swim in the ocean.

Several local citizens of the town passed by—some in cars, some on bicycles, and some walking. The patients would speak to them, and most of them spoke back but hurried on their way. Some ignored the patients altogether. And a few immediately crossed to the other side of the street.

After a few minutes, along came a man pushing a big wooden cart. It was like a huge wheelbarrow with giant wooden wheels, and he was struggling under the weight of the load.

One of the patients asked, "Hey, mister, what's that in your cart?"

The man said, "It's cow manure."

"Really? What are you going to do with it?"

"I'm going to put it on my strawberries."

"You're kidding, right?" asked the surprised patient.

"No, I'm not kidding. I'm really going to put it on my strawberries," he replied.

The patient turned to his friend and said, "Boy, you never know! I put cream and sugar on my strawberries, and they call *me* crazy."

Dear Lord, I want to show your kindness to people around me. Give me your heart of love, compassion, and tenderness toward everyone I meet. Amen.

Guess What?

The free gift of God is eternal life
through Christ Jesus our Lord.

ROMANS 6:23

The story is told that before Christmas one year the kindergarten teacher was inundated with gifts from her little students.

The florist's daughter presented her with a package. The teacher shook it, held it over her head, and said, "I think I can guess what it is—some flowers!"

"You're right!" said the little girl. "But how did you know?"

"Oh, it was just a guess," she said with a smile.

The next student was the son of a candy store owner. The teacher held the gift over her head, shook it, and said, "I think I can guess what this is—a box of candy!"

"That's right! But how did you know that?" asked the boy.

"Oh, just another good guess," said the teacher, smiling.

The next gift was from a little boy whose father managed the local cola bottling company. When the teacher picked up the box, it began leaking. She smiled and asked the boy, "Is it orange soda?"

"Nooo," the boy replied.

The teacher tried again: "Is it lemon-lime soda?" she asked.

"Nooo," the boy answered.

The teacher then said, "Well, I can't guess this one. I give up. What is it?"

The boy grinned and replied, "It's a puppy!"

—*Jennifer Hahn*

As Jennifer points out with this story, sometimes we receive gifts that surprise us, gifts that we might not even want. The Christmas season is one of those times when we may receive a variety of gifts—some we are excited to get; others we're not.

And yet it's important to be thankful for the *giver* if not especially for the *gift*. As the old adage says, "It's the thought that counts." Even more, it's the one who thought to bless us with his special gift that counts.

Father, we are so grateful to you for your gifts of love and sacrifice that came to us wrapped not in shiny paper and glistening bows but in bloody rags. May we always remember that special tree and the gift—your Son, Jesus Christ—that hung upon it. Amen.

December 12

Hot Seat

They share freely and give generously to those in need.
Their good deeds will be remembered forever.

PSALM 112:9

A group of my single friends and I met at our church one cold winter night to drop off our cars before driving together into the city to attend a gospel sing.

On our return drive after the event, one of my guy friends, Bruce, commented, "Boy, this is the type of night that makes me awfully glad my car seats are heated."

We kidded him about how cold the rest of us were going to be, hopping into our icebox-like cars without that heated comfort. By the time we arrived at the church, he was feeling sorry for us.

"Okay, hand me your keys, and I'll start your cars for you."

I liked that idea and complied. I'm five feet two and drive with the seat pulled very close to the steering wheel. I assumed that, with Bruce's six-foot-four frame, he would just lean in the window and start my car, but I watched as he ran over and jumped into my car's front seat. My skinny, five-foot-ten daughter-in-law cannot slide in behind my steering wheel without moving the seat back, so I wondered how Bruce was able to fit. I suspected he must be wedged in like sardines in a can.

Then, as my key made contact with the ignition, I saw a look of horror cross his face as my automatic telescoping steering wheel started to move toward him. He literally dove out of my car, leaving the heater running but without starting the engine.

I laughed for days every time I thought of my sweet friend's good deed. I still love to tease him about the incident, and he calls my car by a new name—Killer.

—Pam Whitley

Thank you, Lord, for friends who care and love to make life better for others. Help us never to take them for granted. Amen.

Stepping Back

May we shout for joy when we hear of your victory
and raise a victory banner in the name of our God.

PSALM 20:5

A few years ago our choir decided to put on a community variety show. We rented a popular old theater called the Grapevine Opry house and were blessed to sell a lot of tickets. Funds from the show went to pay for our upcoming mission trip.

Everything went well until the last big production number from *Grease*. We were all decked out in poodle skirts, bobby socks, penny loafers, and high school letter jackets, singing shooby-doos and doo-wops. Some of us were on the flat stage, while others were on raised platforms.

Toward the end of the song, the choreography called for the entire choir to doo-wop toward the back of the stage, then run back toward the front, ending with a big finale on our knees with hands raised in the air. It was fun to do, but it was a little tricky because the old Opry house stage was not very big.

As we began stepping backward to the rear curtain, we heard a big *kathump*. But in true performance style, we kept on singing and dancing. However, most of us noticed that one of our altos, Kathy, was missing. The soprano next to Kathy had a stricken expression on her face and kept glancing back and down. Kathy had stepped back too far and had fallen backward off the platform!

Just as we hit the last two notes of the song, Kathy rose up from the back of the stage, albeit a little disheveled, ran to her place for the finale, and completed the song on her knees with hands raised in the air. Of course, at that point we weren't sure whether she was raising her hands in victory or surrender!

Father, as Revelation declares, we know we will have the victory over Satan when the grand finale of the world arrives, and we raise our hands in praise to you for that victory. Amen.

December 14

Top Down, Tree Up!

Bring all who claim me as their God, for I have made them for my glory. It was I who created them.

ISAIAH 43:7

In late November 2005, I bought a brand-new 2006 Toyota Solara convertible in "Absolutely Red" with a tan-colored top. Ooh, it was hot! It was the first convertible I had ever owned, so I was feeling pretty spiffy and downright proud of myself. I just loved putting the top down and cruising through the neighborhoods, the wind blowing through my hair, the radio playing old-time rock and roll, and people watching me with a smile and a touch of envy.

About the second week of December, my friend Charlotte and I went shopping for a Christmas tree for my office. We found a pretty, seven-foot "pencil" tree in a square wooden planter box that would work well in my big eight-foot-high window. Of course, after I bought it, we couldn't figure out how to get it into the five-foot-wide trunk of my car because the tree was too tall.

Aha! came the sudden epiphany. I put the convertible top down and set the tree in the backseat with the treetop sticking out where the car top should have been. Charlotte and I drove to my office with the top down, the windows up, and the heater going full blast. Thelma and Louise were on an adventure!

At a stop sign, a Texas cowboy in his pickup truck pulled up beside us. The Stetson-hatted driver glanced over, saw the tree sticking out the top and my friend and I freezing to death, did a double take, and cracked up laughing. Then he pulled out his camera and took a picture. I guess the opportunity was just too good to pass up.

Sometimes in life, when things don't quite fit the way they are supposed to, you have to be creative, like the one who created us.

O Father, thank you for creating humorous moments and joyful days. Amen.

The Worst Way

People judge by outward appearance,
but the LORD looks at the heart.

1 SAMUEL 16:7

The fancy holiday party was in full swing, with the cream of society in attendance. Classy ball gowns, flashy jewelry, tuxedos, and top hats filled the hall. The food had been prepared by one of the top caterers in Washington, DC, and the orchestra was playing all the latest hits. The evening promised to sparkle and glimmer with success.

Couples meandered here and there—some wandering onto the veranda to watch the moon come up over the Potomac, others sitting quietly at small tables talking about politics and kids, and yet others dancing to the music in the ballroom.

Several women sat at a round table, admiring the splendid decor, the holiday decorations, and the wonderful music. Eventually, a tall, none-too-handsome young man approached the table and spoke to one of the ladies.

"Miss Todd, I should like to dance with you in the worst way," he said quietly. "May I have this dance?"

Taking his outstretched hand, she rose, saying, "Certainly, sir. I would be honored."

After negotiating a few clumsy circuits of the room with the tall, ungainly man, Mary was deposited back in her seat, surrounded by her giggling friends.

"Thank you so much, Miss Todd," said the man politely as he turned to leave.

One of the women at the table, grinning at Mary, asked, "Well, Mary, did he dance with you in the worst way?"

"Yes," replied Mary, "in the worst way."

Surprisingly, though, through the years Mary Todd danced many dances with the man who eventually became her husband and the president of the United States—Abraham Lincoln.

As my mother would say, "Handsome is as handsome does." Mr. Lincoln was greatly admired around the world for his actions, if not for his unique appearance.

I pray, dear Father, that you will find my heart pure and focused on you when you examine it. Thank you for looking beyond my outer self to my inner self. Amen.

How Much?

Do to others as you would like them to do to you.

LUKE 6:31

One day in the East Indies, Georges Clemenceau—"The Tiger"—of France was wandering along the main street of a small village, passing time and shopping for Christmas gifts for his friends and family. The little shops along the street offered a variety of trinkets, antiques, and fine artwork for sale, and Georges strolled from shop to shop, looking in the decorated windows.

In one shop window he noticed a small statuette that he liked, so he entered the shop and said to the dealer, "I like your statuette. How much is it, please?"

"Because it's you," the shopkeeper answered, "seventy-five rupees."

"Because it's you," responded Georges, "I'll offer you forty-five rupees."

The shopkeeper raised his hands to heaven in pretend horror. "Forty-five rupees! You're making fun of me! What if anyone happened to hear of it?"

"Forty-five rupees," repeated Georges firmly.

The indignant shopkeeper retorted, "Impossible! I would rather *give* it to you."

"Agreed!" said Georges, taking the statuette and stuffing it into his pocket. Then he said, "You are extraordinarily kind, and I thank you. But it is quite evident that this gift can only come from a friend to a friend. Consequently you won't consider it amiss if I in turn make you a gift?"

"Naturally not," said the shopkeeper with a slight smile.

"Well, friend, here are forty-five rupees to use in good works," said Georges, handing him the money.

The shopkeeper took the rupees, and the men shook hands and parted ways, completely enchanted with each other.

Thank you, Father, for the wonderful gifts you give us every day. In return, I give you the gifts of my heart and my life. Please use them to do good works for others and for your glory. Amen.

If Only He Had Known

Not to us, O Lord, not to us,
but to your name goes all the glory.

PSALM 115:1

One of my favorite Bible stories is about Esther. This tale has all the elements of a classic story—intrigue, danger, love, a villain who's caught, a good guy who's rewarded, a heroine who's saved, and a happily-ever-after ending. What more can you ask for in a story?

The villain is Haman. His biggest foible is how sold he is on himself. He *thinks* he is the most important man in the Persian kingdom next to the king. He *thinks* King Xerxes is going to honor him for being so clever and smart. He *thinks* he is going to get to destroy his enemies, the Jewish nation.

Due to his arrogance and self-absorption, though, Haman's dastardly plan is discovered and destroyed when he ends up in a face-off with his worst nightmare—Esther, the queen of Persia, the king's great love, and God's special servant. I love how God turns the tables on Haman in the end in order to protect his chosen people from annihilation. Haman is, in fact, hanged on the very gallows he'd built for his enemy, Esther's cousin. It's a great "Gotcha!" moment.

People from the city come by and watch Haman's body hanging there, decaying for all the world to see. Haman finally has the grand audience he had always wanted.

It reminds me of a politician in Illinois who died. The magnitude of his achievements was exceeded only by the size of his great ego. His funeral, quite surprisingly, was attended by nearly a thousand people.

A fellow politician said, "That many people? If he had known how big a funeral he was going to have, I think he would have died years ago!"

Forgive me, Father, for thinking I'm important rather than giving you the credit for anything you accomplish through me. May your name alone be glorified. Amen.

Just Follow the Tracks

[Jesus said,] "If any of you wants to be my follower . . . take up your cross daily, and follow me."

LUKE 9:23

Three men were lost in the middle of the Canadian forest. They decided they had to find some food, so the first man left, saying that he was going hunting.

Several hours later, the man came back with a deer across his shoulders. The other two men were amazed and asked him how he managed to get a deer with no weapons. He replied, "I found tracks. I followed tracks. I got deer." They were both confused, but they let it go.

A few days later, the men had eaten all the deer meat, so the second man left and said that he was going hunting. He came back a couple of hours later with an elk over his shoulders. The other two men asked how he had gotten the elk, and he simply replied, "I found tracks. I followed tracks. I got elk."

Later, after they had eaten all the elk meat, the third man said he would go hunting. Feeling cocky, he thought, *This will be a piece of cake. I'm going to get an animal that's better than both of theirs put together!*

The other men waited a couple of hours, but the third man did not come back. They waited another couple of hours, but he was still missing.

Finally, after nine hours, he came back. His clothes were shredded, he was covered in dirt with scrapes and bruises all over his body, and he was bleeding from gashes in his arms and legs.

His friends asked, "What happened?"

He looked at them, wide eyed and confused, and replied, "I found tracks. I followed tracks. I got hit by train."

Heavenly Father, help me always to remember that the only way to you is by following in the footsteps of your Son, Jesus. Keep me on the right path. Amen.

Taking It with You

The love of money is the root of all kinds of evil.

1 TIMOTHY 6:10

There once was a man who worked all his life and saved his money. He loved his money more than anything else, so just before he died, he said to his wife, "Now listen, when I die, I want you to take all my money and place it in the casket with me. I want to take it with me into the afterlife."

"You're kidding, right?" The wife laughed, thinking he was making a joke.

"No, I'm *dead* serious," he replied. He finally managed to get his wife to promise that when he died she would put all his money in the casket with him.

Eventually he died and was laid in a casket. At the funeral, his wife sat near the casket, next to her closest friend. Just before the funeral directors closed the casket at the end of the service, the wife said, "Wait just a minute, please."

She brought a shoe box to the side of the casket, leaned over, kissed her deceased husband, and placed the shoe box next to him. The funeral directors closed and locked the casket and rolled it away to put it in the funeral car to be transported to the cemetery.

Her friend said, "I hope you weren't crazy enough to put all his money in the casket."

"Yes," the wife said. "I promised him I would, and because I'm a good Christian, that's exactly what I did."

"You mean you put every cent of his money in the casket with him?"

"I sure did. I got it all together, put it into my bank account, and wrote him a check."

Lord, help me to store up my treasures with you in heaven rather than here on earth. Amen.

December 20

Not Now, Donald

Respect everyone. . . . Fear God, and respect the king.

1 PETER 2:17

After several long months of preparation, Cindy was at last meeting with an extremely important client. The meeting was scheduled for noon in the American Airlines' VIP lounge at Los Angeles International Airport because her client was stopping there on his way from Houston to London. Cindy was nervous about the meeting, but she was also excited. As luck would have it, her client's flight was coming in a bit late.

As Cindy waited in the VIP lounge, she noticed none other than Donald Trump sitting on a sofa nearby reading the *Wall Street Journal.* Knowing it was probably risky, but being a bold businesswoman, Cindy decided to approach Mr. Trump.

Walking across the lounge, she stopped in front of "the Donald" and said, "Excuse me, Mr. Trump. I'm sorry to interrupt your reading, but I wanted to introduce myself. I'm Cindy Taylor with Ross & Cummings."

Much to her surprise, Mr. Trump turned out to be very nice and welcoming. Encouraged, Cindy explained to him that she was about to close a very important business deal and wondered if he would be gracious enough to just say a quick "Hello, Cindy" to her when she was with her client.

Recognizing a bit of his own assertive business style in Cindy, Mr. Trump agreed to do just that. Cindy was thrilled.

Ten minutes later, while Cindy was speaking with her client, she felt a tap on her shoulder. It was Donald Trump. Cindy turned and looked up at him as he spoke.

"Hi, Cindy. How's it going?"

Cindy glibly replied, "Not now, Donald. Can't you see I'm in a meeting with a client?"

Dear God, I want you to always be part of my interactions with others. Help me to remember to treat people with respect and not just use them for my own purposes. Amen.

A Child Is Born

A child is born to us,
a son is given to us.

ISAIAH 9:6

To announce the church's annual Christmas service to the community, the business committee decided to hang a huge sign outside the church. The theme of the service would be "Unto Us a Child Is Born."

Because there was no sign shop in their small town, the committee appointed one of the deacons to drive to a nearby city and purchase the sign. They wrote the sign's measurements, along with the title, on an index card and gave it to the deacon.

The next day the deacon set out for the city. Pulling into the parking lot of the Quick Signs shop, he began looking for the index card that contained the information he would need for the order. Somehow he had lost the card. *Now what?* he thought.

Glancing down the row of businesses in the shopping center where the sign shop was located, he noticed Western Union at the far end of the center. *That's it!* he thought. *I'll send a telegram to the church and get the information.*

The man walked to Western Union and wrote out a telegram that said, "Lost card. Send information again. Waiting here."

The telegraph operator quickly transmitted the message, and the deacon sat down in a chair to wait for the response. Ten minutes later the response came in. But the deacon was shocked when the telegraph operator read the message and fainted right on the spot.

Reaching over the counter, the deacon picked up the message, which read, "Unto us a child is born—eight feet long, six feet wide."

Father, thank you for this wonderful season of celebrating your Son's birth. May his light shine brightly into every dark corner of the world during this time and always. Amen.

December 22

Home for Christmas

All the people returned to their homes, and David turned and went home to bless his own family.

1 CHRONICLES 16:43

An old man in Phoenix called his son in New York a few days before Christmas and said, "Son, this is Dad. I hate to ruin your day, but I have to tell you that your mom and I are divorcing. Forty-five years of misery is enough! I just can't take it anymore."

"Pop, what are you talking about?" the son shouted.

"It's true. We can't stand the sight of each other any longer," the father said. "Frankly, we're sick of each other, and I'm tired of talking about this, so you can call your sister in Chicago and tell her the bad news. Good-bye."

Frantic, the son called his sister and told her what their dad had said. The sister exploded on the phone: "No way! They are *not* getting divorced! Don't worry. I'll take care of this."

Immediately the daughter called her parents' home in Phoenix and screamed at her father, "Dad, are you crazy? You are *not* getting divorced. Don't you do a single thing until I get there. I'm calling my brother back, and we will both be there tomorrow. Until then, don't you do a thing. *Do you hear me?*" And she hung up.

She called her brother and said, "Get airline tickets. We have to go home and straighten out this mess. I'll see you there."

"Okay, Sis, I'll be there tomorrow."

After the father hung up the phone from the call with his daughter, he turned to his wife and smiled. "It's all set," he said. "Get everything ready. They're coming for Christmas, and they're paying their own way."

Heavenly Father, thank you for this time of year when we get together with our families. And we look forward to the day we can be at home with you forever. Amen.

December 23

A Christmas to Remember

Rescue others by snatching them
from the flames of judgment.

JUDE 1:23

At a party some time ago, I heard someone tell the following story:

I think all ten-year-old boys like fire, and I was no different. It was Christmas Day, and our guests were due to arrive any moment.

In the kitchen Mom was putting the finishing touches on her cookies. My older brother, Cody, was headed for the shower, at Mom's insistence.

Much to my surprise and Cody's disapproval, Dad decided to give me the much-coveted responsibility of starting the Christmas fire.

"Josh, can I trust you to handle this job while I go outside to cut more logs?" Dad asked.

"Absolutely, Dad, no problem," I said, with a bit too much enthusiasm.

My excitement soon turned to frustration when the fire would not stay lit. Out to the garage I went for some newspaper, but instead I returned with a can of gasoline.

As I tossed the fuel toward the logs, I noticed a small glowing ember. For one brief moment, I felt a twinge of regret. Suddenly, a line of fire traveled straight up the fuel into the gas can. I dropped the can and yelled as the fumes ignited my shirt.

Cody arrived first, wearing only a towel. Using the towel, he beat the flame, now spreading across Mom's new rug. Dad came in next and shoved me outside.

Instead of the expected rebuff, Dad yelled, "Stop! Drop and roll!"

I did as I was told, and the fire went out. I glanced up just in time to see our guests walking up the driveway. Stunned looks changed to surprise as they looked from me to the house. Framed by the big bay window, there was Cody in all his glory, putting out the last sparks of the flame with his towel.

It was a Christmas to remember!

—*Susan M. C. Holland*

Father, don't let my pride or concern over what others may think of me get in the way of rescuing those in peril. Amen.

Christmas Treeeat!

A cheerful heart is good medicine,
but a broken spirit saps a person's strength.

PROVERBS 17:22

Candles flickered by the hundreds as numerous lit Christmas trees served as their backdrops. Carols were playing, and the joy and wonder of the birth of Christ filled the Christmas Eve service. But as I looked at the beautiful sight before me, it brought more pain than joy to my sorrow-filled heart.

Seated next to my son's family, I struggled to hold back the tears. The empty seat beside me was a glaring reminder that my husband of thirty-three years was gone. He had died a few months earlier. Truthfully, I was glad when the service was over.

After the service, we picked up my nineteen-month-old grandson, Will, from the nursery. He was tired and hungry. As we headed home, he became very cranky. After all, it was past his mealtime, and eating was a central focus of his life. In an attempt to keep Will distracted, my son said, "Will, what does a sheep say?"

We were all expecting to hear, "Baa!" Instead Will bellowed out, "Eeeeeeat!" We all chuckled.

"Will, tell Grandma what a tiger says!"

With sparkling eyes, Will said, "Eeeeeat!" in his best tiger voice. By then we were all roaring with laughter.

"Will, tell Grandma what a puppy dog says!" Will barked, "Eat, eat, eat."

Of course Will loved being our entertainment, and his delight in amusing us distracted him from thoughts of food. My son continued to ask about different sounds, and Will cried "Eat!" in various tones and elongations. We laughed so hard we had to wipe the tears from our eyes. My heavy heart was lightened by the antics of one precious child.

My soul is also lighthearted and glad at the thought of another Child whose actions gave us abundant life both here and in heaven: Jesus, the Messiah.

—*Pam Whitley*

Thank you, Lord, for redirecting my focus and filling my heart with healing laughter. Amen.

An Unexpected Answer

The LORD says . . .
"When they call on me, I will answer."

PSALM 91:14-15

When the congregation came to church that Christmas Day, I'm sure none of them expected to hear from Mars.

My parents had given our youngest child, David, a battery-operated robot for Christmas. The little boy was delighted with its stiff-legged gait, its flashing lights, and its robotic voice.

Since my husband was the pastor, we lived next door to the church. The church building was too small to seat the entire congregation, so on Christmas Day we held two consecutive services. Because it would be tough for our three children—ages twelve, nine, and five—to sit through both services, we gave them permission to return home after the first service to play with their new toys.

"Stay inside," I instructed them. "Your sister is in charge. If there's a problem, one of you slip quietly into the church and call me. Okay?"

The three of them nodded, and they rushed off to play. I knew our daughter would soon be engrossed in one of her new books and would forget all about the other two. But she would be there if they needed her. In any case, they were right next door. What could go wrong?

During the service, my husband led the congregation to pray. "Let's wait on the Lord," he said. After a moment's silence, the startled congregation heard a mechanical voice through an open window, "Greetings, Earthmen! My name is Telbaz. I come from Mars. Please give my best wishes to everyone."

Mortified, I slipped out the side door to find two giggling little boys crouched under the window as the alien visitor shuffled along the path.

The following year we held our Christmas service in the fellowship hall, which was big enough to hold everyone in one sitting.

—*Shirley M. Corder*

Lord God, how often we pray to you, but how seldom we expect a reply. Please help me to pray and wait for your answer—preferably not from Mars. Amen.

December 26

Gift Exchange with Jesus

Do not judge others, and you will not be judged.

MATTHEW 7:1

It was the day after Christmas in a small Oklahoma town. The holiday festivities were over. Cars loaded with visiting families and presents were leaving town, headed back to the big cities. The snow that had fallen on Christmas Eve was melting and slushy. People were beginning to take down their outdoor decorations, and discarded plastic-wrapped Christmas trees dotted the front yards along Main Street.

Mayor Berkley decided to go for an afternoon stroll through town, just to see what was going on and to keep his finger on the pulse of the community. As he walked through the city park, he suddenly noticed that the plastic doll representing the baby Jesus was missing from among the figures in the city's nativity scene. He searched around the nativity, but he found nothing.

Mayor Berkley started across the park back toward his office to call the local sheriff so he could investigate the incident. Then he saw little Jeremy Thompson riding his bike on the sidewalk in the park. In the basket on his bike lay the Jesus doll, wrapped carefully in a warm blanket.

Smiling, Mayor Berkley said, "Hey, Jeremy, where did you get your passenger, my little friend?"

The little boy did not hesitate and replied honestly, "I got him from the nativity in the park."

"And why did you take him, Jeremy?" asked the mayor.

The boy said, "Well, about a week before Christmas I prayed to the little Lord Jesus, and I told him if he would bring me a bike for Christmas, I would give him a ride around the park on it."

Dear Lord, please help me to remember that things are not always as they first appear. Let me not be quick to judge but careful to give people the benefit of the doubt. I want to show your grace and mercy to those I meet. Amen.

Just Stuffed

[There is] a time to be quiet and a time to speak.

ECCLESIASTES 3:7

My husband and I had moved to New Zealand as missionaries in the fall, just in time to be there for the Christmas holidays. We were delighted to spend time with our new Christian friends, to experience how they celebrated Christmas, and to enjoy the wonderful foods they prepared, such as English trifle and Russian pavlova.

The following week some of our friends, Wally and Maureen O'Donnell, invited us to go out to dinner with them. We met at a delightful restaurant that overlooked the beautiful harbor at Wellington and shared a marvelous meal of leg of lamb, roasted potatoes, vegetables, salad, and fresh bread. After we had been abundantly blessed with great food and stimulating conversation, we finally pushed our plates back in contentment.

As we sat watching the moon come up over the harbor and cast its glimmering beams across the rippling water, my husband and I talked about how we hoped to help the church reach out to the lost and lonely people in and around Wellington. It would be a huge challenge, but it was one we both relished.

Our waitress then came to the table and, addressing my husband, said, "Sir, what may I bring you for dessert?"

My husband said, "Oh, dear! I couldn't eat another thing—I'm just stuffed!"

The waitress ducked her head and giggled, as did Wally and Maureen. We sat, blank faced, not knowing what was so funny.

My husband said, "Okay, I know I must have committed some international faux pas. What was it?"

Wally laughed and said, "Well, my friend, you have just announced to the whole world that you are pregnant! That's what being *stuffed* means in New Zealand."

That turned out to be only one of many linguistic blunders we made during our learning curve as missionaries.

Forgive me, Father, for words I say that should not escape my lips. Help me to govern my words carefully so they reflect well on you. Amen.

December 28

In Stitches

Who can find a virtuous and capable wife?. . . Her hands are busy spinning thread. . . . She makes her own bedspreads. . . . Her children stand and bless her.

PROVERBS 31:10, 19, 22, 28

As a child, I loved to draw. I remember the manila paper (or as I mistakenly called it, "vanilla" paper) and the crayons we used for creating our artistic works at school. Over time, I produced a large collection of artwork that I proudly marched home to my parents. Unknown to me, my mom carefully tucked my masterpieces into a special box, where she kept them for more than thirty years.

One Christmas, my husband and I hosted the family Christmas gathering at our house in Monroe, Louisiana. My parents, my husband's parents, and other family members came from Texas and Kansas for the holiday, and we enjoyed all the traditional foods and festivities.

During the gift exchange, my mother surprised me with a king-size, handmade quilt. She had taken my elementary-school drawings, transferred them to manila-colored fabric blocks, and embroidered the pictures in the same crayon colors I had used when I originally drew them. It was an amazing gift of love and hard work that I still treasure.

She also gave me a scrapbook that contained all the original drawings and the blue ribbon she had won for the quilt at the county fair. Her beautiful handwork included more than sixty of my pictures captured in colorful thread on the quilt, a headboard hanging, and matching pillows.

After the holidays, I received a phone call from a reporter at the local newspaper. She said one of my friends had called to say that the newspaper should do a story about my quilt. Naturally, I was happy to oblige.

I still have the newspaper article in the scrapbook Mom created for me. And I smile every time I see the headline: "Woman Puts Daughter in Stitches."

Father, thank you for the blessing of wonderful mothers. Amen.

Lost and Found

The Son of Man came to seek and save those who are lost.

LUKE 19:10

Our church choir was on a mission concert tour in Scotland. We were scheduled to sing at St. Mary's Church in a small town one evening. Our guide and driver delivered us to the church about an hour before the seven o'clock concert to set up and warm up.

Our director, Charlotte, went to find the person in charge, but she could find only the caretaker. He said he was not aware that a concert was planned for that night. She assured him there was, so he unlocked the door.

We quickly set up our equipment and began warming up. Still no "official" host had come to welcome us. Even more perplexing was the lack of people to hear us sing. Not one single person had arrived by 6:40. Becoming alarmed, Charlotte sent one of the men to find help. Soon he returned with a nun, who assured us no one knew of a concert at the church that night.

"We are supposed to sing at St. Mary's Church," said Charlotte.

"Oh, dear!" said the nun. "We are St. Mary's *Cathedral.* St. Mary's *Church* is downtown."

"Oh, no! Okay, everyone, grab the equipment, and let's go! *Now!*" We all went flying out of the cathedral to our bus—which was locked. Another bus driver said our guide and driver had gone to eat while we were setting up. Now what? It was 6:50.

The other driver said, "Get on my bus, and I'll take you." With no time to question, we rushed onto his bus. When we arrived, Charlotte ran into the church, where she found the sanctuary full of people, patiently waiting.

We clambered out of the bus, lined up outside, and marched into the church at exactly 7:01, singing our opening number. It was a great concert.

Later, our guide said, "I've lost one person on a tour before, but never a whole choir!"

Thank you, dear Father, for always finding us when we are lost. Amen.

December 30

Ring It Out!

Let your unfailing love surround us, LORD,
for our hope is in you alone.

PSALM 33:22

When Dennis and I were dating, people ran the other way when they saw me coming. They were sick of hearing how wonderful I thought he was. I could not wait to see, talk to, and spend time with him. I was in love. Not just in love, but *in love*!

After two years I was hopeful the upcoming holiday season would give Dennis a good excuse to purchase an engagement ring. My late November birthday passed without major fanfare or anything sparkly for my left hand. Surely Christmas would be different!

Because Dennis is a history buff, I purchased a replica of a black powder revolver for his present. As Christmas neared, I pushed him to exchange gifts before we traveled to visit our respective families. Dennis dodged each suggestion, saying we would celebrate when we returned. So I left town with my tail tucked, wondering if I had misread our situation and if God was closing the door.

When I returned, Dennis picked me up for a dinner date, and my hopes soared. Surely the time had finally come. After a lovely dinner, but no ring, we returned to my apartment. I presented him with the gun, and I received a token gift but still no ring. *Whimper.* I kept a smile, but I tried to prepare myself for cutting my losses and moving on. At least God would love me forever.

Just as my hopes fell to the floor, Dennis produced a small black velvet box and went down on one knee. I said yes, of course, and he is thrilled to truthfully brag that a gun was involved in our engagement.

The nice thing is, no matter what happens in our earthly relationships, we always have a heavenly Father who will love us forever, and thankfully, no weapons are involved.

—Lisa Buffaloe

Thank you, Father, for your unfailing love and the hope we have in you. Amen.

December 31

Out with the Old—and the New!

What looked like flames or tongues of fire appeared and settled on each of them.

ACTS 2:3

Gauntlet Brotter was the elderly minister of a spirit-filled church in South Africa. It was time for him to retire, so for two years he had been training a young man named Timba Sambuli to replace him. Gauntlet decided it would be appropriate to make the transition at the New Year's Eve prayer service, using the familiar theme "Out with the Old, In with the New." He invited the congregation to meet under the large tent used for summertime events.

Timba had two American friends named Bob and Tony. In his joy at becoming the new minister, Timba told them about the installation service, and they decided to add some fun to the ceremony.

On New Year's Eve the guys found a spot on a hill about thirty feet from the tent, where they hid to watch. The service went well, until old Gauntlet began calling on God to bless Timba. He called out over and over, "Lawd, come down upon us with the Holy Spirit and fire!" The congregation chanted with him, and the energy of the meeting increased. Singing and chanting soon became dancing and shouting, as they repeated loudly, "Lawd, come down upon us with the Holy Spirit and fire!"

At the height of the chanting, Bob and Tony set off two Roman candles, pointing them at the tent. The balls of fire *zoomed* through the tent, exploding in the midst of the church service. One fiery ball exploded where Gauntlet and Timba were dancing. In a flash they both dived from the podium out opposite sides of the tent, hollering, "O Lawd! Thank you, Lawd! We see your fire!"

That's when the New Year's theme changed to "Out with the Old . . . *and* the New!"

Thank you, Lord, for your Spirit, who guides us and interprets our prayers. May your Spirit empower us to touch the world around us in the coming year. Amen.

About the Author

Mary Hollingsworth is the author of more than one hundred Christian adult, gift, and children's books; animated videos; and CD-ROMs. Sales of her books now top seven million copies, including *My Little Bible* (Word, 1991), which received both the Gold and the Platinum Book Awards presented by the Evangelical Christian Publishers Association, and *The International Children's Story Bible* (Word, 1990), which received the Gold Medallion Book Award. She also wrote *Just Imagine!* with Barney the dinosaur (Lyons Group, 1992)—the first picture book featuring Barney, which sold more than 1.3 million copies. Mary's books have appeared on bestseller lists in the Christian market more than one hundred times. One of her books, *Hugs for Women* (Howard, 1998), was on the *CBA Marketplace* list for fifteen months and was a finalist for the 1999 Inspirational Gift Book of the Year Award from the Inspirational Network. In May 2002, Mary was awarded the Spiritual Development Award from Howard Books, a division of Simon & Schuster, in recognition of her extensive Christian publishing career. She has also had more than one hundred other works published, including magazine articles, poetry, plays, and songs. As a freelance production editor for more than ten years with Thomas Nelson, Inc., Mary supervised the production of bestselling books by Women of Faith and such well-known authors as Billy Graham, Max Lucado, Charles Swindoll, Patsy Clairmont, Chuck Colson, Luci Swindoll, Pat Robertson, Dee Brestin, Kathy Troccoli, and others. In her spare time, Mary enjoys traveling, collecting miniature and rare books, writing poetry and lyrics, and singing. She telecommutes from her home in Bedford, Texas, where she serves as the managing director of Creative Enterprises Studio and lives with her two dogs, Jazz and Samson.

Permissions

The devotional on January 3, titled "The Perk from Above," is reprinted by permission of Luci Swindoll. All rights reserved.

The devotional on January 4, titled "All the Way to the Tub," is printed by permission of Dianna Booher, www.booher.com. All rights reserved.

The devotional on January 8, titled "Name That Wife," is taken from *If the Pasta Wiggles . . . Don't Eat It*, copyright © 1995, Vine Books, Ann Arbor, and is reprinted by permission of Martha Bolton. All rights reserved.

The devotional on January 9, titled "The Muscle Man," is printed by permission of Edith Moore-Parkman. All rights reserved.

The devotional on January 10, titled "Oh, How I Love Jesus!" is printed by permission of Stephanie Terry. All rights reserved.

The devotional on January 12, titled "The Big Snow," is printed by permission of C. Anne Morrison. All rights reserved.

The devotional on January 13, titled "Actions Speak Louder," is printed by permission of Sandra Heska King. All rights reserved.

The devotional on January 14, titled "I Have a Great Plan!" is printed by permission of Jennifer Stair. All rights reserved.

The devotional on January 15, titled "Senior I.D.," is printed by permission of Grace G. Booth. All rights reserved.

The devotional on January 16, titled "How Do We Define Ourselves?" is printed by permission of Renea McKenzie. All rights reserved.

The devotional on January 17, titled "Credit Where Credit Is Due," is printed by permission of Al Speegle Jr. All rights reserved.

The devotional on January 18, titled "Marshmallow Wars," is printed by permission of Lisa Buffaloe. All rights reserved.

The devotional on January 28, titled "What's Your Line?" is printed by permission of Diane E. Kay. All rights reserved.

The devotional on January 30, titled "Cleansing and Clothespins," is printed by permission of Mary Hake. All rights reserved.

The devotional on February 1, titled "Where Is God?" by J. John and Mark Stibbe, is reprinted by permission from *A Bucket of Surprises*, J. John and Mark Stibbe, copyright © 2002, Monarch Books, London. All rights reserved.

The devotional on February 3, titled "Out of Sight," is printed by permission of Shirley M. Corder. All rights reserved.

The devotional on February 6, titled "What Powdered-Sugar Doughnuts?" is printed by permission of Max Elliot Anderson. All rights reserved.

The devotional on February 7, titled "Serving with Grace," is printed by permission of Kathleen A. Brown. All rights reserved.

The devotional on February 9, titled "Laughing in the Pits," is printed by permission of Lisa Buffaloe. All rights reserved.

The devotional on February 13, titled "Sing to the Lord," is printed by permission of Barbara Ferguson. All rights reserved.

The devotional on February 15, titled "Anatomy 101," is printed by permission of Christine Thomas. All rights reserved.

The devotional on February 20, titled "Grandma-saurus," is printed by permission of Susan Sundwall. All rights reserved.

The devotional on February 21, titled "Comfort Zone," is printed by permission of Stevie Stevens. All rights reserved.

The devotional on February 25, titled "To Kiss a Frog" by Bruce Larson, is reprinted by permission. *Ask Me to Dance*, Bruce Larson, copyright 1977, Thomas Nelson Inc., Nashville, Tennessee. All rights reserved.

The devotional on February 26, titled "Read the Instructions? You're Kidding!" is printed by permission of Rebecca Willman Gernon. All rights reserved.

The devotional on March 1, titled "The Race," is printed by permission of Pam Whitley. All rights reserved.

The devotional on March 2, titled "Soggy Seats," is printed by permission of Pam Whitley. All rights reserved.

The devotional on March 3, titled "The Frantic Fowl," is printed by permission of Raymond N. Hawkins. All rights reserved.

The devotional on March 4, titled "Request a Shower from God," is printed by permission of Janelle Shantz Hertzler. All rights reserved.

The devotional on March 6, titled "The *Rs* Have It," is printed by permission of Mary Brawner. All rights reserved.

The devotional on March 9, titled "The Painful Truth," is printed by permission of Naomi Cassata. All rights reserved.

The devotional on March 10, titled "Imagination? No Problem," is printed by permission of Susan Sundwall. All rights reserved.

The devotional on March 11, titled "Remember Names," is printed by permission of Pamela S. Davis. All rights reserved.

The devotional on March 13, titled "Love Your Neighbor," is printed by permission of Lisa Bartelt. All rights reserved.

The devotional on March 15, titled "Wash Your Hands!" is printed by permission of Cynthia Phagan Bittick. All rights reserved.

The devotional on March 16, titled "Bleating Buffaloe," is printed by permission of Lisa Buffaloe. All rights reserved.

The devotional on March 22, titled "What's in a Name?" is printed by permission of Melanie Jongsma. All rights reserved.

The devotional on March 24, titled "Fill 'Er Up!" by Charles Swindoll, is reprinted by permission. *The Tale of the Tardy Oxcart*, Charles Swindoll, copyright 1998, Thomas Nelson Inc., Nashville, Tennessee. All rights reserved.

The devotional on March 31, titled "Expect the Unexpected," is printed by permission of Genevra Bonati. All rights reserved.

The devotional on April 1, titled "Serpent in the Basement," is printed by permission of Marilyn Eudaly. All rights reserved.

The devotional on April 3, titled "Never Too Stuck," is printed by permission of Lisa Buffaloe. All rights reserved.

The devotional on April 4, titled "When Will It Be Fixed?" is printed by permission of Jennifer Stair. All rights reserved.

The devotional on April 6, titled "Stuck," is printed by permission of Stevie Stevens. All rights reserved.

The devotional on April 7, titled "Blew Our Family Away," is printed by permission of Paula Hemingway. All rights reserved.

The devotional on April 9, titled "Headless Superheroes," is printed by permission of Pam Whitley. All rights reserved.

The devotional on April 10, titled "Skuzzy," is printed by permission of Sue Ferguson. All rights reserved.

The devotional on April 12, titled "Clean Sandwich," is printed by permission of Felicia Washington. All rights reserved.

The devotional on April 16, titled "Roar of the Dandelions," is printed by permission of Catrina Bradley. All rights reserved.

The devotional on April 17, titled "An 8-Track Girl in an iPod World," is printed by permission of Lisa M. Garvey. All rights reserved.

The devotional on April 19, titled "Animal Antics," is printed by permission of Diane E. Kay. All rights reserved.

The devotional on April 22, titled "Now That Tastes Good!" is printed by permission of Elaine Williams Cavalier. All rights reserved.

The devotional on April 24, titled "Distracted," is printed by permission of Heather Lawley. All rights reserved.

The devotional on April 27, titled "New Ideas" by J. John and Mark Stibbe, is reprinted by permission from *A Barrel of Fun*, J. John and Mark Stibbe, copyright © 2004, Monarch Books, London. All rights reserved.

The devotional on April 28, titled "Yuck-cumbers and Omelets," is printed by permission of Diane E. Kay. All rights reserved.

The devotional on May 1, titled "Floored," is printed by permission of Pam Whitley. All rights reserved.

The devotional on May 2, titled "Silly Goose," is printed by permission of John McCutcheon. All rights reserved.

The devotional on May 3, titled "A Clean Sweep," is printed by permission of Stevie Stevens. All rights reserved.

The devotional on May 4, titled "Flip-Flops and Mountain Streams," is printed by permission of Marion C. Ueckermann. All rights reserved.

The devotional on May 7, titled "I Proved It!" is printed by permission of Sandra Heska King. All rights reserved.

The devotional on May 8, titled "Feeding Sheep from a Piñata," is printed by permission of Al Speegle Jr. All rights reserved.

The devotional on May 14, titled "I See That Finger," is printed by permission of Max Elliot Anderson. All rights reserved.

The devotional on May 15, titled "Pretending," is printed by permission of Colleen Luntzel. All rights reserved.

The devotional on May 17, titled "Fairy Faith," is printed by permission of Diane E. Kay. All rights reserved.

The devotional on May 18, titled "Oozing Joy," is printed by permission of Sandy Lackey Wright. All rights reserved.

The devotional on May 20, titled "Rub-a-Dub-Dub," is printed by permission of Tanya Magnus. All rights reserved.

The anecdote from Marvin Phillips in the devotional on May 24, titled "Give It to Him!," is reprinted with the permission of Howard Books, a Division of Simon & Schuster, Inc. from *Never Lick a Frozen Flagpole!* by Marvin Phillips. Copyright © 1999 by Marvin Phillips.

The devotional on May 30, titled "Upside Down," is printed by permission of Sue Bohlin. All rights reserved.

The devotional on June 2, titled "Sooty and Shielded," is printed by permission of Lisa Buffaloe. All rights reserved.

The devotional on June 4, titled "The Warrior and the Mice," is printed by permission of Marty Prudhomme. All rights reserved.

The devotional on June 8, titled "Well Prepared?" by Kathy Peel, is reprinted by permission. *Do Plastic Surgeons Take Visa?* Kathy Peel, copyright 1992, Thomas Nelson Inc., Nashville, Tennessee. All rights reserved.

The devotional on June 9, titled "Squeaking Sheets," is printed by permission of Stevie Stevens. All rights reserved.

The devotional on June 11, titled "I Love to Tell the Story," is printed by permission of Jennifer Stair. All rights reserved.

The devotional on June 12, titled "Making Lemonade," is printed by permission of Marty Prudhomme. All rights reserved.

The devotional on June 13, titled "The Fun in Funny," is printed by permission of Barbara Ferguson. All rights reserved.

The devotional on June 15, titled "My Turkey's Cooked . . . or Not," is printed by permission of Al Speegle Jr. All rights reserved.

The devotional on June 16, titled "Like Little Children," is printed by permission of Kathleen A. Brown. All rights reserved.

The devotional on June 18, titled "How's Your Light?" is printed by permission of Elaine Williams Cavalier. All rights reserved.

The devotional on June 19, titled "Birthday Bloopers," is printed by permission of Marion C. Ueckermann. All rights reserved.

The devotional on June 20, titled "Simplicity" by Charles Swindoll, is reprinted by permission. *The Tale of the Tardy Oxcart*, Charles Swindoll, copyright 1998, Thomas Nelson, Inc., Nashville, Tennessee. All rights reserved.

The devotional on June 24, titled "The Way," is printed by permission of Sue Ferguson. All rights reserved.

The devotional on June 27, titled "A Journey to Remember," is printed by permission of Mary Hake. All rights reserved.

The devotional on July 2, titled "Tiller-Riding Buffaloe," is printed by permission of Lisa Buffaloe. All rights reserved.

The devotional on July 5, titled "Family Ties," is printed by permission of Paula Hemingway. All rights reserved.

The devotional on July 7, titled "Pride Goes before the Fall," is printed by permission of Jennifer Stair. All rights reserved.

The devotional on July 9, titled "Spell-Check, Please," is printed by permission of Coleene VanTilburg. All rights reserved.

The devotional on July 11, titled "Listen Up!" is printed by permission of Carrie Bezusko. All rights reserved.

The devotional on July 13, titled "Where's Donn?" is printed by permission of Max Elliot Anderson. All rights reserved.

The devotional on July 17, titled "A Better Boy," is printed by permission of Shari Johnston Gunter. All rights reserved.

The devotional on July 31, titled "Did God Hear You?" was adapted for this book by Mary Hollingsworth from *Behavior of Belief* by Spiros Zodhiates, copyright 1973, and is printed by permission of AMG Publishers, Chattanooga, Tennessee. All rights reserved.

The devotional on August 2, titled "Moving Day," is printed by permission of Stevie Stevens. All rights reserved.

The devotional on August 4, titled "Who Are You Going to Call?" is printed by permission of Lisa Bartelt. All rights reserved.

The devotional on August 8, titled "Perspective" by Erwin Lutzer, is taken from *Failure: The Backdoor to Success*, copyright 2008, and is printed by permission of Moody Publishers, Chicago, Illinois. All rights reserved.

The devotional on August 9, titled "Skin-Deep Beauty," is printed by permission of Jennifer Nagy. All rights reserved.

The devotional on August 15, titled "Be Alert," is printed by permission of Sue Ferguson. All rights reserved.

The devotional on August 17, titled "In the Driver's Seat," is printed by permission of Pam Whitley. All rights reserved.

The devotional on September 7, titled "Centered," is printed by permission of Kathleen A. Brown. All rights reserved.

The devotional on September 14, titled "An Unmentionable Mishap," is printed by permission of Jennifer Stair. All rights reserved.

The devotional on September 20, titled "Godly Potato Chips," is printed by permission of Gwen Williams. All rights reserved.

The devotional on September 30, titled "Where Are You?" is from *Growing Spiritually*, E. Stanley Jones, copyright © 1981, Abingdon Press, Nashville. Used by permission.

The devotional on October 1, titled "Rescued Lamps and Lives," is printed by permission of Peggy Nelson. All rights reserved.

The devotional on October 6, titled "Garlic in the Church," is printed by permission of Raymond N. Hawkins. All rights reserved.

The devotional on October 8, titled "Joy Remembered," is printed by permission of Kathleen A. Brown. All rights reserved.

The devotional on October 11, titled "The Sum of All Trials," is printed by permission of Jerri Kelley. All rights reserved.

The devotional on October 15, titled "Mission: Possible," is printed by permission of Paula Hemingway. All rights reserved.

The devotional on October 17, titled "Radiant Beauty," is printed by permission of Erin Hobbie. All rights reserved.

The devotional on October 19, titled "Trained to Hear God's Voice," is printed by permission of Gloria J. Wallace. All rights reserved.

The devotional on October 23, titled "Waging War," is printed by permission of Jennifer Mersberger. All rights reserved.

The devotional on October 31, titled "God's Left Hand," is printed by permission of Foy O. Jackson. All rights reserved.

The devotional on November 1, titled "Follow My Example," is printed by permission of Jennifer Stair. All rights reserved.

The devotional on November 3, titled "My Weekend Barbecue," is printed by permission of Al Speegle Jr. All rights reserved.

The devotional on November 4, titled "Booming Voice," is printed by permission of Pamela S. Davis. All rights reserved.

The devotional on November 5, titled "These Shoes Weren't Made for Walking," is printed by permission of Lisa M. Garvey. All rights reserved.

The devotional on November 7, titled "Joy Thread," is printed by permission of Sandy Lackey Wright. All rights reserved.

The devotional on November 9, titled "Car-Seat Caper," is printed by permission of Pam Whitley. All rights reserved.

The devotional on November 12, titled "Equipped for Disaster," is printed by permission of Sue Ferguson. All rights reserved.

The devotional on November 19, titled "Rush Hour," is printed by permission of Kathleen A. Brown. All rights reserved.

The devotional on November 22, titled "Where There's Smoke, There's Turkey," is taken from *Who Put the Pizza in the VCR: Laughing Your Way through Life's Little Emergencies*, copyright 1996, Ann Arbor and is reprinted by permission of Martha Bolton. All rights reserved.

The devotional on December 2, titled "From the Heart of a Child," is printed by permission of Gwen Williams. All rights reserved.

The devotional on December 3, titled "War in Heaven," is printed by permission of Shirley M. Corder. All rights reserved.

The devotional on December 4, titled "Looking for the Bonus," is printed by permission of Gloria J. Wallace. All rights reserved.

The devotional on December 7, titled "The Ugliest Christmas Tree," is printed by permission of John Ray Greif. All rights reserved.

The devotional on December 8, titled "Will I Ever Learn?" is printed by permission of Diane E. Kay. All rights reserved.

The devotional on December 9, titled "Gingerly Snack," is printed by permission of Pam Whitley. All rights reserved.

The devotional on December 12, titled "Hot Seat," is printed by permission of Pam Whitley. All rights reserved.

The devotional on December 23, titled "A Christmas to Remember," is printed by permission of Susan M. C. Holland. All rights reserved.

The devotional on December 24, titled "Christmas Treeeat!" is printed by permission of Pam Whitley. All rights reserved.

The devotional on December 25, titled "An Unexpected Answer," is printed by permission of Shirley M. Corder. All rights reserved.

The devotional on December 30, titled "Ring It Out!" is printed by permission of Lisa Buffaloe. All rights reserved.

Scripture Index

For Women
(continued)

The One Year® Devotional of Joy and Laughter

For Men

The One Year® Devotions for Men on the Go

The One Year® Devotions for Men

For Families

The One Year® Family Devotions, Vol. I

For Couples

The One Year® Devotions for Couples

The One Year® Love Language Minute Devotional

The One Year® Love Talk Devotional for Couples

For Teens

The One Year® Devos for Teens

The One Year® Devos for Sports Fans

For Personal Growth

The One Year® Walk with God Devotional

The One Year® At His Feet Devotional

The One Year® Daily Insights with Zig Ziglar

For Bible Study

The One Year® Praying through the Bible

The One Year® Through the Bible Devotional

It's convenient and easy to grow with God the One Year way.

CP0145